A Companion to
Chaucer's *Canterbury Tales*

Chaucer reading to a courtly audience. Corpus Christi College 61 fol. 1v. By permission of the Parker Library, Corpus Christi College, Cambridge University.

A COMPANION TO CHAUCER'S *CANTERBURY TALES*

Margaret Hallissy

Greenwood Press
Westport, Connecticut • London

Library of Congress Cataloging-in-Publication Data

Hallissy, Margaret.
    A companion to Chaucer's Canterbury tales / by Margaret Hallissy.
      p.   cm.
    Includes bibliographical references and index.
    Text in English, with some passages in the original Middle
English.
    ISBN 0–313–29189–6 (alk. paper)
    1. Chaucer, Geoffrey, d. 1400. Canterbury tales. 2. Christian
pilgrims and pilgrimages in literature. I. Title.
PR1874.H27 1995
821′.1—dc20   95–16017

R
821.1
CHAUCER

British Library Cataloguing in Publication Data is a

Copyright © 1995 by Margaret Hallissy

Library of Congress Catalog Card Number: 95–16017
ISBN: 0–313–29189–6

First published in 1995

Greenwood Press, 88 Post Road West, Westport, CT 06881
An imprint of Greenwood Publishing Group, Inc.

Printed in the United States of America

The paper used in this book complies with the
Permanent Paper Standard issued by the National
Information Standards Organization (Z39.48–1984).

10 9 8 7 6 5 4 3 2 1

Copyright Acknowledgments

The author and publisher are grateful for permission to reprint excerpts from the following copyrighted material:

Larry D. Benson (Editor), *The Riverside Chaucer*, Third Edition. Copyright © 1987 by
Houghton Mifflin Company. Reprinted with permission.

For Jerry Hallissy

For everi wight that hath an hous to founde
Ne renneth naught the werk for to bygynne
With rakel hond, but he wol bide a stounde,
And sende his hertes line out fro withinne
Aldirfirst his purpos for to wynne.

For a man who has a house to build
Does not hurry to begin the work
With hasty hand, but he will wait a while,
And send his heart's line out from within
First, to achieve his goal.

— *Troilus and Criseyde*, I, 1065–1069

Contents

List of Illustrations

FIGURE

PHOTOS

Preface

For my entent is, or I fro yow fare,
The naked text in English to declare
Of many a story.

For my intent is, before I leave you,
To declare the naked text in English
Of many a story.

— *Legend of Good Women*, G Prol., 85–87

My purpose in writing this book is to keep a new reader company on his or her first pilgrimage through Geoffrey Chaucer's *Canterbury Tales*. Since the book is intended for the first-time reader, whether student or general reader, it assumes no previous experience with Chaucer's work and no background in medieval studies. Its purpose is to clothe the "naked text" of Chaucer's many stories with a helpful garment of explication.

The first decision a modern reader of *The Canterbury Tales* must make is whether to approach the "naked text" in the original Middle English or in modern English translation. Most students are introduced to Chaucer in translation. At first glance this appears practical, analogous to reading *Don Quixote* in English rather than Spanish. But Chaucer's language is English, not a foreign tongue. My experience is that college students in a Chaucer class, with a well-annotated text and a helpful instructor, learn to read Middle English competently in a matter of weeks. Indeed, this process enhances their enjoyment of the work.

In the hope of approximating this group experience in a companion volume, the decision has been made to move back and forth between Middle and modern English in the following fashion. Long quotes are presented in Middle English, followed by my modern English paraphrases;

short quotes are in my modern English paraphrases only. Both sets of paraphrases are intended to follow the Middle English as closely as possible and are such as might be supplied by the instructor in a class on *The Canterbury Tales*. They depend—as does all Chaucer scholarship—on the annotations and glossary in Larry Benson's standard modern edition, *The Riverside Chaucer*, 3rd ed. (Boston: Houghton Mifflin, 1987); punctuation has been altered where needed to clarify the meaning. No attempt has been made to approximate the rhythm or meter of the original; that has been expertly done by others.

The line references to *The Riverside Chaucer* follow a system familiar to Chaucer scholars but new to novices. *The Canterbury Tales* is an unfinished work. Since Chaucer did not arrange the component parts of his manuscript himself, the proper order must be inferred on the basis of clues within the text. Textual scholars organize the parts of the *Tales* according to a system of fragments and groups. Lines of text, then, are indicated not only by line number but also by the fragment and group in which the line is found. For example, the first line of the *Tales* is designated as I, A, 1, meaning that it is the first line in fragment I, group A. These numerical references grow more detailed as the text progresses, for complex editorial reasons. For the beginning reader, the key to locating material in *The Riverside Chaucer* is to look for the fragment, group, and line numbers at the top of each page of text. If the reader begins with the simplest ones in the "General Prologue," the more difficult ones later in the *Tales* will seem less formidable.

My hope is that the user of this book will develop sufficient confidence in his or her ability to cope with Middle English to go on from it to read Chaucer in the original. If the reader chooses to use a translation, several are listed in Suggestions for Further Reading following the section entitled Chaucer's Language. The translation by Ronald L. Ecker and Eugene J. Crook is the best one to use in tandem with *The Riverside Chaucer*; its language approximates the Middle English very closely. On the other hand, if the reader chooses to work with a modern translation only, the Nevill Coghill translation is the one to use. The illustrated edition is particularly desirable for a first-time reader, as its visual material is not only beautiful to look at but also is illuminating in the medieval sense of shedding light on the text.

The ideal way to use this book is as a do-it-yourself course on Chaucer. Reading this book along with *The Canterbury Tales*, tale by tale, will give the reader the flavor of an undergraduate college course. The appendixes briefly discuss those tales that are out of fashion with modern readers and that are currently read more by Chaucer scholars than by the intended audience for this book. To study a single tale, the reading is best approached in this order:

1. The "General Prologue," at least to line 42
2. The portrait of the tale-teller (if any)
3. Chaucer's tale, in Middle or modern English
4. Chaucer's World
5. Chaucer's Language
6. The General Prologue chapter, up to the discussion of the portraits of the individual pilgrims
7. The discussion of the portrait of the pilgrim tale-teller, if he or she is characterized in the "General Prologue"
8. The chapter on the tale
9. Chaucer's tale again (surely in Middle English this time!)

For further study, the Suggestions for Further Reading section is provided after each chapter, as an entry into the vast arena of Chaucer scholarship. Some tales are more complex than others, have attracted a greater volume of criticism, or deal with currently controversial issues. These factors are reflected in the length and complexity of the bibliographies. The books and articles listed have been selected to extend the reader's knowledge beyond this book's first reading, but they do not venture into the more esoteric regions of criticism. The critical approach taken in this volume is to situate Chaucer in his time, in hope of clarifying what the responses of his first audience might have been. Other critical methods add layers of sophistication to this necessary groundwork.

In *The Western Canon* (New York: Harcourt, 1994), a masterly interweaving of the relationships between the works of twenty-six great writers, Harold Bloom poses the ultimate reader's question: "What shall the individual who still desires to read attempt to read, this late in history?" (15). Bloom thinks that reading individuals should read Chaucer, placing him second in importance only to Shakespeare. But, like all great writers, Chaucer demands a proportional greatness in his readers, a willingness to make the intellectual effort to match wits with a giant. It is my hope that this volume will help readers undertake that challenge.

Like Chaucer himself, the maker of this book has a day job, as professor of English at Long Island University in Brookville, New York. In that role

I have been teaching graduate and undergraduate courses in Chaucer for some years; in the process, I have gained insight into what new readers need to know to become comfortable with this unfamiliar material. Through the support of the Research Committee of the C. W. Post Campus, time was provided for this book, for which I hereby express appreciation. Thanks are also due to my generous and cooperative colleague, Dr. Edmund Miller, chair of the English Department, for his helpful scheduling, making it possible for me to teach the material in this book at an appropriate stage in its writing. In this way I was able to imitate Chaucer's ideal academic, the Clerk of Oxford, he who would "gladly learn," then "gladly teach."

A Companion to
Chaucer's *Canterbury Tales*

Chaucer's World

Here bygynneth the Book of the Tales of Caunterbury.
Here begins the Book of the Tales of Canterbury.
(Subtitle preceding "General Prologue")

In the image that serves as the frontispiece for this book, Geoffrey Chaucer reads to a courtly audience. The arrangement of the figures places the poet at the center of his social group, not apart from it. As a rendering of the way literature was experienced in the Middle Ages, the image is important to an understanding of Chaucer's masterwork, *The Canterbury Tales*. Before the introduction of the printing press to England by William Caxton in 1476, texts were copied by hand one by one, and were therefore expensive and scarce, available to few. So the transmission of literature involved a single text, an oral reader (who might or might not also be the author), and a listening audience. Unlike the modern reader, who typically reads silently and alone, the medieval reader was a member of a group, interacting with other listeners and with the reader, experiencing the work much as moderns do theater, television, or film. Because of this mode of transmission, medieval works often incorporate references to a narrator and an audience. Direct addresses to the listeners and conversational tags remind the modern reader that *The Canterbury Tales* are imagined orally, as stories told by an individual to a group.

Just as he is depicted in the frontispiece, Geoffrey Chaucer was a man at the center of his society. England in the fourteenth century was a society in transition. During the course of Chaucer's lifetime, changes were taking place in its structure that would affect him directly. Son of a vintner, or wine-merchant, Chaucer was a member of what future historians would call the middle class. Like the modern middle class, their medieval counterparts were affluent enough to support themselves increasingly well, but not affluent enough to guarantee their children a life of cultured leisure, as the hereditary nobility could. This situation determines a crucial fact of Chaucer's life: he had to work for a living.

It is easy to imagine Chaucer as a man involved with the court; his literary abilities alone would have made him a valuable addition to any sophisticated gathering. But Chaucer was no pet poet subsidized by a royal patron; his role in the court was as a salaried employee. As page, yeoman or personal servant, diplomat, controller of the Customs, and clerk of the King's Works, Chaucer held the equivalent of modern civil service positions. Although he experienced financial difficulties at times, in general his pay, and surely his responsibilities, increased over the course of his career.

Chaucer's work as a public servant was as demanding and time-consuming as any modern career. While his salaried occupation necessarily curtailed the amount of time he could devote to his writing, it had the advantage of placing him in contact with a wide variety of people from all social classes, "sundry folk" (I, A, 25) like his Canterbury pilgrims. The civil servant's experience of the world contributed to the poet's ability to create realistic characters. Chaucer several times depicts himself, self-mockingly, as a bookworm, always in his library; but the demands of his paid position meant that in reality he could only have been a part-time bookworm. His experience of literature was balanced by an active public life.

In several of his jobs, especially as controller of the Customs and clerk of the King's Works, Chaucer was responsible for managing money. As a man who lived on his salary, he was necessarily conscious of finances. Much that is known about him and his wife Philippa has to do with records of payments to both: it is as if a modern author were to be known to future historians by his and his wife's paycheck stubs. Between the financial aspects of his work and his own need for steady income, Chaucer became highly attuned to the realities of money and interested in the finances of his characters to a degree uncommon to medieval authors. How his characters get their money and how they spend it is a matter of consuming interest to their creator.

Another major fact about Chaucer's professional life is that, especially in his diplomatic positions, it expanded his experience of the world by causing him to travel and to hone his language skills (see Chaucer's Language). Like any educated man of his day, Chaucer could read Latin and French. French was the language not only of literature but also of diplomacy; anyone functioning in an international political capacity in the Middle Ages would have to be fluent in French. On one particularly important diplomatic journey, to Italy in 1372–1373, he was introduced also to the literature of that country. He became a careful reader of the works of the greatest Italian writers of his age: Dante, Petrarch, and Boccaccio. Chaucer's job required him to move easily between four languages; this linguistic fluency increased his exposure to a variety of literatures while enriching his knowledge of people and ideas.

In addition to the facts of his career, another noteworthy fact about Chaucer is that he was married, and to a woman with important court connections and a salary of her own. Like Geoffrey, Philippa Chaucer worked for a living, as lady-in-waiting to the queen. This position was prestigious, not menial; Chaucer's own connections with royalty were supplemented by his wife's. The Chaucers had four children. Aside from that, little is known about Philippa other than her career landmarks: positions granted, moneys paid. A curiously modern, two-wage-earner marriage like Chaucer's and Philippa's must have been affected by the frequent separations required by both their careers. It is tempting to see Chaucer's wife as decisive in the development of her husband's unusual ability to characterize women; but it is impossible to speculate on what kind of influence she had. Philippa is the mystery woman of Chaucer scholarship.

The society in which Geoffrey and Philippa lived was strikingly homogeneous by modern standards. Modern Americans, though divided by language, ethnicity, and religion, still can agree on many common principles; medieval Englishmen, united by the same factors, could agree on many more. Chaucer shared an all-pervasive belief system with the members of his original audience. Key terms in Chaucer's vocabulary crucial to the understanding of his work point to commonplaces of medieval thought, great generalizations immediately understandable to his contemporaries but requiring explanation for the modern reader.

The first great assumption was the existence of an afterlife. To fourteenth-century Christians, life in this world was a preparation for another, better world. Medieval people imagined human life as a journey or a pilgrimage, with heaven as the destination. In choosing a path to heaven, two alternative routes presented themselves: religious life and secular life. Of the two, religious life, membership in a religious order bound by vows of poverty, chastity, and obedience, was perceived as superior, a surer path to heaven (if the vows were kept). In secular life, life in the world, temptation was ever-present. Without the stricter commitment of religious vows, the worldly man or woman might overindulge in the love of money, the lust of the flesh, the will to self-aggrandizement. Any of these sins might cause an individual to lose heaven and be damned to hell for all eternity.

Belief in the superiority of the religious life over the secular was reinforced by the age's general tendency to think in terms of hierarchy. Medieval thought was infused with a passion for setting things in order, ranking everything in a neat continuum of higher to lower. In both religious and secular life, individuals were situated according to what Chaucer calls *estat*, *degree*, or *condicioun*: a place of one's own in a preordained and static hierarchy. As it is to this day, the Catholic church in the fourteenth century was organized hierarchically, with the pope at the top, followed on a descending scale by cardinals, bishops, priests, nonordained members of religious orders, and laity. In secular life, the king ranked above all the grades of nobility; nobility outranked commoners; within the expanding ranks of commoners some were economically and socially superior to others; and on the bottom were serfs or villeins, bound to the land. This organization of the universe was believed to be not of human but of divine origin. Therefore every human group was expected to organize itself according to the same orderly hierarchical pattern: religious orders had their superiors, to whom the members vowed obedience; and in the family, the husband ruled his wife and children.

The all-pervasive concept of order was considered immutable. *Estat* or *degree* or *condicioun* was assumed as a given, an essential part of one's nature against which it was not only futile but also sinful to rebel. Chaucer refers to this complex of beliefs when he uses the term *auctoritee*. Only king and pope had no earthly superior. While the lower must obey the higher, the higher had the reciprocal duty of exercising their proper *maistrye* and *governaunce* over the lower with prudence and justice, ever mindful of the ultimate authority of God. It was, however, all too obvious that behavior often did not correspond to rank. A continuing debate raged over whether true nobility resided in birth or behavior. Innate nobility of character in members of the higher classes, their *gentilesse*, was demonstrated by their refined behavior, their *curteisye*. These same virtues, however, might also be possessed by their social inferiors, possibly even to a greater degree. Poor behavior marked a man as a *cherl* whatever his bloodlines.

Proper behavior in one's *estat* was also signaled by clothing, *array*. Clothing was expected to reflect an individual's social position with accuracy and precision. Kings and queens were expected to wear sumptuous garments, as were popes, whose religious rank mirrored the highest secular position. Nobles and bishops similarly proclaimed their *estat* through fine *array*. Uniformity of dress signified membership in a variety of groups: religious orders wore the habit or common dress; a noble's retainers wore his livery; members of crafts guilds proclaimed group solidarity through similar garb. Ideally, *estat* should equal *array*; medieval people thought it crucial that clothing symbolism be employed authentically. But because the fourteenth century was a time of rapid economic progress for the nonnoble classes, many people of bourgeois origins could afford clothing similar to that worn by the nobility. Wearing garments unsuitable to *degree* was considered inappropriate; laws were even passed to make it illegal. Well aware of this controversy, Chaucer is attentive to the clothing of his characters. His clothing imagery always deserves the reader's close attention, as it signals conformity or nonconformity of the character to *estat* norms. This matter of *array* was taken seriously, as any kind of rebellion, however trivial, seemed to threaten the stability of the whole.

The medieval passion for order had its corollary in an equally intense fear of disorder. Principles of disorder in Chaucer's work are variously labeled as *cas* or chance, *aventure* or unplanned happenings, or, simply, Fortune. A recurrent image in *The Canterbury Tales* as in other medieval works, the goddess Fortuna and her wheel (see photo 2), embodied the uneasy feeling that, despite all of man's careful planning and attempts to control his fate, uncontrollable factors intervened. The individual striving for earthly success was imagined as climbing onto Fortuna's wheel at the bottom. As the wheel ascends, he is achieving more and more. Finally, he reaches the top. Just then Fortuna, blindfolded to indicate the arbitrariness of her actions, turns her wheel, and the man on top falls. This image expresses the medieval belief in the mutability of all things. In this imperfect world, *weal*, or well-being, is inevitably followed by *wo*. Only in heaven is there joy eternal.

The ideal medieval hierarchy of values always kept this crucial fact in mind. Man's earthly pilgrimage, if successful, ends in everlasting *weal*. Absorption in the things of the world distracts the medieval Christian from the true goal of the earthly journey. Yet at the same time, the world is fascinating, sinners are more interesting than saints, and a Miller's tale is more fun than a Parson's. Ultimately, however, literature is to be judged not according to the pleasure principle, but according to its *sentence*, the moral lesson it teaches. The tension between the serious, or *ernest*, purpose of literature, its usefulness as a road map to the heavenly city, and its function as *game*, sophisticated entertainment along the way, is present throughout the tales. In his "Retraction," Chaucer rejects his gaming tales in favor of his earnest ones. In doing so, he sets his affairs in order according to the norms of his age. While scholars do not agree that the "Retraction" was indeed Chaucer's last piece of writing, it nevertheless represents his judgment of the ultimate place of literature in the life of both poet and audience: as one of the "things of the world," inferior to the "things of God."

Chaucer was working on *The Canterbury Tales* when he died, at the turn of the new century in 1400. He finished his own pilgrimage before he finished his pilgrims'. From whatever heaven receives the souls of dead poets, he invites the modern reader to join him on the journey to Canterbury.

SUGGESTIONS FOR FURTHER READING

Bibliography

Brewer, Derek. *Chaucer and His World*. London: Eyre Methuen,1978.

Gibaldi, Joseph. *Approaches to Teaching Chaucer's Canterbury Tales*. New York: Modern Language Association, 1980.

Howard, Donald R. *The Idea of The Canterbury Tales*. Berkeley: University of California Press, 1976.

————. *Chaucer: His Life, His Works, His World*. New York: Dutton, 1987.

Huppé, Bernard. *A Reading of The Canterbury Tales*. Albany: State University of New York Press, 1964.

Hussey, Maurice. *Chaucer's World: A Pictorial Companion*. Cambridge: Cambridge University Press, 1967.

Kelly, Harry A. *Love and Marriage in the Age of Chaucer*. Ithaca, N.Y.: Cornell University Press, 1975.

Kolve, V. A. *Chaucer and the Imagery of Narrative: The First Five Canterbury Tales*. Stanford, Calif.: Stanford University Press, 1984.

Loomis, Roger Sherman. *A Mirror of Chaucer's World*. Princeton, N.J.: Princeton University Press, 1965.

Lumiansky, R. M. *Of Sondry Folk: The Dramatic Principle in The Canterbury Tales*. Austin: University of Texas Press, 1955.

Mann, Jill. *Chaucer and Medieval Estates Satire*. Cambridge: Cambridge University Press, 1973.

————. *Geoffrey Chaucer*. Atlantic Highlands, N.J.: Humanities Press, 1991.

Miller, Robert P., ed. *Chaucer: Sources and Backgrounds*. New York: Oxford University Press, 1977.

Robertson, D. W., Jr. *A Preface to Chaucer: Studies in Medieval Perspectives*. Princeton, N.J.: Princeton University Press, 1962.

Ruggiers, Paul G. *The Art of The Canterbury Tales*. Madison: University of Wisconsin Press, 1965.

Videography

A Prologue to Chaucer. Films for the Humanities and Sciences #WU 998.

Chaucer. Films for the Humanities and Sciences #WU 1295.

Chaucer Reads Chaucer: "The Miller's Tale." Films for the Humanities and Sciences #WU 1742.

Chaucer: The General Prologue to the Canterbury Tales. Films for the Humanities and Sciences #WU 4081.

Geoffrey Chaucer and Middle English Literature. Films for the Humanities and Sciences #WU 906.

The Middle Ages. Video Enrichment Clearvue/EAV 9VH0496.

Chaucer's Language

And for ther is so gret diversite
In Englissh and in writyng of oure tonge,
So prey I God that non myswrite the,
Ne the mysmetre for defaute of tonge.

And since there is such great diversity
In English and in writing of our tongue,
So I pray to God that no one miswrite you,
Nor mismeter you for default of tongue.
                              — *Troilus and Criseyde*, V, 1793–1796

Near the end of his great romance *Troilus and Criseyde*, Chaucer prays for
the integrity of his book once it passes out of his hands and into the wider
world. Publication in Chaucer's day meant that a copyist, working by hand,
duplicated one manuscript from another. If several copies were made, either
from the author's copy or from subsequent copies, the copies might be
identical neither to each other nor to the original copy. So the book's
"maker," its author, depends on the "writer," the scribe, to transmit his work
correctly. In modern publishing, copies are made mechanically from proofs
corrected by the author; even so, errors creep in. All the more this was so
in medieval manuscript production. A scribe might be, as Chaucer notes,
unskillful from *defaute of tonge*, imperfect knowledge of the language; he
might be inattentive and *myswrite*, copy incorrectly. At the other extreme,
a scribe might be too creative, usurping the prerogative of the "maker" by
altering the text according to his own imaginative vision. Chaucer prays
that none of these mishaps befall his work, because he knows how likely it
is that they will, given the human propensity to err, the vagaries of medieval
publishing, and the *gret diversite* of the English language in his time.

Linguists call Chaucer's language "Middle" English to distinguish it from the Old English that preceded it and from the modern English that followed it. Speakers of modern English would not at first be able to read Old English:

> Faeder ure
> þu þe eart on heofonum
> Si þin nama gehalgod.

With study, they would learn to recognize the first sentence of the "Lord's Prayer":

> Our Father
> Who art in heaven
> Hallowed be thy name.

Despite its different word meanings, variant spellings, and syntactical differences, Middle English is much closer to modern English than is Old English. Only two centuries after Chaucer, the language available to Shakespeare is in fact modern English. Often Shakespeare's language presents no difficulty to the modern reader. A son mourning his dead father might speak of him today much as Hamlet did of his father:

> He was a man, take him for all in all,
> I shall not look upon his like again.
>
> (I, ii, 187–188)

Sometimes, however, variant meanings and unfamiliar syntax require the student of *Hamlet* to read with such care and thought that many new to the experience call it "translating." But it is not. Shakespeare's English is the language written and spoken today.

Chaucer's English requires more habituation than does that of Shakespeare. Not only was the language itself as Chaucer says, "diverse," but so were Chaucer's own linguistic abilities. Chaucer would probably have been taught French as a child, and his involvement in government and international diplomacy expanded his knowledge of the language spoken by the ruling classes in all European countries. Formal schooling in the Middle Ages required the student to learn Latin, the language of classical literature. Thus both French and Latin were professional, working languages for Chaucer. Having mastered these two related languages and read extensively in their literatures, Chaucer could easily learn Italian, allowing him to read the works of his contemporaries, Dante, Petrarch, and especially Boccaccio. Not only could Chaucer read French, Latin, and Italian, he could also translate from them into English. He translated portions of *The Romance of the Rose* from the French, and Boethius' *Consolation of Philosophy* from the Latin. In addition, the strong influence of Boccaccio's *Decameron* on Chaucer's own work is evidence of his mastery of Italian.

But the richness of Chaucer's vocabulary cannot solely be attributed to his own considerable language skills. By the fourteenth century, the English language itself had acquired the diversity of which Chaucer writes. The basic stock of Anglo-Saxon words had been enriched by contributions from French and Latin. The direction of the development of the English language was changed forever by a single event: the Norman Conquest. In 1066, Count William of Normandy in France, believing that his claim to the English crown was stronger than that of the reigning King Harold, invaded England, conquering and killing Harold at the Battle of Hastings. With the new King William came a new French-speaking aristocracy. Those members of the English nobility who were not killed at the decisive battle decreased in influence, and so did their language. French became the language of the rulers, the "in-group," and English the language of the ruled, the "out-group." Since French was spoken by the political, social, and cultural elite, those who aspired to join their ranks had to learn to speak their language. Not only was the language itself influential as a separate written and spoken language, but also linguistic borrowings from it to English were added to, and eventually in some cases even replaced, Old English terms.

In addition to French, Latin influenced the speech and writing of educated people in the Middle Ages. To be educated was, until the very recent past, to learn to read Latin. Latin was the language of university education in the Middle Ages, of advanced study in philosophy, theology, law, and medicine. The clerk, the learned man, was by definition one who knew Latin. Thus an educated fourteenth-century Englishman like Chaucer could read, write, speak, and translate from Latin. Latin was also, and remains today, the universal tongue of the Catholic church; although liturgies are now celebrated in the language of the worshipers, papal encyclicals and other official documents are still written in Latin. Thus both religion and higher education contributed to the widespread influence of Latin on English, through the agency of religious and secular authorities. Spoken languages, whether Italian or Spanish or English, were considered inferior, the vehicle for everyday conversation or less serious writing. Consequently, although writers working in comic genres such as the *fabliau*, or bawdy tale, used the spoken languages, when a writer wanted to be taken in earnest, he used one of the "important" languages: French or Latin. Even if a medieval writer worked solely in English, more serious high-style passages might incorporate more French- or Latin-derived terminology, while comic low-style diction tended toward the Anglo-Saxon word stock.

Chaucer often uses linguistic details as a means of characterization. The Prioress only knows the French spoken at Stratford at Bowe, not Parisian French; like so many other details in her portrait, this indicates her superficial, worldly ways. The virtuous Parson sees the French language as a vehicle for the expression of worldly vanities; he quotes, in French, a lyric of a French love song about time wasted on trivia instead of the "good work" that leads to salvation (X, I, 246).

Latin, the language of higher education, marks its user as a member of an elite, a possessor of secret, special knowledge. Being restricted to the few, the language is exclusionary. It can, then, be the vehicle for private jokes, or an instrument for wielding power over the unlearned. The meaning of the Latin inscription on the Prioress's brooch, "*Amor vincit omnia*" (I, A, 162), would be clear only to the educated members of the medieval audience; only they would know that the Latin term *amor* referred to profane love, as opposed to the *caritas*, or spiritual love, that should prevail between good Christians. Those ecclesiastical conmen the Friar, the Summoner, and the Pardoner all use the Latin terminology of church and law court to impress the unlearned, the better to gull them. Chaunticleer takes advantage of his wife's ignorance of Latin to deceive her by deliberately mistranslating a misogynistic phrase. In contrast, the sweet innocence of the "little *clergeoun*" of the "Prioress's Tale" is shown in his ignorance of the meaning of the Latin hymn to the Virgin; his song is one of pure devotion unmixed with intellectual snobbery. These references to French and Latin show language skills as status markers: good French carries social prestige, and any Latin at all, even a few little tags that show only minimal command of the language, confers power.

Oddly for the greatest English poet of his day, Chaucer's references to the English language are often apologetic, suggesting a narrator's imperfect command of the language. The Man of Law damns Chaucer with faint praise for writing in "such English as he can" (II, B[1], 49). Yet that same narrator later expresses doubts about the adequacy of his own English to describe his villainess Donegild. Both the Knight and the Squire worry about the inadequacy of their English to convey their thoughts. In the prologue to the "Second Nun's Tale," the narrator several times refers to how things are said in English, as if the speaker was making a special effort to use an acquired language. The Parson knows a phrase in theological Latin but does not know its English translation. The sense conveyed by

Chaucer's references to the English language is that it is one language among several others, at times even an imperfect tool for the task at hand.

Despite his profession of linguistic hesitancy, Chaucer is in full command of English and exploits its versatility to the fullest. In just three lines, in the "Lenvoy de Chaucer" at the end of the "Clerk's Tale," Chaucer's word choice shows "diversity of tongue":

> Ye archewyves, stondeth at defense,
> Syn ye be strong as is a greet camaille;
> Ne suffreth nat that men yow doon offense.

> You archwives, stand at defense,
> Since you are as strong as a great camel,
> Do not allow men to do offense to you.

(IV, E, 1195–1197)

The words "wife," "stand," "strong," "great," and "men" are all derived from Anglo-Saxon; the prefix "arch-" from Greek; "defense," "suffer," and "offense" are from French; and "camel" is from Latin.

In addition to possessing a large vocabulary, Chaucer could move easily from one level of diction to another. He employs elevated high-style diction when dealing with abstract concepts, as in this philosophical passage on universal order from the "Knight's Tale":

> "That same Prince and that Moevere," quod he,
> "Hath stablissed in this wrecched world adoun
> Certeyne days and duracioun
> To all that is engendred in this place. . . .
> Ther nedeth noght noon auctoritee t'allegge,
> For it is preeved by experience,
> But that me list declaren my sentence."

> "That same Prince and that Mover," said he,
> "Has established in this wretched world below
> Certain days and duration
> To all that is engendered in this place. . . .
> No authority is needed to confirm this,
> For it is proven by experience,
> Except to make my point even clearer."

(I, A, 2994–2997, 3000–3002)

In contrast, when he requires an earthy low-style effect, he abandons elevated diction and employs simpler colloquialisms:

"Go fro the wyndow, Jakke fool," she sayde;
As help me God, it wol nat be 'com pa me.'
I love another—and elles I were to blame—
Wel bet than thee, by Jhesu, Absolon.
Go forth thy wey, or I wol cast a ston,
And lat me slepe, a twenty devel wey!"

"Go from the window, Jack fool," she said;
"So help me God, it will not be 'Come kiss me!'
I love another—or else I were to blame—
Much more than you, by Jesus, Absolon.
Go forth, away, or I will throw a stone,
And let me sleep, in twenty devils' names!"

                                                    (I, A, 3708–3713)

And, as the reader of Chaucer in Middle English immediately notices, Chaucer has a good stock of vulgarisms for the human anatomy and for basic bodily functions. Surely he was a master of the "great diversity / In English and in the writing of our tongue."

But he might well worry that scribal error or misguided editing might cause his carefully planned English line to *mysmetre*. Chaucer typically, though not invariably, uses the four-stress line, as in the following examples:

A Knýght ther wás, and thát a wórthy man

                                                    (I, A, 43)

A Frére ther wás, a wántowne and a mérye

                                                    (I, A, 208)

But a correct count of the number of stressed and unstressed syllables in a line of Middle English depends on correct transcription of the author's words. Omissions or substitutions by a careless scribe would throw off the meter. While Chaucer is often flexible in his own adherence to metrical rules, he prays that his scribe will not "mismeter" through making unauthorized changes. Chaucer wants his words to stand as he wrote them.

Learning to read Chaucer's language, Middle English, is an intellectual pleasure that enhances the modern reader's appreciation of Chaucer's writing. Before readers automatically reach for a modern translation, they should consider approaching *The Canterbury Tales* in the language in which Chaucer wrote. As the Preface notes, one of the hoped-for results of the use of this book is to offer readers experience with Middle English sufficient to give them confidence to begin working with the original.

SUGGESTIONS FOR FURTHER READING

Editions and Translations

Benson, Larry D., ed. *The Riverside Chaucer*. 3rd edition. Boston: Houghton Mifflin, 1987.

Coghill, Nevill, trans. *Geoffrey Chaucer: The Canterbury Tales*. 1951. London: Penguin, 1977.

————. *Geoffrey Chaucer: The Canterbury Tales, An Illustrated Edition*. London: Cresset, 1986.

Ecker, Ronald L., and Eugene J. Crook, trans. *Geoffrey Chaucer: The Canterbury Tales*. Palatka, Fla.: Hodge and Braddock, 1993.

Discography

Selections from Chaucer: The Canterbury Tales. Read in Middle English by Nevill Coghill and Norman Davis. Spoken Arts, Inc., no. 919.

Language

Burnley, David. *The Language of Chaucer*. London: Macmillan, 1983.

Davis, Norman, Douglas Gray, Patricia Ingham, and Anne Wallace-Hadrill, comps. *A Chaucer Glossary*. Oxford: Clarendon, 1979.

Kokeritz, Helge. *A Guide to Chaucer's Pronunciation*. Toronto: University of Toronto Press, 1978.

1. The goal of the pilgrimage: Canterbury Cathedral. Modern pilgrims travel from London to Canterbury via the M2 motorway or by train from Victoria Station. Photograph by Gerald J. Hallissy.

The General Prologue

Er that I ferther in this tale pace,
Me thynketh it acordaunt to resoun
To telle yow al the condicioun
Of ech of hem, so as it semed me,
And whiche they weren, and of what degree,
And eek in what array that they were inne

Before I pass further into this tale,
I think it according to reason
To tell you all the condition
Of each of them, as it seemed to me,
And who they were, and of what degree,
And also what array they wore.

(I, A, 36–41)

The "book of the Tales of Canterbury," as Chaucer calls his masterwork, begins with images connoting spring and new life: rain, earth, wind, sun, and birds. April's sweet showers have pierced the dry land of March to the root. Moisture bathes each flower, stimulating growth. The wind breathes upon the land, putting the spirit of life into it. The sun is in just the right place in the zodiac. Little birds sing; and because nature is exciting in spring, the birds seem never to sleep. When the difficulties of winter travel are over, when all these signs of a new season appear, then people long to go on pilgrimage.

The pilgrimage in the Middle Ages was primarily a spiritual journey. All religions have sacred sites, and pilgrimages still take place. A Catholic pilgrim today might go to Lourdes, where the Virgin Mary is said to have appeared to St. Bernadette; a Jewish pilgrim might visit Israel; a Muslim might visit Mecca. The pilgrim's motives might include repentance for sin, thanksgiving for divine favors, the need to get in touch with one's religious roots, or a combination of these. But, like pilgrims today, the medieval traveler to the holy places was also not averse to having a good time in the company of like-minded associates. In *The Canterbury Tales*, the pilgrimage is also a vacation.

Like vacation acquaintances in all time periods, the Canterbury pilgrims experience each other in a lighthearted way. The pilgrimage offers them time and space away from their everyday cares; they are on holiday, thus open to each other in a way they would not be in any other context. A spirit of play animates their interactions, a spirit of acceptance informs their attitudes. People who would otherwise be separated by social class or occupation or gender are brought together by chance in quest of a mutual goal: to visit the shrine of St. Thomas Becket in Canterbury.

Thomas Becket (1118—1170) began his career as a friend and political ally of King Henry II. In 1154, Henry made Thomas his chancellor, his right-hand man in ruling the kingdom. Had Henry left Thomas in that position, Becket would have been an effective chancellor but a mere footnote in the story of Henry's reign. Becket's role was considerably expanded by Henry's decision to employ his chancellor in another, more challenging capacity. A major issue in the lifetime of Henry and Thomas was the balance of power between church and state. In 1162, in an attempt to consolidate his power over both, Henry appointed his longtime friend Thomas as archbishop of Canterbury, thus making him the most powerful ecclesiastical official in England. Henry assumed that Thomas would continue to serve Henry's own political interests in that job, much as he had done as chancellor.

But Thomas perceived his new role differently. Whether his new clerical status solidified his commitment to the church as a spiritual institution more important than any earthly kingdom, or whether he was inclined to seek power of his own through his new ecclesiastical office, Thomas's motives remain obscure and are debated to this day. What is certain, however, is that Thomas and Henry, caught on opposite sides of this power struggle between church and state, became deadly enemies. The crisis came when Henry complained vehemently that he wished to be rid of the annoying Thomas. Several of Henry's followers took him at his word and on December 29, 1170, murdered Thomas as he was at prayer in the cathedral at Canterbury. Thus Thomas became, in Chaucer's words, "a holy blissful martyr" (I, A, 17).

The modern pilgrim can visit the exact spot on which this famous medieval crime took place. The pilgrimage to Canterbury today is by car or by train from London. The town of Canterbury is an interesting mixture of medieval architecture and modern mercantilism; but the cathedral itself, a masterwork of medieval architecture, is as worthy a goal of pilgrimage today as it was to Chaucer's pilgrims (see photo 1). In a nearby gift shop, the modern pilgrim can obtain a Canterbury Cross, a token of accomplishment, henceforth to be worn proudly as a sign that one has completed this earthly journey to the martyr's shrine.

Modern historians see Thomas Becket as a complex character with an ego rivaling Henry's own. But the medieval Catholic church saw him as a saint, canonizing him in 1173. In the Catholic church, then as now, a saint is one in whom Christian virtue is so manifest that the church officially proclaims its belief that he or she is in heaven with God, and therefore worthy of veneration by the Christian community here on earth. Visiting the saint's shrine is a traditional indicator of the believer's devotion. If the saint had already (through the power of God) granted a favor, then it seemed only fair to journey to the saint's shrine to thank him or her. Moreover, the beauty of the cathedral would give pilgrims a foretaste of the ultimate goal of their life's journey: the heavenly Jerusalem. Hence the Canterbury pilgrimage.

In the spring, pilgrims long to go to shrines in faraway places, and especially from all over England they go to Canterbury. Their purpose is to thank St. Thomas, whom they credit with having "helped them when they were sick" (I, A, 18); given the sorry state of medieval medicine, supernatural help in times of illness was most welcome. So it happens that this group of pilgrims assembled. Joined by a religious purpose, but otherwise a various group, they meet at a London inn, the Tabard, in Southwark, a section of London.

At the Tabard, the reader meets the narrator, a pilgrim named Geffrey who is similar but not identical to the poet Chaucer. Geffrey is a perceptive and sociable fellow. He gets to know everyone in the pilgrimage party quickly and has in general an accepting, nonjudgmental attitude toward them all. The reader depends on Geffrey throughout as, to use a modern metaphor, the camera lens through which all the other characters are seen. Unlike the sophisticated poet Chaucer, Geffrey is naive. Often the reader must infer what Chaucer might believe, as opposed to what Geffrey says.

Geffrey, having arrived at the Tabard "ready to wend on my pilgrimage / To Canterbury with full devout heart" (I, A, 21–22), eagerly meets his fellow pilgrims. There are twenty-nine of them in all,

> *a compaignye*
> *Of sondry folk, by aventure yfalle*
> *In felaweshipe.*

> a company
> Of sundry folk, by chance fallen
> In fellowship.

(I, A, 24–26)

Several key terms here explain why *The Canterbury Tales* is so diverse a collection.

Medieval books were sometimes composed of several unrelated manuscripts, odd assemblages that often do not satisfy the modern perception of art as requiring a strong unifying principle. At the other extreme from the apparently random compilations were medieval collections of *exempla*, stories giving examples of some general principle (the "Monk's Tale" is one of these; see Appendix V). What Chaucer was striving for in *The Canterbury Tales* was a happy medium: a group of tales that are sufficiently related to each other to form a real book; and different enough from each other to provide variety. A strong unifying principle of the tales is "fellowship" or "company," the sense of a group united by a common goal: the pilgrimage to Canterbury. An equally strong principle of diversity is the "sundriness" of the "folk," the variety of the people fallen together in fellowship "by chance."

The twenty-nine Canterbury pilgrims who meet at the Tabard Inn represent a cross-section of medieval society. Only the highest social classes, who would travel with their personal entourage, not with a ragtag group of chance acquaintances, are missing. All the other *estats* are represented. With his descriptions of the individual pilgrims, Chaucer also gives us a sampling of representative types of the *estats*, or social classes, in the fourteenth century. A visual schematic of these class relationships is provided in Figure 1.

Medieval sources commonly discuss their society as being divided into three groups: those who work, those who fight, and those who pray. Each group has its own special task, which it performs on behalf of the whole. The workers, whether professional or menial, are responsible for all economic functions; the fighters defend all the others; and the pray-ers provide spiritual sustenance. Within these three subdivisions, hierarchies exist. Among the workers, for example, a physician outranks a tradesman, who in turn outranks an agricultural laborer. Comparable social status prevails between members of the three orders: a monk, for example, occupies a position in society similar

Figure 1.
Chaucer's pilgrims and the "Three Estates."

"Those who work"	"Those who fight"	"Those who pray"

Landed gentry
  Franklin
	Knight	*Religious orders*
		  Monk

Professionals
  Sergeant of the Law
  Doctor of Physic
	Squire	Prioress
		Friar
		Nun's Priest

Tradespeople
  Merchant
  Wife of Bath
  Five Guildsmen
  Harry Bailly
  Miller
		Second Nun
		
		Parish clergy
		  Parson
		
		Student
		  Clerk of Oxford

Secular employees
  Manciple
  Reeve
		Church employees*
		  Pardoner
		  Summoner

Laborers
  Shipman
  Yeoman
  Cook		

Peasants Plowman		

*May be laypersons or in minor orders.

The commonplace medieval system of classification is discussed in detail by historian Georges Duby.

to that of a lay professional. The choice of a religious life might carry social advantages as well; the Parson, though brother to the Plowman, outranks him by virtue of the superiority of the clerical function. While the basic tripartite scheme is generally accepted among medievalists, the hierarchies within each order and the parallels between them, as schematized in Figure 1, are my interpretations and are open to debate. The fourteenth century was a time of rapid social change; society was not as static as any printed chart might suggest. What the chart does present to the modern reader is the diversity of *estats* represented by the Canterbury pilgrims and a sketch of their social relationships to each other.

In addition to the three orders, another characteristically medieval way of imagining the world was as a pyramid, with the highest social classes, a small group, on top, and the lower classes, a larger group, on the bottom. In the fourteenth century, while the top and bottom of this hierarchical pyramid remained stable—kings stayed kings, and few peasants improved their lot—there was motion in the middle. What historians were later to term the middle class had its roots in the rising bourgeoisie of the fourteenth century. More and more money was finding its way into the pockets of people of no particular distinction of birth; at the same time, the landed gentry was becoming relatively cash-poor by comparison. When Chaucer describes the *condicioun* or *degree* of his pilgrims (I, A, 38, 40), he situates them in society with respect to a dramatic shift in economic power away from the traditional nobility. The new rich of the Middle Ages were people very much like Chaucer's modern readers, who make their way in the world not by hereditary right but by their own efforts: what they learn and what they earn.

Again like many moderns, the fourteenth-century person was likely to express his or her sense of self by *array*: clothing. Chaucer devotes considerable attention to what his characters are wearing. While precise description lends an air of realism, it is not just to set the stage that Chaucer costumes his characters. Clothing had a precise function in medieval society: as a visible sign of one's position in society. Royalty dressed regally, in fur and jewels, silks and embroidery, bright colors, in voluminous trains and headgear of lavishly draped expensive fabric. Peasants dressed poorly, in simple styles fashioned of harsh, cheap cloth in drab colors—browns, greys, russets—as if to reflect in their *array* the earth to which they were bound. In between, in the unruly middle class, people who could afford it engaged in conspicuous consumption much as the affluent do today, showing off their earning capacity by means of their *array*.

This practice was considered not only socially unacceptable but also unlawful. During the fourteenth century, laws were repeatedly passed with the intent of curbing the unseemly display of the wealthy middle classes. These sumptuary laws, laws regulating consumption, attempted to define the level of dress appropriate to a person's social class. Obviously, the upper classes were getting nervous: a wealthy tradesman's wife might dress as well as a land-poor lord's, and what would become of social distinction then? From the viewpoint of the makers of the sumptuary laws, *array* should indicate precisely one's fixed position in a predetermined hierarchical order; but from the viewpoint of the violators of the laws, clothing expresses one's definition of oneself. If a carpenter is so successful that his wife can wear a dress with a train and look like a lady, then more power to him. By the same token, less power to the lord and lady whose proper *array* is being usurped. It is within this social context that Chaucer describes the *condi-cioun*, *degree*, *estat*, and *array* of his pilgrims.

THE KNIGHT

Chaucer starts with a Knight, as is only fitting, since the Knight is the person of highest *degree* on the Canterbury pilgrimage. Any knight's function is to fight in defense of the rest of society. Chaucer's Knight is exemplary in that role. He behaves with all the qualities proper to his *estat*, "troth and honor, freedom and courtesy" (I, A, 46). "Troth" means not only truthfulness but also fidelity to the pledged word. "Honor" means adherence to norms for decent and proper behavior. "Freedom" means not the absence of constraint as moderns would define it, but generosity, liberality, lavishness in gift-giving, a disinclination to hoard the spoils of war. "Courtesy" refers to that complex set of social behaviors that makes a rugged military man also acceptable in the highly civilized and ritualized medieval court. The medieval knight was not expected to be merely a fighting machine, but was also required to function competently in peacetime.

As a soldier, the Knight has participated in an improbable number of fourteenth-century battles. Some of these were the so-called holy wars, the Crusades. According to the religious beliefs of the Middle Ages, the church founded by Christ was the one true faith, and only by means of adherence to that faith could anyone go to heaven after death. Religious tolerance was not a value held dear by medieval people; quite the contrary. Those who held other beliefs were, to medieval Christians, simply "hea-thens" (I, A, 49), and wars to destroy them or recapture lands from them were considered not only justifiable but meritorious as well. The extent of these battles in Chaucer's day is suggested by the geographical expanses covered by the Knight as he "fought for our faith" (I, A, 62): Prussia, Lithuania, Russia, Granada, Spain, Turkey, Morocco. The medieval Chris-tian did not perceive such conflicts as many moderns would perceive them, as illegitimate attempts to stamp out cultural diversity, but rather as defenses of God's church. To them, there would have been no contra-diction in the character who could "slay his foe" on the one hand, and on the other, be "worthy . . . wise . . . meek as a maid . . . a true, perfect, gentle knight" (I, A, 63, 68, 69, 72).

To anyone who was not his foe, he was invariably kind and polite:

He nevere yet no vileynye ne sayde
In al his lyf unto no maner wight.

He never yet said any villainy
In all his life unto any one.

(I, A, 70–71)

Reflecting his appropriate behavior is his appropriate *array* (I, A, 73–78). His eagerness to rush to a pilgrimage of thanksgiving immediately after a battle is indicated by the fact that he still wears military garb, a coarse cloth tunic stained with the rust from his armor. Similarly, his horse befits the rider's status, being "good but not gay," serviceable but not lavishly appointed (I, A, 74). Medieval knights often decorated their steeds flamboyantly, a practice, Chaucer suggests, which was often at odds with military utility.

THE SQUIRE

The Knight is accompanied by his son, who serves as his squire. A squire is a knight-in-training, a young man whose education consists of apprenticeship to an older man, a master of the knightly function. One typical duty of a squire is to "carve before his father" at the table (I, A, 100), so that he might learn the proper ways to carve meat at dinner—a manly duty surviving in some modern American households, especially during ritual holiday dinners like Thanksgiving. Except for this brief allusion to the acquisition of this culinary skill, the Squire is described less in terms of his future as a knight—his father's portrait has already served to define that *estat*—than as a typical example of the medieval courtly "lover" and "lusty bachelor" (I, A, 80).

Modern critics use the term *courtly love* to describe a set of beliefs and practices that informed the love poetry and narrative romances of the Middle Ages and later. The courtly lover and his lady were stock characters in literature for hundreds of years. Like all medieval relationships, the courtly love relationship was hierarchical. In contrast to real life, in which men were assumed to be superior to women, in courtly love literature the lady dominated the lover. The lady was beautiful, pure, noble, and inaccessible (often because she was married). The lover was handsome, accomplished, and frustrated by the lady's aloofness. His quest to gain the lady's favors was all the more ardent for being ultimately futile, because if the lady yielded, she would, of course, no longer be the pure and spiritual being he had so desired. The contradictory nature of this relationship caused the lover great distress: he is often described as listless, pale, wan, sleepless, likely to die for love. The lady, however, was oblivious to his suffering. These beliefs were to influence literary portrayals of love for hundreds of years, even surviving in our own cynical age.

Chaucer's Squire is characterized in terms of this tradition. Twenty years old, he is strong and handsome, of a good height and with curly hair. Having fought in several battles and conducted himself properly, he is well on his way to knightly fame. Unlike his father the Knight, whose motivation for valor is left unexplained, the Squire has the classic motivation of the courtly lover: by demonstrating his prowess in battle, he "hope[s] to stand in his lady's grace" that is, to receive the lady's approval as a reward for his accomplishment (I, A, 88). In keeping with his identification with the courtly bachelor are his *array* and behavior. Wearing a short smock with long wide sleeves and embroidered with fresh flowers, he sings and plays the flute all day. He possesses such accomplishments as would be likely to please a lady: he rides his horse well; he can write songs, joust, dance, and draw. Sleepless, he is presumably kept awake by thoughts of his lady. All the elements of his description work together to form a character who is "courteous" (I, A, 99), suited to the elegant life of courts—possibly in contrast to his worthy father, whose stained tunic suggests a man more comfortable on the battlefield than in a lady's chamber.

THE YEOMAN

The Knight and his Squire travel in company with a Yeoman. Like his two companions, the Yeoman also exemplifies a stock medieval character type: the rustic countryman. Indeed, every element of the Yeoman's *array* signals his rural origins. He is dressed in green, his face is brown—exposure to sun was a sure indicator of lower-class *estat* into our own century—and he carries a well-tended bow and arrow. Like the forest that is his natural habitat, he is associated with woodcraft; he even has a nut-shaped head. In addition to his archery equipment, he has an arm guard, a shield, a sword, a horn, and a dagger. As befits his temporary status as a pilgrim, he wears a medal of St. Christopher, the patron saint of travelers. So formidably equipped for yeomanry is this Yeoman that the narrator Geffrey's conclusion is a piece of comic understatement: "He was a forester, I guess" (I, A, 117). It is as if a modern character was described as wearing a wet suit, carrying a surfboard, and standing on the beach, and the narrator concluded, "He was a surfer, I guess." Chaucer often pokes fun at his alter ego Geffrey by allowing him just such naive comments as these.

In creating the Knight, the Squire, and the Yeoman, Chaucer is working with stereotypes. This Knight is much like other knights, and the Squire and Yeoman are typical of their respective social classes and occupational categories, their *estats*. Chaucer creates other characters in much this same way: the Physician, the Franklin, and the Miller are representatives of their social groups. But some characters differ dramatically from the stereotype and mark Chaucer's accomplishment of a literary feat unusual for his historical period: the creation of a highly individualized character.

THE PRIORESS

Chaucer's Prioress, Madame Eglentyne, is the first of these. The Prioress is also the first of Chaucer's characters to be given a name of her own; she is not just a generic nun but a unique woman. To understand Madame Eglentyne, it is necessary to take a brief excursion into the topic of convent life in the Middle Ages.

Medieval women were perceived as having two basic life choices: religious life or secular life as married women. Since an unmarried woman had no real place in medieval society, any woman who could not marry, or who chose not to, affiliated with a religious order. A woman might become a nun for several reasons. She might be the real thing: a person with a genuine vocation to place her relationship with God above all else. She might be attracted to the ordered, peaceful life of prayer, work, and study that the convent offered. Women could pray and work in any *estat*; but at a time when intellectual opportunities were available only to the few, the convent provided a level of education that was not available elsewhere to women. Less in accord with the intended purpose of convent life was the custom of using it as an alternative of last resort for women who were for any reason unmarriageable: those whose families could not afford a dowry (money and/or land settled upon a girl at marriage); or those who were simply too unattractive to snare a mate. Since Chaucer's Prioress is specifically described as attractive, she may have been consigned to a convent for reasons of family convenience, because it is clear that she lacks a true religious calling. In Madame Eglentyne, Chaucer depicts charm without substance. Although the Prioress is appealing, she represents the decline of convent life in the Middle Ages, from a haven for saints and scholars to a finishing school for proper, but vapid, ladies.

The Prioress is exceedingly well-mannered. She smiles sweetly and demurely, and uses only the mildest oath. She knows how to chant the liturgy, intoning it through her nose in a seemly manner. She can speak

French, a genteel accomplishment then as now, but only as it is taught in England, not as it is spoken in Paris; in other words, there is a superficiality even to such limited learning as she has. Many behavior manuals available in the fourteenth century stressed proper behavior at table, and the Prioress has learned these social graces. She doesn't drop bits of food on the way to her mouth, nor does she allow bits of food to fall onto her breast; she does not "wet her fingers in the deep [bowls of] sauce" (I, A, 129) when she dips a bit of food into them; she wipes her upper lip clean of grease before she drinks from her wine glass; she reaches for her food politely rather than grabbing for it in a rude, lower-class manner. All this detail shows that she was "well taught" (I, A, 127) on how to behave in company. But what has this to do with the religious life? The fact that the Prioress knows such "courtesy" (I, A, 132) suggests that she is attracted more to fashionable society than to the convent.

Other details of Madame Eglentyne's portrait show that in conducting herself as a courtly lady she is implicitly violating the spirit of her religious commitment. "Great deportment," a pleasant, "amiable," "stately . . . manner" (I, A, 137–140), are all qualities more suitable to the courtly lady than to the nun. A nun is not supposed to "counterfeit the manners / Of court" or worry if she is being "held worthy of reverence" in society (I, A, 139–141). The cumulative effect of all these details would indicate to the medieval reader that the Prioress's values were secular, not religious; and the point would be reinforced by her behavior with animals.

In the medieval convent, pets were either strongly discouraged or downright forbidden. Since the nun was supposed to direct her love toward God alone, a pet would be a distraction, a worldly affection that the nun should reject. But the Prioress is emotionally overinvolved with animals, particularly small, cute ones:

> She was so charitable and so pitous
> She wolde wepe, if that she saugh a mous
> Kaught in a trappe, if it were deed or bledde.

> She was so charitable and so full of pity
> That she would weep, if she saw a mouse
> Caught in a trap, if it were dead or bled.

(I, A, 143–145)

This behavior often appeals to animal lovers in Chaucer's modern audience, but "charity" for the medieval nun is supposed to mean love directed upward toward God, not directed downward toward what medieval people regarded as lower beings.

Even worse than weeping for a mouse is the Prioress's behavior with her dogs. Some medieval religious orders allowed cats; but dogs were never allowed. Despite this prohibition,

> *Of smale houndes hadde she that she fedde*
> *With rosted flessh, or milk and wastel-breed.*
> *But soore wepte she if oon of hem were deed.*

> She had small hounds that she fed
> With roasted flesh, or milk and white bread,
> And she wept bitterly if one of them were dead.

(I, A, 146–148)

Little lapdogs were popular accessories of the flirtatious courtly lady; she could cuddle cutely with them, thus displaying her "tender heart" (I, A, 150) and in general looking utterly adorable. Such behavior would be silly and trivial even in a marriageable young girl, and it is entirely inappropriate for a nun. The Prioress's feeding the small hounds with roast meat and white bread—both culinary treats in the Middle Ages—shows that her convent is extravagant (religious rules prescribed humble fare) and that leftovers are not being given to the poor. The Prioress weeps for dead pets, but she should be weeping for the sorry state of her own spiritual development. Her "conscience" (I, A, 150) is misinformed about the proper object of her tender-hearted solicitude.

Her sense of appropriateness is also defective in the matter of her *array*. Nuns were supposed to be indifferent to their appearance and unconcerned with clothing. The habits or uniform apparel adopted by religious orders (the wearing of which was abandoned only in the mid-twentieth century) were based on the garb of widows. Simple, modest, and inexpensive, the nun's habit was supposed to contrast with the lavish *array* of wealthy women in secular life. Thus the Prioress violates the spirit of religious life by wearing an attractively pleated wimple or head-dress, an elegant cloak, and an expensive set of coral prayer beads. Most questionable of all is her brooch. If lavish and costly clothing was forbidden to a nun, all the more was jewelry. Worse, this gold brooch contains an inscription: "*Amor vincit omnia*," love conquers all (I, A, 162). What kind of love is suggested by this brooch? The love of God or the love of a man? Chaucer leaves the matter tantalizingly unresolved. But in presenting a character who conforms to the stereotype of the courtly lady, with her small nose, her grey eyes, her small, soft, red mouth, Chaucer calls our attention to the moral ambiguity surrounding a person whose appearance and behavior fit her more for secular life than for religious life.

THE MONK

The Prioress is only the first of a group of characters through whom Chaucer, gently but firmly, points to problems in the life of the medieval church. Like the Prioress, the Monk is ill-suited to religious life. Like her, he demonstrates a mismatch between man and vocation in two ways: *array* and behavior. But unlike the Prioress, who seems innocently unconscious of her deviations from the norms of religious life, the Monk has a fully developed philosophy of rebellion.

In appearance, Chaucer's Monk is "a manly man, able to be an abbot" (I, A, 167). No ascetic, he wears the best clothing and eats the best food. The narrator Geffrey observes the Monk's *array*:

> *I seigh his sleves purfiled at the hond*
> *With grys, and that the fyneste of a lond;*
> *And for to festne his hood under his chyn,*
> *He hadde of gold ywroght a ful curious pyn;*
> *A love-knotte in the gretter ende ther was.*

> I saw his sleeves lined at the hand
> With gray fur, and that the finest in the land;
> And to fasten his hood under his chin
> He had a very curious pin wrought of gold;
> There was a love-knot in the larger end.

(I, A, 193–197)

According to the sumptuary laws, fur-trimmed clothing was supposed to be worn only by the nobility; then as now, fur signaled wealth and status. Decorations of precious metal worn on the clothing—like the Monk's gold brooch in the shape of a love-knot—were also common among the upper classes. Like the Prioress's gold brooch, the Monk's sends a worldly message of wealth and love.

The Monk's deviation from *estat* norms goes beyond *array*. He likes to hunt (an upper-class sport), and he keeps "many a fine horse . . . in stable" (I, A, 168) for that purpose. But since monks took vows of poverty, meaning rejection of ownership of worldly possessions, keeping a stable of hunting horses is a violation of his religious rule. He has access to money and a taste for luxury. Clothing and possessions have always indicated wealth, but to medieval people, being "full fat" (I, A, 200), exhibiting the evidence of a hearty diet, was as much a status symbol as being thin is today. The consumption of rich foods was believed to manifest itself in just such an oily, glowing complexion and plump frame as the Monk has. "Steaming like a furnace" (I, A, 202), the Monk has assimilated unto himself the characteristics of cooking food. Geffrey admires the Monk's hearty appetite for life's good dinners:

> He was nat pale as a forpyned goost.
> A fat swan loved he best of any roost.
>
> He was not as pale as a pining ghost;
> He loved a fat swan best of any roast.

(I, A, 205–206)

But Geffrey's seemingly unconscious reference to a pale, emaciated ghost reminds the reader that, by virtue of his commitment to the religious life, the Monk is supposed to be an ascetic. Asceticism means the deprivation of the body for the sake of the soul. Medieval people, especially religious, were encouraged to fast, so that their minds might turn away from earthly things toward the Lord. Some medieval saints even starved themselves to death in an excess of this practice. (Today we might label their condition anorexia.) The Monk's devotion to the pleasures of the hunt and the table are manifestations of a larger refusal to follow either the letter or the spirit of monastic life.

As mentioned earlier, in the discussion of the Prioress, one symptom of the decline of religious life in the fourteenth century was the practice of using religious orders as a kind of occupation of last resort for those members of society without other options. If convents began to fill up with unmarriageable daughters, monasteries, too, experienced an influx of men with no genuine calling to the religious life. Such monks would be religious in name only, evading their vows whenever possible. Chaucer's Monk not only does this—most conspicuously in the matter of the vow of poverty—but also in the matter of obedience.

Monks then and now take vows of obedience, both to the superior as head of their monastery (the abbot) and to the rule of their order. The rule of a religious order is a set of bylaws for the organization. All members agree to submit to the uniform way of life described in their order's rule, much as one who joins an organization today agrees to observe its regulations. A major difference between modern organizations and medieval religious orders, however, is that violation of monastic rules was considered sinful.

Chaucer's Monk, exhibiting a degree of independent-mindedness unacceptable in an age valuing *auctoritee*, proclaims his belief that he can legitimately remain a member of his order while flouting all its rules.

> *The reule of Seint Maure or of Seint Beneit—*
> *By cause that it was old and somdel streit*
> *This ilke Monk leet olde thynges pace.*

> The rule of St. Maurus and St. Benedict—
> Because they were both old and somewhat strict,
> This same monk let these old things pass.

(I, A, 173–175)

St. Maurus and St. Benedict wrote rules for religious orders. To medieval people, the fact that rules were "old" gave them the more weight and authority, and the fact that they were "strict" was all the more justification for the effort expended in observing them. To medieval people, it is wrong of the Monk to let these "old things pass" as if they had no significance.

Unlike moderns, medievals did not believe that they had the right to make decisions for themselves. They believed that all must obey their hierarchical superiors and any written regulations appropriate to their *estat*. So when the Monk decides he does not "give . . . a pulled hen"—care a bit—about the "text" forbidding monks to hunt, or to leave their "cloister" or enclosure (I, A, 177, 181), he is committing a sin of intellectual rebellion. But he is so convincing that the gullible Geffrey agrees with him. Geffrey even chimes in with his own criticisms of the monastic life, showing how the Monk's evil influence can corrupt even a sweet innocent like Geffrey. Too impressed by the "manly man" (I, A, 167) with his fine horse and commanding presence, Geoffrey has momentarily forgotten the principles guiding religious life:

> *What sholde he studie and make hymselven wood,*
> *Upon a book in cloystre alwey to poure,*
> *Or swynken with his handes, and laboure,*
> *As Austyn bit? How shal the world be served?*

> Why should he study and make himself mad,
> Always poring upon a book in cloister,
> Or work with his hands, and labor,
> As Augustine bid? How shall the world be served?

(I, A, 184–187)

Why should a monk study? Why work? Every medieval reader would know why: because these activities—study and work—are two of the three key elements (the other is prayer) to which a man commits himself when he takes monastic vows. A monk should do what St. Augustine bid because that eminent early church theologian wrote the rule to which the Monk has committed himself. "How shall the world be served?" All know the answer to this rhetorical question: Not by monks, who have pledged themselves precisely to abandon the service of the world, and to serve God alone.

THE FRIAR

Chaucer depicts the fourteenth-century church as heavily populated with worldly religious like the Monk and the Prioress. Such another is the Friar. In the portraits of both Prioress and Monk, Chaucer concentrates on clothing details; in his depiction of the Friar, he relies on behavior. The ascetic life of poverty, chastity, and obedience has no more appeal for this Friar than it did for the Prioress or the Monk. Instead, he is preoccupied with the issues that also engage moderns: sex and money.

Like the Prioress and the Monk, the Friar is a member of a religious order; like them, he is supposed to be committed to poverty, chastity, and obedience; like them, he violates his vows. With the Friar's portrait it becomes even more apparent that Chaucer saw abuses in the church of his day. But his criticism is filtered through the gentle and approving Geffrey. A dual vision emerges: Chaucer's as opposed to Geffrey's. Where the poet sees corruption, the narrator sees interesting facts. Geffrey, a man in a holiday mood, reports but does not judge; Chaucer leaves it up to his readers to do so.

Because members of religious orders were expected to enclose themselves within their convents or monasteries, Chaucer must explain their being on pilgrimage at all. Like the Monk, an "outrider" (I, A, 166) in charge of taking care of business outside the monastery, the Friar has a job that involves travel. He is a "limiter" (I, A, 209) who travels from place to place begging for contributions to his order. Properly done, this was legitimate; it was the equivalent of the fund-raising work of charitable organizations today. But abuses could arise if the individual entrusted with financial responsibility was dishonest; and this is the case with the Friar.

When a friar leaves his monastery, he is not supposed to seize the opportunity to violate his vows. But this Friar's portrait is basically a list of sins. "He was a noble supporter of his order," Geffrey says (I, A, 214), but the effect is ironic, for everything Geffrey describes the Friar doing is illegitimate. First, the Friar violates his vow of chastity. Knowing "much of dalliance and fair language" (I, A, 211), he is a smooth operator with the ladies. "He had made full many a marriage / Of young women at his own cost" (I, A, 212–213), not out of generosity to impoverished maidens, but because that is what one does for women whom one has impregnated but cannot marry. The Friar likes the pleasures of the tavern as well as the bed. The "franklins" or landowners and the "worthy women of the town" (I, A, 217) knew him well, as did the innkeepers and bartenders in the local taverns. When Geffrey comments that the Friar likes the company of such people better than that of lepers and beggars, the medieval audience would have noted that such worldly values are inappropriate in a follower of Christ.

These personal moral faults, serious enough in themselves, are magnified by the Friar's misuse of his sacramental authority:

> *For he hadde power of confessioun,*
> *As seyde hymself, moore than a curat,*
> *For of his ordre he was licenciat.*
> *Ful swetely herde he confessioun,*
> *And plesaunt was his absolucioun:*
> *He was an esy man to yeve penaunce,*
> *Ther as he wiste to have a good pitaunce.*

> For he had powers of confession
> As he said himself, more than a curate,
> For he was licensed by his order.
> He heard confession very sweetly,
> And his absolution was pleasant;
> He was an easy man to give penance,
> Wherever he hoped to get a good pittance.

(I, A, 218–224)

A sacrament in the Catholic church is an act believed to have supernatural efficacy. Penance, one of the seven sacraments, involves confessing one's sins to a priest and requesting God's forgiveness as mediated through that priest. A local priest, a curate, had "power of confession," the power to hear and forgive sins, by virtue of his priesthood. So did the "licensed" Friar. Why would the Friar try to convince believers that he had "power of confession / . . . more than a curate," in effect setting himself up as a competitor? His motive is to solicit contributions in return for hearing confessions "sweetly" and giving absolution "pleasantly." Confessing one's sins was supposed to be uncomfortable; if making a donation could make it easier, many would consider the money well spent. But the confessor's proper role is to correct the sinner and impose a penance, a punishment harsh enough to act as a deterrent. The Friar's acceptance of a donation (a "pittance") in return for mitigating the distressing aspects of the sacrament is, then, contrary to its purpose and constitutes an abuse of the "power of confession." The Friar has thoroughly rationalized this sinful behavior, however. He regards giving money to a "poor order" of friars as a "sign that a man is well shriven," thoroughly forgiven of his sins (I, A, 225–226). Some people cannot weep and pray, so they give money. This self-serving attitude makes him "the best beggar in his house" (I, A, 251).

In addition to taking money for hearing confessions, the Friar has a side business selling "knives / And pins" (I, A, 233–234) like a traveling salesman. Because he dresses very well, "not like a cloisterer / With a threadbare cope, like a poor student" (I, A, 259–260), it is clear that he does not return all the money he collects to his order. Instead, he skims off the top, taking money even from a "poor widow [who] had not a shoe" (I, A, 253) to put good clothes on his own back. Since the Friar is a cloisterer, he should be wearing a threadbare cope; as in the case of many other characters in Chaucer, violation of clothing norms signals other forms of deviancy as well. The Friar's *array*, like his overall approach to life, indicates an increasing problem in the medieval church: members of religious orders were using the wealth donated to their orders for their own personal gain.

THE MERCHANT

With the Merchant's portrait, Chaucer's commentary on religious life is briefly interrupted with a description of a character in secular life. The Merchant is less well-developed a character than, for example, the Prioress or the Monk; but his portrait highlights a major theme in Chaucer's writing: money and commerce. Experienced in the economic world, Chaucer is the most practical of medieval writers. At a time when much literature was highly abstract, Chaucer is concrete. Like the Merchant himself, Chaucer is concerned with the "increase of . . . winning" (I, A, 275)—profit, and the various factors that affect it.

As a man of the business world, however, Chaucer also must have known many men like the Merchant who, despite giving the appearance of being affluent, were actually "in debt" (I, A, 280). The Merchant is active in trade, buying and selling, bargaining, much involved in the attempt to make money. But such enterprises were fraught with risk; there would be no need to worry about keeping the sea safe between Middleburg and Orwell were it not for pirates, and even without pirates all sea trade was subject to the vagaries of tides and weather. So one involved in a high-risk occupation like the Merchant might conceal mountains of debt beneath a "stately" demeanor (I, A, 281). In the Merchant's commercial world, all is not what it appears to be.

THE CLERK OF OXFORD

The Clerk lives in another world, the world of the medieval educational system. Then as now, the city of Oxford was the site of a great university. Like the religious life, the world of the schools often attracted men with no particular aptitude for the scholarly life; but the Clerk is not one of these. The Clerk represents the genuine commitment to the life of the mind that should motivate students medieval and modern.

Two main traits characterize the Clerk: poverty and sincerity. Because university life removes a man from the kind of money-making activities a man like the Merchant might pursue, the Clerk is poor. This is obvious in his *array* and appearance: unlike the well-dressed Prioress, Monk, and Friar, the Clerk wears a threadbare outer garment; unlike the plump Monk, the Clerk's body is so thin as to look "hollow"; even his horse is "lean . . . as a rake" (I, A, 287–288). The reason for this is that the Clerk "had not yet gotten himself a benefice," or church office, which would provide him with an income (I, A, 291). Although the "yet" implies that he might do so in the future, at this point he is not "worldly" enough to have such a position (I, A, 292). He would rather use what little money he has to further his education:

> *For hym was levere have at his beddes heed*
> *Twenty bookes, clad in blak or reed,*
> *Of Aristotle and his philosophie*
> *Than robes riche, or fithele, or gay sautrie.*

> For he would rather have at his bed's head
> Twenty books, clad in black or red,
> Of Aristotle and his philosophy
> Than rich robes, or a fiddle, or a merry harp.

(I, A, 293–296)

Until the invention of the printing press reduced the cost of books, books were hand-copied and very expensive. So the Clerk's twenty books represents a large library for a poor student; no wonder the Clerk has "but little gold in coffer" (I, A, 298). But he would rather spend his money this way than on the trappings of elegant university life. He is not an empty-headed young gentleman who is only at the university to enjoy himself. Chaucer's Clerk is a real student, the genuine article, as is also shown in his speech.

The hallmark of the Clerk's speech is sincerity. A "sober" or serious man (I, A, 289), he considers every word and refrains from idle chatter:

> Of studie took he moost cure and moost heede.
> Noght o word spak he moore than was neede,
> And that was seyd in forme and reverence,
> And short and quyk and ful of hy sentence.

> Of study he took most care and most heed.
> He spoke not one word more than was needed,
> And that was said in proper form and reverence
> And short and quick and full of high sentence.

(I, A, 303–306)

"High sentence" is a medieval term for the highest and most important purpose of speech: to teach a moral lesson. If it is true to his description in the "General Prologue," we can expect the "Clerk's Tale" to be didactic, which it is; but we might also expect it to be "short and quick," which it decidedly is not (perhaps Chaucer's little joke). From his description the Clerk seems solemn and a bit dull; but in the context of a society in which Chaucer sees so many hypocrites, the Clerk stands out as an ideal role model for academics: "Gladly would he learn and gladly teach" (I, A, 308).

THE SERGEANT OF THE LAW

The Oxford Clerk has removed himself from the world of profit and loss inhabited by the Merchant; with the Sergeant of the Law we return to that world. The legal profession in the Middle Ages, much like its counterpart today, allowed a man of common birth to make an excellent living on the basis of professional training. Chaucer describes his Lawyer in terms of legal competence (which shows in turn that Chaucer was familiar with the operations of courts and lawyers himself). The Lawyer is admirable, "rich in excellence" (I, A, 311), "discreet," and "of great reverence" (I, A, 312)—just the kind of lawyer one might employ today. This Lawyer really knows his law, as one would expect of one who had often been a "Justice . . . in the Assizes" (I, A, 314), the district civil court. He knows all the cases and legal decisions (I, A, 323) from the time of King William I (1066–1087), a major feat of memorization. Such expertise is well-rewarded:

For his science and for his heigh renoun,
Of fees and robes hadde he many oon.

Because of his learning and his high renown,
He had many fees and robes.

                                                          (I, A, 316–317)

A successful lawyer like him makes money and has good clothing. "Robes," all hand-made, were, like books, expensive in the Middle Ages. Such a man would have sufficient income to invest in real estate too. Every property was a potential purchase, subject to his sole ownership, possession in "fee simple" (I, A, 319), a term used in real estate law to this day to indicate total and complete ownership.

With his portrait of the Lawyer, Chaucer calls the reader's attention to the rising affluence of a new professional class. But Chaucer undercuts his portrait of this man so "rich in excellence" (I, A, 311) by suggesting that, as in the case of the Merchant, all is not entirely as it appears to be. Twice the narrator describes the lawyer as "seeming": "He seemed rich" (I, A, 313), "He seemed busier than he was" (I, A, 322). "Seeming" suggests a deceptiveness in the Lawyer's character. Why, for example, would a man who had a rich wardrobe wear a simple outer garment on this pilgrimage? By these few suggestions of a disparity between the Lawyer's appearance and his reality, nowhere fully developed, Chaucer is perhaps alluding to distrust some feel for members of the legal profession.

THE FRANKLIN

As would be expected considering the Lawyer's high social position, he is accompanied by the Franklin, a country gentleman whose main character trait is his devotion to food. Medieval people were ambivalent about food as they were about other sensory pleasures. On the one hand, they were fond of great ceremonial meals featuring huge amounts of food and many elaborate courses. On the other hand, "feast" was opposed to "fast," the belief that to deny the body was to nourish the soul. In every way, the Franklin's description contrasts with the religious tradition of asceticism that was so much a part of medieval Christianity.

As "Epicurus' own son" (I, A, 336), a follower of the pagan philosopher Epicurus (c. 340–c. 270 B.C.), the Franklin believes that physical pleasure equals happiness. His portrait indicates that food is his main source of earthly joy. Specific items from the medieval menu are mentioned as being his particular favorites: bread, wine, ale, several varieties of "fish and flesh" (I,

A, 344). He requires seasonal "dainties" (I, A, 346), foods cooked in "poignant and sharp" (I, A, 352), heavily spiced sauces; he is a gourmet, sparing no expense on fresh foods and fine seasonings. As an extension of his personal love for food, the Franklin is a veritable St. Julian, patron saint of hospitality: he likes to have dinner guests, and his house is all ready for them.

> *His table dormant in his halle alway*
> *Stood redy covered al the longe day.*
>
> His table dormant in his hall always
> Stood ready for use all day long.
>
>   (I, A, 353–354)

Medieval people, even great householders, customarily did not have a table standing permanently in a room set aside exclusively for the purpose of dining, as houses of any size do today. Instead, they would set up a trestle table in the great hall or the largest public space in the house, dismantling it between meals so that the room could be used for other purposes. Ownership of a *table dormant* thus indicates more than typical commitment to food and to hospitality.

The Franklin's food habits situate him in an upper-class *estat*; he is a great "householder" (I, A, 339), a man of wealth and property. Nowhere does Chaucer mention noble birth; the Franklin is characterized by his affluence and the way he chooses to display it. The social contacts made by such entertaining might well contribute to his becoming "knight of the shire" (I, A, 356), representative of his district in Parliament. Political power follows social prestige, and in Chaucer's day both were consequences of the increasing prosperity of those born outside the nobility.

THE FIVE GUILDSMEN

Farther down the social scale, but no less important as an economic indicator, are the Guildsmen: the Haberdasher, Carpenter, Weaver, Dyer, and Tapestry-Maker. The medieval guild, a forerunner of the modern trade union, was a group of skilled craftsmen banded together for mutual economic protection. A guild would set wage standards, engage in quality control, train apprentices, and accept new members. Since despite their diverse trades all these Guildsmen wear the livery or uniform of a single guild, it can be assumed that they are members of a guild large enough to encompass a variety of crafts. The affluence of tradesmen such as these followed from the reduction of population caused by the recurrent waves of plague during the fourteenth century. Simply because there were fewer of them, skilled tradesmen could command higher prices for their labor.

The resulting prosperity of people such as the five Guildsmen, however, led to social adjustments that their hierarchical superiors found painful. An impoverished member of the nobility might have less cash available for conspicuous consumption than a rich tradesman. This led to the issue of *array* appropriate to one's *estat*. Medieval people believed that *array* should signify the social class of its wearer. When the consumerism of the *nouveaux riches* began to threaten the *estat*-consciousness of the nobility, laws were passed to prevent the likes of the Guildsmen from aping the manners of their betters. The details of the Guildsmen's collective portrait indicate, however, that such laws were ineffective. The Guildsmen have "fresh and newly decorated gear"; their knives are mounted "not with brass" as would befit their lower social class but "all with silver," as were their belts and pouches (I, A, 365–368). Decoration, being unnecessary, connotes luxury, all the more so when it is of precious metal.

Similarly, the Guildsmen's wives indulge in the kind of conspicuous consumption that is symptomatic of social climbing. They like to be called "madame" as if they were of noble blood, and they lay claim to precedence in religious processions. To appear worthy of such honors, they wear "mantel[s] royally borne" (I, A, 378), capes so long that they had to be carried in a stately fashion, by pages, as if the wearers were royalty. As in the modern wedding ceremony, the wearing of flowing garments and trains lends dignity to the occasion. The Guildsmen's wives wear enough drapery to require train-bearers, another indicator of high *estat*. Many medieval commentators saw this blatant usurpation of the prerogatives of the upper classes as a sign of frightening social upheaval.

THE COOK

Bringing their own Cook with them on pilgrimage is another sign of the Guildsmen's affluence. This Cook is characterized in terms of his profession: the foods the Cook could cook (chicken, boiled with the marrow-bone, stew, pie); the culinary techniques he had mastered (roasting, seething or simmering, broiling, and frying); his knowledge of spices and of London ale. But Geffrey notices that the Cook's attention to hygienic standards is less than ideal: he has an unappetizing sore on his shin. Since many diseases were believed to be communicated through food, the

Guildsmen's pretentiousness in retaining their own Cook might become a disadvantage.

THE SHIPMAN

Nowhere is Geffrey's general attitude of approval more noticeable than in the description of the Shipman. Even the term *shipman* is a euphemism, for this man of the sea seems rather to be a pirate:

> *Of nyce conscience took he no keep.*
> *If that he faught and hadde the hyer hond,*
> *By water he sente hem hoom to every lond.*

> He took no heed of delicate conscience;
> If he fought and had the upper hand,
> He sent them home by water to every land.

(I, A, 398–400)

He had no delicate conscience; when he got the upper hand in a fight he drowned his opponents. Despite the Shipman's noticeable character flaw, however, Geffrey seems rather to like him too. Despite his sinister appearance, his "brown hue" or sunburned skin, his "dagger hanging on a cord / . . . about his neck," Geffrey sees the Shipman as "a good fellow" (I, A, 392–395). He admires the Shipman's knowledge of seamanship and his familiarity with all the harbors and havens. The obvious disparity between the description of the Shipman and Geffrey's genial attitude constitutes part of the characterization of Geffrey himself, and contributes to the reader's growing sense that Chaucer the poet might have a more censorious point of view than Geffrey the pilgrim.

THE DOCTOR OF PHYSIC

So far, we have met several less than perfect people who might well need such a pilgrimage to pray for forgiveness. The Monk, the Prioress, the Merchant, the Franklin, the Guildsmen and their Cook, and the Shipman are poor representatives of the Christian church on its journey through this life to the afterlife. Even measured by a more lenient ideal than that of the religious pilgrimage, the next pilgrim, the Doctor of Physic or Physician, falls short. This man fails to meet the highest standards of professional ethics. Here is a character type not unknown in modern medicine: the well-trained doctor who is only in it for the money.

Medical training in the Middle Ages was book-learning, not experimental or experiential training. The medieval reverence for old books meant that, even in science, the older the source, the better. Like all his medieval peers, the Physician has studied medical authorities who were ancient even then. The list includes such venerables as Hippocrates, who was born circa 460 B.C., and Galen, who lived in the second century A.D., in addition to such relative newcomers as John of Gaddesden and Bernard of Gordon, both of whom lived in Chaucer's own century. According to medieval beliefs, however, the older authorities would be better sources for medical wisdom than the newer.

In addition to old books on medicine and surgery, the typical medieval physician would know astrology. The position of the planets at the time of treatment was believed to be crucial; so a good doctor would have to be able to cast his patient's horoscope, employing this "natural magic" (I, A, 416) in the service of a cure. The physician must work to restore the balance of "humours," the "hot, or cold, or moist, or dry" qualities of the body (I, A, 420–421), a proper balance of which was believed to constitute health and an imbalance, illness. Possessor of this body of knowledge, Chaucer's Physician is defined as a well-educated medieval doctor.

But although he has knowledge and skill, he lacks dedication. Geffrey mentions, as if in passing, that the Physician's "study was but little on the Bible" (I, A, 438). The Physician is not a religious man. It is a mystery, then, why he might want to go on pilgrimage to Canterbury. He is engaged in his profession for the profit in it. Not that he is incompetent: "He was a true, perfect practitioner" who, once he knew the "cause" and the "root" of the patient's "harm," prescribed a "boote," a remedy (I, A, 422–424). It is not the Physician's behavior but his motivation that is wrong. He prescribes properly, but he also has a long-term alliance with the pharmacists "to send him drugs" (I, A, 426) for his patients, for the profit of both Physician and pharmacist. This behavior would be comparable to that of a modern physician who prescribed only the products of a drugstore in which the physician had a direct financial interest. Yet the Physician prescribes correctly. He is a good doctor in the sense of being skilled, but a bad one in that he uses his skills strictly for profit.

So successful is he that he is rich enough to wear luxurious fabrics, taffeta and silk, in bright colors, red and blue. Dyes were expensive in the Middle Ages, so brightly colored clothing became a status symbol. For such as he, the plague is a money-making opportunity:

He kepte that he wan in pestilence.
For gold in phisik is a cordial,
Therefore he lovede gold in special.

He kept what he earned during pestilence.
For gold in physic is a cordial,
Therefore he especially loved gold.

                                                    (I, A, 442–444)

If a doctor survived the plague himself, he would be wealthy (especially if he only treated patients who could pay and avoided the sickly poor). Geffrey treats himself to a little joke here: ground gold as a treatment ("in physic," or medicine) was believed to be good for a patient's heart; therefore, the Physician loves gold. Money is a "cordial," good for a Physician's heart.

THE WIFE OF BATH

Finances are similarly important in the description of the Wife of Bath. Two significant details alert the reader to her dual sources of income. First, she is a superlative weaver, better than those of Ypres and Ghent, two Belgian towns famous for their cloth-making industries. So the Wife is a working woman of the rising middle class, with a trade of her own. Second, she has had "five husbands at church door" (I, A, 460), that is, five legal marriages performed in the most public place in the medieval town. The church-door ceremony guarantees her inheritance rights. If she has had five husbands and is now a widow, she has inherited as well as earned income. These two details tell the medieval audience that she is a woman of independent means, perhaps even wealthy; her clothing reinforces that impression.

As a widow, the Wife of Bath should be dressed like one; instead, she is dressed in a showy costume: heavy coverchiefs, red stockings, new shoes, a broad hat, an overskirt, spurs on her feet. While some of this excess of cloth might be a way of exhibiting her own wares, her flamboyant *array* is just one aspect of her defiance of behavioral norms for women, a theme that will be developed fully in her prologue. In this abbreviated introduction to Chaucer's most fully developed character, her central traits emerge: assertiveness, rebelliousness, and sexuality.

Signaling her temperament, the Wife's face is "bold" and "red of hue" (I, A, 458). Boldly she seeks precedence in parish affairs: she allows no other to precede her at the Offering of the Mass, the point in the medieval liturgy at which all eyes are upon the bearer of the bread and wine to the altar. Boldly she joins a pilgrimage at a time when good women, especially widows, were advised to protect their virtue by staying at home. The Wife "knew much of wandering by the way" (I, A, 467); she has been to many of the pilgrimage sites still favored by pilgrims today, Rome and Jerusalem among them. She has a traveler's equipment, too, an ambler (a horse suitable for long journeys), and "sharp spurs" to urge him on (I, A, 473).

But the Wife's most noticeable trait is suggested by her complexion: her full-blooded sexuality. Alisoun's lustiness makes her Chaucer's most memorable creation. She has had five husbands, and, as Chaucer slyly suggests, that's not counting "other company in youth" (I, A, 461), other men she didn't marry. She knows all about "remedies of love" or solutions to love problems, and the "art" of love, the "old dance" of men and women (I, A, 475–476). Here is a woman of wide experience who presents herself to the Canterbury pilgrims as an authority on male-female relationships. Of all the Canterbury pilgrims, she is the one whose portrait is most clearly linked to her prologue and tale. Portrait, prologue, and tale form a well-woven unity worthy of the cloth-maker of Bath.

THE PARSON

In complete contrast to the earthy, lusty Wife is the Parson. Of all Chaucer's ecclesiastics, only the Parson measures up to the highest standards of perfection in his priestly vocation. In portraying the Parson, Chaucer is able not only to create a character but also to critique a system. Chaucer was not a religious rebel, but he was a critic. An astute observer of his world, he saw a flawed church and sinful churchmen. In creating one worthy Parson, he simultaneously describes the unworthiness of others. "A good man . . . of religion," like this Parson, is one poor in money but "rich in holy thought and work" (I, A, 477–479). To know what to preach, he must be "a learned man, a clerk"; to preach "Christ's gospel truly," he must practice it (I, A, 480–481). In describing his Parson, Chaucer is drafting a job description of the ideal Parson: an exemplary priest whose virtues serve as a pattern for the Christian life.

What this Parson does not do is as telling as what he does do. He doesn't curse for his tithes—that is, excommunicate people for not contributing a tenth of their incomes to their church. He does not seek a soft job saying prayers for the dead at St. Paul's Cathedral in London, leaving his rural "sheep encumbered in the mire" (I, A, 508) without their pastor; "he was a shepherd and not a mercenary" (I, A, 514). Although he is virtuous himself, he does not take a holier-than-thou attitude toward others. He does not concern himself with social status or flatter the rich; he corrects sinners "of high or low estate," and he expects no particular "pomp and reverence" in anyone's behavior toward him (I, A, 522, 525). By summarizing behaviors that the Parson avoids, Chaucer criticizes other parsons for engaging in those same behaviors.

What the Parson does do is summarized in the last two lines of his portrait:

> But Cristes loore and his apostles twelve
> He taughte; but first he folwed it hymselve.

> But Christ's lore and that of his apostles twelve
> He taught; but first he followed it himself.

(I, A, 527–528)

Putting Christian principles into practice is the area in which Chaucer perceives clerical failure. The adjectives describing this Parson show his perfection in his calling: he is "benign," "diligent," "patient," "holy," "virtuous" (I, A, 483–484, 515). One virtuous behavior is described specifically:

> Wyd was his parisshe, and houses fer asonder,
> But he ne lefte nat, for reyn ne thonder,
> In siknesse nor in meschief to visite
> The ferreste in his parisshe, muche and lite,
> Upon his feet, and in his hand a staf.

> His parish was wide, with houses far asunder,
> But, despite rain or thunder, he did not neglect
> To visit in sickness or in mishap
> The farthest house in his parish, great and small,
> Upon his feet, and in his hand a staff.

(I, A, 491–495)

The visual image of a walking man carrying a staff, traveling long distances to see the least of his parishioners, must have reminded the medieval audience of a common image in religious art: Christ the Good Shepherd. While many modern members of religious groups may not like to think of themselves as sheep—animals who appear docile, dependent, and malleable—medieval believers, accustomed to the use of both hierarchical and pastoral metaphors, focused on the caring protection such a shepherd would provide.

The leader modeling himself on Christ the Good Shepherd would give "noble example" (I, A, 496) to his followers: first he practices, then he preaches. Such a leader would be "gold," his followers a lesser metal, "iron"; and

> *if gold ruste, what shal iren do?*
> *For if a preest be foul, on whom we truste,*
> *No wonder is a lewed man to rust.*

> if gold rust, what shall iron do?
> For if a priest, in whom we trust, be foul,
> It is no wonder if a common man rusts.

(I, A, 500–502)

It is a shame, says Chaucer, if priests forget their exemplary role. There cannot be a "shiten" (dirty) "shepherd, and a clean sheep"; rather a priest must give "example . . . / By his cleanness, how his sheep should live" (I, A, 505–506). This is the whole point of priesthood: example. Clerical status must not merely confer privilege but require service. It is a telling criticism of the medieval church that Chaucer includes only one good religious in a group of eight: that ratio, eight to one, may suggest what Chaucer thought of the professional ecclesiastics of his day.

THE PLOWMAN

Like his brother the Parson, the Plowman is a good man by the different norms of his lower *estat*. A peasant farmer, he engages in the earthiest possible task, hauling dung. But even the lowliest, the medieval believer knew, could be first in the kingdom of heaven if, like the Plowman, he performed his duties with the right spiritual attitude:

> *A trewe swynkere and a good was he,*
> *Lyvynge in pees and parfit charitee.*
> *God loved he best with al his hoole herte*
> *At alle tymes, thogh him gamed or smerte,*
> *And thanne his neighebor right as hymselve.*

> He was a true worker and a good one,
> Living in peace and perfect charity,
> He loved God best with all his whole heart
> At all times, even if it hurt,
> And then his neighbor just as himself.

(I, A, 531–535)

A plowman who could "dig and delve / For Christ's sake" (I, A, 536–537), who paid his tithes in labor or property, is as good a man as the Parson. (Chaucer probably intends the familial relationship to underline this.) While the Plowman never gets a tale of his own, he stands as a representative of virtue in low places.

THE MILLER

Though higher on the social scale than the Plowman by virtue of his status as an independent tradesman, the Miller is paradoxically even more a creature of the earth than the hauler of dung. A "stout," "thick" man, "big . . . of brawn and also of bones," "short-shouldered" and "broad," the Miller is powerful enough to be a successful wrestler, or to rip a door off its hinges or "break it at a running with his head" (I, A, 545–546, 549, 551). With his red spade-like beard, his hairy nose-wart, and his wide, black nostrils, he is remarkably unattractive. Because medieval people believed that beauty was allied to virtue and, conversely, that physical ugliness indicated moral corruption, the Miller's dishonesty would have come as no surprise to them. Any miller could cheat his customers as this one did, by using his "thumb of gold" (I, A, 563) on the scale to charge for a false weight. Raucous, loud, and vulgar, the Miller, playing bagpipes, leads the parade of pilgrims out of London. Discordant speech and sound, plus thick physicality, make the reader expect exactly what we get from him: a dirty story of human behavior at its earthiest.

THE MANCIPLE

The Miller's portrait is followed by that of several of his fellow crooks and tricksters: two in secular life, the Manciple and the Reeve; and two in religious life, the Summoner and the Pardoner. All are guilty of medieval versions of white-collar crime: manipulation of finances for personal profit. Of the four, the two in secular life are lesser villains. Operating within the world of getting and spending, they compete only with other profiteers; at least they do not exploit simple believers. The Summoner and the Pardoner, on the other hand, exemplify abuses in the church of Chaucer's day. Of the two, the Pardoner, a conscious and deliberate sinner, is arguably the worst of Chaucer's sinners.

Each of these four malefactors engages in his own complex financial scam. The Manciple is the financial manager of an educational institution, an Inn of Court or law school. His job is to buy provisions for the school.

His scam is to buy for less than he is reimbursed by the school, and pocket the difference. But since the Manciple's victims are lawyers, famous for fraudulent dealings themselves, Geffrey asks,

> Now is nat that of God a ful fair grace
> That swich a lewed mannes wit shal pace
> The wisdom of an heep of lerned men?

> Now isn't that a very great grace of God
> That such a common man's wit shall surpass
> The wisdom of a heap of learned men?

(I, A, 573–575)

Geffrey is amused at the deception of a whole "heap" of educated deceivers by one less educated than they.

THE REEVE

Financial manipulation is also the stock in trade of the Reeve, a manager or overseer of an estate. His job is to sell the produce of the farm, the grain, sheep, cattle, dairy products, pigs, horses, livestock, and poultry. Like the Manciple, he skims off the profits that should be returned to his employer:

> He koude bettre than his lord purchace.
> Ful riche he was astored pryvely.
> His lord wel koude he plesen subtilly,
> To yeve and lene hym of his owene good,
> And have a thank, and yet a cote and hood.

> He could purchase better than his lord.
> He secretly provided for himself quite richly.
> He could subtly please his lord
> By giving and lending him his own goods,
> And have his thanks, and even a coat and hood.

(I, A, 608–612)

In the absence of written confirmation of transactions, it would be easy for the Reeve not to reimburse his lord for the full amount of a sale of the lord's farm products. With the money he has thus illicitly withheld, the Reeve engages in yet another layer of financial deception. Now more cash-rich than his employer, the Reeve lends his boss the money stolen from him. In return, the Reeve gets not only the lord's thanks, but also gifts—a coat and hood. Thus the Reeve abuses a position of trust for personal gain. The

Reeve has forsaken the honest toil of carpentry, a "good craft" (I, A, 613) and a productive one, and has substituted for it the barren manipulation of money.

THE SUMMONER

While the Manciple is not described physically at all and the Reeve only briefly, the Summoner's appearance is stressed. In keeping with medieval theories on physiognomy, the pseudoscience of reading character in the face, the Summoner would be seen as a man whose ugly body houses an equally ugly soul. So revolting that "of his visage children were afraid" (I, A, 628), he seems to suffer from a skin disease similar to severe acne that causes a facial rash and hair loss, and was unresponsive to the medical treatments of the day:

> *Ther nas quyk-silver, lytarge, ne brymstoon,*
> *Boras, ceruce, ne oille of tartre noon,*
> *Ne oynement that wolde clense and byte,*
> *That hym myghte helpen of his whelkes white,*
> *Nor of the knobbes sittynge on his chekes.*

> Neither quicksilver, lead ointment, nor brimstone would help him,
> Borax, ceruce, nor oil of tartar,
> Nor ointment that would cleanse and bite
> That might cure him of his white whelks,
> Nor of the knobs sitting on his cheeks.

> (I, A, 629–633)

While medieval people believed that such an affliction might be caused by dietary excess (the Summoner enjoyed garlic, onions, leeks, and strong wine, all of which were believed to contribute to skin problems), the main point of his physiological condition is as a metaphor for spiritual corruption. Modern medicine distinguishes physical illness from moral guilt, but medieval people saw disease as a symptom of and a punishment for sin.

What is the Summoner's sin? Again, as in the case of several other pilgrims, he is guilty of practicing his profession dishonestly. The job of the summoner was, as his title implies, to summon people to the courts which tried offenses against the church. In the American legal system today, a process-server has the analogous task of delivering a court summons. If upon finding the person being summoned, the modern process-server accepted a bribe and then lied to the court saying he could not locate the person, his offense would be similar to that of Chaucer's Summoner, who would accept bribes in cash or gifts from offenders against church law:

> *He wolde suffre for a quart of wyn*
> *A good felawe to have his concubyn*
> *A twelf month, and excuse hym atte fulle.*

> For a quart of wine, he would allow
> A good fellow to have his concubine
> For twelve months, and excuse him fully.

(I, A, 649–651)

The Summoner justifies his behavior on the basis of his contempt for the church judgments he is committed to enforce. For example, consider his handling of "cursing," or excommunication. Excommunication was a serious matter for medieval Christians. To excommunicate was to sever a church member from the community of believers; it deprived him or her of the sacraments essential to salvation. But the Summoner reduces this crucial spiritual matter to a cash transaction. For him, a bribe is a sufficient remedy for the "archdeacon's curse" (I, A, 655), and a cash payment (to him) is punishment enough:

> *But if a mannes soule were in his purs;*
> *For in his purs he sholde ypunysshed be.*

> But if a man's soul were in his purse,
> Then he should be punished in his purse.

(I, A, 656–657)

A man's soul is in his purse: this idea sums up the Summoner's attitude toward life. Cynical, greedy, worldly, he knows that the Christian cannot serve both God and money, and deliberately, in full consciousness, he chooses money.

THE PARDONER

Abuse of an ecclesiastical position for personal gain is the Pardoner's sin too. The Pardoner's job can only be understood after a brief excursion into two elements of medieval popular religion: the sale of relics and the sale of pardons or indulgences.

The Pardoner's wallet is "brimful of pardon, come from Rome all hot" (I, A, 687). What the Pardoner carries is a pardon or indulgence, a document testifying to the spiritual benefit gained from performing a virtuous deed. Medieval Christians believed that the individual soul would be judged after death and sent to heaven, hell, or purgatory, depending on its good or bad deeds in life. Both heaven and hell were permanent states; purgatory was temporary. The soul consigned to purgatory was destined for heaven but not pure enough to go there yet, requiring a time of purgation, or spiritual cleansing. Imagining purgatory as a kind of prison, and the punishment endured therein as limited to a quantifiable amount of time, gave rise to the concept that good deeds performed in this life could shorten the term of purgation for an individual soul. This time off for good behavior (to continue the prison metaphor) could be ensured on earth by means of performing good deeds of various sorts.

Making a cash contribution to a religious order or institution is just such a good deed. Abuses arose, however, in assigning a cash price to a spiritual benefit. A pardon such as the Pardoner sells would assure the believer of, for example, a year off from purgatory, in return for a contribution to the hospital which the Pardoner represents. Now, following the mathematical model, a contribution five times as large would give five years off one's purgatorial sentence, and so forth. The link between money and time off from purgatory seems to mean that the rich could buy their way to heaven. Clearly, this was an abuse of the religion founded by Christ, a poor man.

As if this were not bad enough, the Pardoner also sells relics. A relic is an object associated with a saint, perhaps even a part of a saint's body. The relic is supposed to remind the believer of the saint, much as a photograph brings its subject to mind today; to unsophisticated believers, however, it was only a short step to believing that a relic possessed magical powers derived from the saint. So such items commanded a good price and were treated as objects of great value by being stored in reliquaries made of precious metals, intricately carved, and studded with jewels. But not all relics were authentic. The Pardoner says that he has a piece of the Virgin Mary's veil and a piece of St. Peter's sail. The extreme unlikelihood of these fragile objects surviving for thirteen centuries makes it obvious that the Pardoner's relics are false and that his sole interest is in selling this profitable product to the naive:

> But with thise relikes, whan that he fond
> A povre person dwellynge upon lond,
> Upon a day he gat hym moore moneye
> Than that the person gat in monthes tweye.

But with these relics, when he found
A poor parson dwelling upon land,
In one day he got more money for himself
Than the parson got in two months.

(I, A, 701–704)

As the reader will recall, Chaucer's good churchman, his Parson, is a poor man who gives of his own meager resources to help others. One reason why such a Parson lacks funds is that his gullible parishioners are likely to spend their own limited funds on items like the Pardoner's false relics. The Pardoner, then, sells false relics. But even if the Pardoner's pardons were authentic, he sells them, too, in an abusive fashion by manipulating the simple faith of the poor. The Pardoner is a successful salesman because "he was in church a noble ecclesiast," a really talented preacher (I, A, 708). His prologue and tale will demonstrate the skill as a preacher which makes him an excellent pitchman for his phony wares.

Clever and interesting though the Pardoner is, the modern reader must remember that, by medieval standards, he is an evil man, a mortal sinner. Medieval theology made a distinction between mortal sin and venial sin. A sin was venial, or minor, if it represented a flaw in the sinner's relationship with God. A mortal sin was a major breach. In a modern analogy, a venial sin is like a marital argument, but a mortal sin is like a divorce. To sin mortally requires full consciousness of the seriousness of one's actions, followed by a free choice to do the evil action anyway. Both the Summoner and the Pardoner sinfully exploit the faith of others. But while the Summoner's prologue adds little to his characterization, the Pardoner is fully developed in his, as a conscious hypocrite perverting the good intentions of others to his own evil end. It is an irony that he is on this journey at all, as the pilgrimage to Canterbury is, ideally, a journey of faith.

Having introduced all the pilgrims assembled at the Tabard Inn in Southwark, Geffrey issues a warning to the reader. Geffrey says he will "speak plainly" (I, A, 727), clearly and accurately report what the pilgrims say, not edit or censor it:

Whoso shal telle a tale after a man,
He moot reherce as ny as evere he kan
Everich a word.

Whoever shall retell another man's tale,
He must repeat, as closely as ever he can,
His every word.

(I, A, 731–733)

His tale-tellers are, he reminds us, of various *estats* or *degrees*. Common men might speak "rudely" (I, A, 734), and he must repeat their every word anyway. So, reader, don't blame poor Geffrey if you find anything offensive, any "villainy," in the tales; his "wit is short," and he can only "rehearse," or repeat, what he hears (I, A, 726, 746, 732).

Having thus applied this warning label, Chaucer introduces another character, Harry Bailly, our Host, the tavern-keeper of the Tabard Inn. "Bold of his speech," a "merry man," Harry decides to drop everything and join the "merry . . . company" of pilgrims (I, A, 755, 757, 764). Sociable as his occupation would suggest, Harry proposes an entertainment and sets up ground rules. Each pilgrim shall tell two tales on the way to Canterbury and two coming back; the teller of the best tale will win a "supper at all our cost" (I, A, 799) upon their return to the Tabard; and Harry will be the moderator, reporter, and judge of the proceedings. All agree to Harry Bailly's terms.

The introduction of the character of Harry Bailly is a masterstroke on Chaucer's part. Harry is a principle of organization, a link holding the tales together and binding them to the pilgrimage frame. He will appear in his role as moderator and judge at various points in the links between the tales, becoming a significant personality in his own right (see Appendix I). Thus Harry Bailly provides a principle of order unifying a diverse group of pilgrims and tales, keeping them on the right path to their goal: Canterbury Cathedral.

"Forth we ride" (I, A, 825), Canterbury pilgrims and readers medieval and modern, on our journey. As luck would have it, or as if there were a guiding principle of order overseeing this pilgrimage, lots are drawn and "the cut fell to the Knight" (I, A, 845) to tell the first tale. This is only appropriate, for he is the highest ranking pilgrim, the first to be introduced.

> And he bigan with right a myrie cheere
> His tale anon, and seyde as ye may heere.

> And he began, with a right a merry cheer,
> His tale anon, and said as you may hear.

(I, A, 857–858)

SUGGESTIONS FOR FURTHER READING

Bloom, Harold, ed. and intro. *Geoffrey Chaucer's "The General Prologue."* New York: Chelsea House, 1988. This collection of essays illustrates a variety of critical approaches.

Bowden, Muriel. *A Commentary on the General Prologue to The Canterbury Tales*. 2nd ed. New York: Macmillan, 1967. Bowden's exhaustive interpretation of each of the portraits is an essential source for the close study of this text.

Braswell-Means, Laurel. "A New Look at an Old Patient: Chaucer's Summoner and Medieval Physiognomia." *Chaucer Review* 25, no. 3 (1991): 266–275. Medieval physiognomical theories illuminate Chaucer's portraits, especially with reference to the Summoner's skin disease; Braswell-Means's article is an example of the application of medieval scientific ideas to Chaucer's description of the pilgrims.

Duby, Georges. *The Three Orders: Feudal Society Imagined*. Trans. Arthur Goldhammer. Chicago: University of Chicago Press, 1980. Duby demonstrates the all-pervasiveness of the tripartite formula (those who work, those who fight, and those who pray) as a descriptor of medieval society.

Eberle, Patricia J. "Commercial Language and the Commercial Outlook in the *General Prologue*." *Chaucer Review* 18, no. 2 (1983): 161–174. Eberle discusses the role of the "language of the marketplace" in the descriptions of the pilgrims.

Hodges, Laura F. "A Reconsideration of the Monk's Costume." *Chaucer Review* 26, no. 2 (1991): 133–146. Hodges argues that, contrary to prevailing critical opinion, the Monk's *array* is acceptable when judged by "varying dress regulations of the religious orders" of the Middle Ages.

Mann, Jill. *Chaucer and Medieval Estates Satire*. Cambridge: Cambridge University Press, 1973. Mann shows how the "General Prologue" is "an example of a neglected medieval genre . . . the literature dealing with the 'estates' of society."

2. The goddess Fortuna and her wheel. MS. Douce 332, fol. 58r. By permission of the Bodleian Library, University of Oxford.

The Knight's Tale

For fallyng nys nat but an aventure.
For falling is nothing but chance.

(I, A, 2722)

By chance the Knight tells the first tale; and chance shapes its plot. In the visual arts of the Middle Ages, a key image was that of the goddess Fortuna and her ever-turning wheel (see photo 2). Men striving for worldly advancement were imagined as climbing onto Fortuna's wheel at the bottom. Reaching the top of the wheel symbolized success. But the goddess Fortuna is a woman and thus, according to medieval beliefs, changeable by nature. At any time, without warning, she could spin her wheel, sending the overachievers at the top crashing to the bottom. So, medieval people thought, was the nature of human success: a brief and transitory interlude of "joy" before inevitable "woe" (I, A, 2841). This dreary world-view was not expected, however, to engender despair in the medieval Christian, for transience was characteristic only of earthly happiness, not of the eternal bliss of heaven. The characters in the "Knight's Tale," being pre-Christians, have no inkling of the everlasting reward promised to the Canterbury pilgrims at the end of their life's journey. The only consolation available to them is the consolation of philosophy. Their story shows that chance, fate, Fortuna's spinning wheel, *aventure*—however one names the unpredictable—are part of a larger universal order.

The "Knight's Tale" is a romance, a popular literary form for several hundred years before Chaucer. The romance is a tale of love and courage featuring noble characters who experience only the most elevated emotions described in the loftiest diction, or high style. Compared to modern narrative forms such as the short story or novel, the romance has several distinguishing features. For one thing, the narrative pace of the romance is slow, stately, and dignified. While moderns often praise a novel for being a page-turner that the reader could not put down, medieval people valued slow pace, as in a procession. Again like the procession, the longer a romance narrative was, the more importance was attached to the events narrated. Sometimes the story line stops entirely, interrupted by a long, detailed description. This word-painting can be thought of as the verbal artist's attempt to approximate the work of the visual artist, inviting the reader to stop and look. Long speeches perform a similar function: they ask the reader to stop and listen, to think carefully about serious thoughts, what medieval people termed "high sentence."

The most noticeable difference between modern fictional forms and the medieval romance, however, is in characterization. Romance characters fall into recognizable types: the brave young hero, the beautiful heroine, the wise ruler. As types, they lack individuality. In the novel, characters are sharply drawn; Huck Finn cannot be confused with Jim, and, although there are four Bennet daughters in Jane Austen's *Pride and Prejudice*, each has distinguishing traits. But if the first-time reader has difficulty telling Palamon and Arcite apart, this cannot solely be attributed to inexperience with medieval literature. Palamon and Arcite are indeed very similar, in fact all but indistinguishable. This is deliberate on Chaucer's part and an element of the overall plan of the tale: since each of these young men is equally worthy of winning the lovely Emelye, the outcome is attributable solely to *cas*, *aventure*, or Fortune.

The action is set in ancient Athens. Theseus, its duke, has just returned from conquering the Amazons, the kingdom of women, those upstarts who thought they could do without men. To solidify the peace he has taken to wife Hippolyta, queen of the Amazons. As the story begins, Theseus is returning to Athens with his bride and her sister Emelye. In the interests of brevity, the Knight will omit the story of the conquest of the Amazons; but medieval people would have known these "old stories" (I, A, 859) much as we know the tale of Cinderella or Sleeping Beauty. So the Knight-narrator can get right into the action.

Theseus is interrupted on his progress into Athens by a "company of ladies" (I, A, 898), dressed in black, weeping and lamenting. They are the widows of men killed at the siege of Thebes, the unsuccessful attempt to overthrow the rule of Oedipus's successor Creon (the same revolt that triggers the plot events in Sophocles' *Antigone*). In consequence, these "wretched women" (I, A, 921) have fallen from the high position they once held as wives of powerful men. Victims of "Fortune and her false wheel" (I,

A, 925), they appeal to Theseus, a man at the top of that wheel. What they want is that their husbands' bodies, which now lie "on a heap" for dogs to eat, be released to them to be "buried or burned" (I, A, 946) according to proper funerary custom.

Moved by pity, Theseus immediately returns to Thebes, conquers Creon, and restores the remains of the dead to the grieving widows. Pillagers, ransacking the bodies of the enemy dead, find "two young knights lying side by side / . . . of the royal blood of Thebes, / And born of two sisters" (I, A, 1011, 1018–1019). These two are Palamon and Arcite. Though badly wounded, "neither fully quick [alive] nor fully dead" (I, A, 1015), they survive, and Theseus takes them as prisoners to Athens. Theseus returns home and is "crowned as a conqueror"; but Palamon and Arcite, the conquered, are imprisoned "in a tower, in anguish and in woe" (I, A, 1027, 1030). Fortune's turning wheel has so dictated their respective fates.

Time passes, with Palamon and Arcite still in prison. But one May morning, Theseus' sister-in-law Emelye walks in the garden adjoining the prison. A proper romance heroine, she is ideally beautiful and engaged in gracefully symbolic activities:

> *Hir yelow heer was broyded in a tresse*
> *Bihynde hir bak, a yerde long, I gesse.*
> *And in the gardyn, at the sonne upriste,*
> *She walketh up and doun, and as hire liste*
> *She gadereth floures, party white and rede,*
> *To make a subtil gerland for hire hede;*
> *And as an aungel hevenysshly she soong.*
>
> Her yellow hair was braided in a tress
> Behind her back, a yard long, I guess.
> And in the garden, as the sun rose,
> She walked up and down, and, as she wished,
> She gathered flowers, partly white and red,
> To make an intricate garland for her head;
> And she sang, as heavenly as an angel.

(I, A, 1049–1055)

The conventional romance heroine always has long blonde hair. From prom corsages to bridal bouquets, flower customs have long marked key events in a young woman's life. Emelye gathers flowers and sings: these idealized behaviors, along with her preternatural beauty, make her seem an angel in the garden to the imprisoned knights in their tower.

"By *aventure* or *cas*," as luck would have it (I, A, 1074), it is Palamon who, looking out through a barred window, first sees Emelye:

> *And therwithal he bleynte and cride, "A!"*
> *As though he stongen were unto the herte.*

> And right away he blanched and cried, "Ah!"
> As though he were stung unto the heart.
>
> (I, A, 1078–1079)

His cry alerts Arcite, who assumes that his fellow prisoner is lamenting his captivity. Arcite offers Palamon the consolation of philosophy:

> *"For Goddes love, taak al in pacience*
> *Oure prisoun, for it may noon oother be.*
> *Fortune hath yeven us this adversitee."*

> "For God's love, take in patience
> Our prison, for it may not be otherwise.
> Fortune has given us this adversity."
>
> (I, A, 1084–1086)

But Palamon assures him that his problem is not imprisonment but love:

> *"This prison caused me nat for to crye,*
> *But I was hurt right now thurghout myn ye*
> *Into myn herte."*

> "This prison did not cause me to cry,
> But I was hurt just now through my eye
> Into my heart."
>
> (I, A, 1095–1097)

Palamon's explanation of his love-injury reflects a medieval belief about falling in love that still shapes romantic fantasies. A visitor to any card store around Valentine's Day will find images of Cupid with his bow and arrow, vestiges of medieval beliefs on the origins of love. Falling in love was believed to be just as Palamon describes it: on first sight of the beloved, Cupid shot the arrow of love through the eye of the lover into his heart. Such love at first sight has become a romantic ideal. But Cupid is a notorious trickster, and so two lovers may fall in love with the same lady. Not only do Palamon and Arcite both love Emelye, but both love her identically, according to the conventions of the courtly love tradition.

Convention is custom, an expected and accepted element of a tradition, to be obeyed or violated. Thus, the modern bride makes a statement either by wearing the traditional white dress or by wearing something else. In the arts, convention shapes audience expectations; unconventional developments depend on the audience's knowledge of the conventions to which they are contrasted. The macho western hero such as John Wayne often played shapes later characterizations of men in film; the Marilyn Monroe stereotype of the dizzy blonde, women. In fashion, defiance of convention is a convention in itself and drives the entire industry.

As noted earlier, the conventional set of beliefs within which Palamon and Arcite are depicted is the courtly love tradition. Arising during the eleventh century in Provençal, courtly love was basically a highly idealized version of heterosexual love. To the courtly lover, the lady is pure, beautiful, and inaccessible. The perfect love object, she can never be reduced to a mere object of physical gratification. The courtly lover is her abject worshiper. As the medieval Christian adored the Virgin Mary, so the lover adores his lady. While the lady represents an unattainable goal, not a potential partner, the lover can, by dint of long service, hope to achieve some subtle sign of the "mercy" and "grace" (I, A, 1120) of which Arcite speaks. So crucial is the lady not only to the lover's well-being, but also to life itself, that without the lady's favor the lover will surely die. Without Emelye, says Arcite, "I am but dead" (I, A, 1122).

Both Arcite and Palamon have been imprisoned by the power of love just as surely as by the power of Theseus. But Emelye is herself immune to love: she has seen neither of the knights, nor is she aware that they have seen her, much less that they are in love with her. Given the circumstances, Palamon and Arcite's debate about which of them is more entitled to regard himself as Emelye's lover seems entirely futile. Palamon claims justly that he saw her first; Arcite rebuts with the claim that Palamon didn't know whether she was "a woman or a goddess" (I, A, 1157), and so cannot be in love with the real Emelye. Their hair-splitting arguments, presented in two parallel speeches, are beside the point in that Emelye loves neither of them. Besides, neither prisoner is in any position to court a lady. But the argumentative speeches do show that these two nearly identical young men, who, "born of two sisters" (I, A, 1019), were not only blood cousins but also sworn brothers, have now become mortal foes.

"Damned to prison / Perpetually" (I, A, 1175–1176), the two knights seem doomed. But fate, chance, *aventure* intervenes in the form of a visit from Duke Perotheus, friend of Theseus and ally of Arcite. Perotheus prevails upon Theseus to release Arcite from prison; Theseus agrees, but, as a condition of release, he banishes Arcite. "Now is my prison worse than before!" laments Arcite (I, A, 1224). Palamon, jailed, is paradoxically better off than exiled Arcite; he can happily live in prison, since he can see Emelye, and

> *"For possible is, syn thou hast hire presence,*
> *And art a knyght, a worthy and an able,*
> *That by som cas, syn Fortune is chaungeable,*
> *Thow maist to thy desir somtyme atteyne."*

> "It is possible, since you are in her presence,
> And are a worthy and an able knight,
> That by some chance—since Fortune is changeable—
> You may sometime attain to your desire."

> (I, A, 1240–1243)

But Palamon doesn't agree. In yet another set of parallel speeches, Palamon argues that it is Arcite who is blessed by Fortune. Arcite could

> *"Assemblen alle the folk of oure kynrede,*
> *And make a werre so sharp on this citee*
> *That by som aventure or some tretee*
> *Thow mayst have hire to lady and to wyf*
> *For whom that I moste nedes lese my lyf."*

> "Assemble all the folk of our kindred
> And make so sharp a war on this city
> That by some chance or by some treaty,
> You may win, as lady and as wife,
> She for whom I must lost my life."

> (I, A, 1286–1290)

The contrasting fortunes of these two identical knights lead Palamon to muse on the vagaries of *aventure*. What justice prevails in a universe in which chance has so great a role? Innocence is punished; guilt is not. The larger philosophical issue of the role of Fortune in human affairs will become an important theme.

The situation, then, at the end of Part One, is that Palamon remains in prison in Athens and Arcite returns to Thebes, free but desolate. Like any conventional literary lover of the period, he languishes from grief:

> *His slep, his mete, his drynke, is hym biraft,*
> *That lene he wex and drye as is a shaft;*

His eyen holwe and grisly to biholde,
His hewe falow and pale as asshen colde,
And solitarie he was and evere allone,
And waillynge al the nyght, makynge his mone. . . .
So feble eek were his spiritz, and so lowe,
And chaunged so, that no man koude knowe
His speche nor his voys.

His sleep, his meat, his drink, are taken from him,
So he grew lean and dry as a shaft;
His eyes were hollow and grisly to behold,
His color sickly pale as cold ash,
And he was solitary, and always alone,
And wailing all the night, making his moan. . . .
So feeble were his spirits, and so low,
And he was so changed, that no man could recognize
His speech or his voice.

(I, A, 1361–1366, 1369–1371)

So ill is Arcite, lovesick for Emelye, that he is unrecognizable. Paradoxically, this misfortune gives him the opportunity to return to Athens and to Emelye, there to live incognito as a menial laborer in Theseus' household. Since medieval people believed that noble birth would manifest itself despite appearances, he rises up through the ranks and is made a squire of Theseus' chamber.

After seven years, "whether by *aventure* or destiny" (I, A, 1465), Palamon breaks out of prison. Like Arcite, he cannot break out of the prison of his love for Emelye; and so he does not avail himself of the chance to flee, but plans to return to Athens with an army of fellow Thebans to fight Theseus for the hand of Emelye. To accomplish this, he has to get out of Athens undiscovered. So he hides in a grove and awaits the cover of darkness.

At this point, the role of chance becomes pronounced to the point of unbelievability. Arcite, behaving like the conventional courtly lover, is walking in the same grove in which Palamon is hiding. "To do his observance to May" (I, A, 1500), month of love and fertility, he praises the season but laments his own misfortunes—aloud, so that Palamon, in hiding, hears him. By his tale of love for Emelye, Palamon knows his otherwise unrecognizable enemy and challenges him to a duel. The sad irony that these two cousins and blood brothers are now mortal foes is highlighted when each helps the other to arm for the duel which, they expect, will kill one of them.

The Knight-narrator does not describe the duel, but he uses the imagined time to reflect on the multiple layers of chance and circumstance that have governed the tale thus far and will continue to do so:

> *The destinee, ministre general,*
> *That executeth in the world over al*
> *The purveiaunce that God hath seyn biforn,*
> *So strong it is that, though the world had sworn*
> *The contrarie of a thyng by ye or nay,*
> *Yet somtyme it shal fallen on a day*
> *That falleth nat eft withinne a thousand yeer.*

> Destiny, minister-general
> That executes all over the world
> The foreknowledge that God has seen before,
> It is so strong that, though the world had sworn
> The contrary of a thing, by yes or no,
> Yet sometimes something happens on a day
> That does not often happen in a thousand years.

(I, A, 1663–1669)

Coincidences do happen. Some events seem fated. Destiny is the agent that carries out events foreknown by an all-seeing God. Destiny is so strong that, even if the whole world had sworn that a particular event was impossible, it still could happen once, even if not for another thousand years. Thus the Knight defends the many chance happenings in his tale. But in literature coincidence often seems contrived. So it can seem absurdly improbable that, just as Palamon and Arcite begin to fight, Theseus, out hunting with a large company including his wife and Emelye, happens upon that same grove. Theseus stops the duel but is enraged with both young knights, for Palamon has broken out of prison and Arcite has been engaged in a seven-year-long deception. Theseus condemns both to die.

Upon this announcement, Hippolyta, Emelye, and the company of ladies begin to weep:

> *Greet pitee was it, as it thoughte hem alle,*
> *That evere swich a chaunce sholde falle,*
> *For gentil men they were of greet estaat,*
> *And no thyng but for love was this debaat.*

> It was a great pity, they all thought,
> That ever such a chance should happen,

> For they were gentlemen of great estate,
> And this debate was for nothing but love.

(I, A, 1751–1754)

Theseus has earlier responded to a company of weeping women, and he does so again. The ladies plead with Theseus to relent, and he does, reasoning logically

> *that every man*
> *Wol helpe hymself in love, if that he kan,*
> *And eek delivere hymself out of prisoun.*

> that every man
> Will help himself in love, if he can,
> And also deliver himself out of prison.

(I, A, 1767–1769)

Theseus is not one of those leaders who is too proud to reverse a decision. With philosophical detachment, he reflects on the "high folly" of love and decides to "have . . . mercy" upon the young men (I, A, 1799, 1774). As Theseus notes with humor, only now does Emelye know that Palamon and Arcite are involved in "all this hot fare" (I, A, 1809) for love of her. Theseus admits that both young men are worthy to marry Emelye—the audience remembers from the beginning of the tale that they are "of the royal blood / Of Thebes, and born of two sisters" (I, A, 1018–1019). So they are both equally deserving of a woman of the royal blood of Athens. Obviously, Emelye cannot marry both of them. How should Theseus resolve this problem?

In modern times we would expect Emelye to make such a choice. But her preference is not the key factor. For one thing, she has only just discovered the existence of the two knights and the fact that they are in love with her. Even if she knew them better, she would be hard pressed to distinguish between these twin-like gentlemen. In any case, no one would expect Emelye herself to decide on a husband. An unattached woman of high rank would have her marriage arranged by her male protector, usually her father. Here Theseus, her brother-in-law, plays this role. Since Theseus deems Palamon and Arcite equal, he rules that the hand of Emelye will be won in the lists.

The lists, or tournaments, were formal, ritualized mock-battles that provided an opportunity for knights to demonstrate military ability and manly prowess in the absence of an actual war. Similar to modern sporting events, they also filled a need to channel male violence and competitive energies into forms less destructive than battle. So, instead of allowing Palamon and Arcite to fight to the death in the grove, Theseus' decision to postpone the battle for fifty weeks and to reconvene it as a tournament cools passions and reduces the possibility of death. But again like modern sporting events, the possibility of injury always exists and indeed adds to the excitement of the competition. The better of these two virtually identical knights will win the beautiful Emelye. A typical romance heroine, Emelye is the reward for male prowess.

Nothing is more typical of the slow, stately pace of the romance than the fact that the action does not now proceed briskly to this climactic competition. Instead, all narrative movement stops to allow for a series of long descriptive passages. To house the great tournament, Theseus causes a "noble theater" to be built (I, A, 1885). This larger-than-life structure, a mile in circumference, contains not only the playing field and rows of seats characteristic of its modern counterpart, the sports arena, but also three "oratories" (I, A, 1905), or shrines, one to each of three pagan deities: Venus, Mars, and Diana.

The pre-Christian characters of the "Knight's Tale" would have delighted in such shrines to their favorite gods and goddesses, much as the medieval Christian loved the many side chapels in medieval churches dedicated to saints. Like those chapels, the three oratories have wall-paintings and wall-carvings featuring the iconography of the god or goddess to whom the shrine was dedicated. Like those chapels too, the shrines would focus on a statue of the deity. All action stops as each shrine is described in parallel fashion. First the wall-paintings, or wall-carvings, are described in detail; then the statues. This is done similarly three times. The images highlight characteristic features of the god or goddess, just as medieval images of Christian saints often included objects or settings associated with them. St. Joseph, for example, is often depicted in his carpentry shop using the tools of his trade; similarly, the descriptions of Venus, Mars, and Diana function as iconographic representations of each deity's traditional roles. To illustrate Chaucer's method, we will look briefly at these three descriptions.

Venus, the love goddess, is associated with the suffering and pain of love,

> The broken slepes, and the sikes colde,
> The sacred teeris, and the waymentynge,
> The firy strokes of the desirynge
> That loves servantz in this lyf enduren.

> The broken sleeps, and the cold sighs,
> The sacred tears, and the sorrowful cries,

> The fiery strokes of the desire
> That love's servants endure in this life.

> (I, A, 1920–1923)

Her statue is, appropriately, naked; she wears a rose garland in her hair and doves flutter above her head. Her little son Cupid, blind and winged, carries his trademark bow and arrow. Thus Venus is associated pictorially with wayward emotion.

Similarly, the image of Mars stresses all the misfortunes connected with the dark angry god of war:

> *The smylere with the knyf under the cloke;*
> *The shepne brennynge with the blake smoke;*
> *The tresoun of the mordrynge in the bedde.*

> The smiler with the knife under his cloak;
> The stable burning with black smoke;
> The treason of the murdering in the bed.

> (I, A, 1999–2001)

"Armed" and "grim" with a wolf at his feet, Mars is a menacing character, a "dark imagining" (I, A, 2042, 2047, 1995).

Diana, goddess of chastity, is depicted in the context of several mythological adventures. One of these, the metamorphosis of Actaeon, stresses Diana's transcendent purity; Actaeon was changed into a hart "for vengeance, because he saw Diana all naked" (I, A, 2066), and his own dogs ate him. Diana, a versatile goddess, is also a huntress and protectress of women in childbirth. Thus her statue shows her with her hunting dogs, her bows and arrows, and a woman in labor, crying out for Diana's help. Diana's chastity is a source of considerable power; she is as mighty a deity in her sphere as the others are in theirs.

The theater having been thoroughly described, the action resumes. The day of the tournament arrives at last. Theseus had decreed that the great battle was not to be a single combat between the two knights, but rather that they were to be accompanied by "a hundred knights / Armed for lists" (I, A, 1851–1852). So it is. In parallel passages, the two groups, representing "knighthood" and "chivalry" (I, A, 2103, 2106), are described. The pageantry surrounding the occasion adds to its high seriousness. Medieval people loved such elaborate display. A man's worth was measured by the number and rank of the supporters he could muster for an occasion like this. Palamon and Arcite each bring one hundred men; each noble company is led by an even more noble king: Lygurge, king of Thrace, fights for

Palamon; Emetreus, king of India, fights for Arcite. Each of these kings receives long and detailed parallel descriptions of his own; both are impressive men impressively arrayed but as undistinguishable from each other as are Palamon and Arcite themselves.

It should be obvious at this point that, in the romances especially, medieval people enjoyed detailed description as much as narrative movement. The modern reader often finds that these passages move too slowly; but to the medieval audience, the slow pace conferred dignity. Just as a graduation, a wedding, or a funeral cannot be quick without loss of meaning, so the epic descriptions lend weight and importance to the events described. The obvious parallelism of the descriptions helps to organize a large mass of material. But it also serves another function. The audience is reminded by the virtually identical descriptions of the two kings supporting Palamon and Arcite that the two lovers are both equally worthy of Emelye; so only fate, chance, *aventure* will determine the outcome.

Like any medieval knight before a great battle, each of the participants prays for success. Each chooses one of the three shrines so carefully described earlier. Three more parallel descriptions follow, consisting of the prayer and the deity's response. Palamon prays at the temple of Venus:

> *"I kepe noght of armes for to yelpe,*
> *Ne I ne axe nat tomorwe to have victorie,*
> *Ne renoun in this cas, ne veyne glorie*
> *Of pris of armes blowen up and doun;*
> *But I wolde have fully possessioun*
> *Of Emelye."*

> "I care not to boast of feats of arms
> Nor do I ask tomorrow to have victory,
> Nor renown in this case, nor vainglory
> Of deeds of arms proclaimed all over.
> But I would have full possession
> Of Emelye."

> (I, A, 2238–2243)

The statue of Venus "made a sign" that his prayer was answered, but "the sign showed a delay" (I, A, 2266, 2268). Satisfied by this mixed message, Palamon leaves Venus' temple.

Emelye, as might be expected, prays to Diana that she may remain a virgin:

> *"Chaste goddesse, wol wostow that I*
> *Desire to ben a mayden al my lyf,*
> *Ne nevere wol I be no love ne wyf."*

> "Chaste goddess, well you know that I
> Desire to be a maiden all my life
> And never be a love or wife."

(I, A, 2304–2306)

She prays that Palamon and Arcite may reconcile their conflict in another way, and that their "hot love and . . . desire" may be "quenched" without requiring her to "be a wife and be with child" (I, A, 2319, 2321, 2310). Whether this is a pose of conventional maidenly reluctance or a genuine commitment to permanent virginity is not clear; but what is clear is that Emelye's prayer is answered in the negative. Two fires are burning on Diana's altar:

> *For right anon oon of the fyres queynte*
> *And quyked agayn, and after that anon*
> *That oother fyr was queynt and al agon.*

> For right away one of the fires was quenched
> And quickened again, and, right after that
> The other fire was quenched entirely.

(I, A, 2334–2336)

The statue of Diane speaks but without explaining the sign of the fires:

> *"Thou shalt ben wedded unto oon of tho*
> *That han for thee so muchel care and wo."*

> "You shall be wedded unto one of those
> Who had so much care and woe for you."

(I, A, 2351–2352)

Emelye, then, will marry; but which knight, and why the mysterious behavior of the fires?

Arcite's prayer, to Mars, the god of war, makes a specifically military request:

> *"I moot with strengthe wynne hire in the place,*
> *And wel I woot, withouten help or grace*
> *Of thee ne may my strengthe noght availle.*
> *Thanne help me, lord, tomorwe in my bataille."*

"I must win her in this place with strength,
And well I know without the help or grace
Of you, my strength may not avail.
Then help me tomorrow, lord, in my battle."

(I, A, 2399–2402)

With much rattling of his coat of mail, Mars indicates that Arcite will have the victory in battle. Thus Arcite leaves the shrine satisfied; but so did Palamon. Although both have been promised victory by their respective deities, only one can win Emelye.

How can this apparent contradiction be resolved? Only through the intercession of the gods. Just as Palamon and Arcite have royal champions supporting them on earth, so each has his ally in the realm of the gods: Palamon's is Venus, goddess of love; Arcite's is Mars, god of war. Both love and war are powerful forces on earth; both Venus and Mars are powerful deities on Mount Olympus. But Jupiter, highest of the gods, reigns supreme over them both. The rivalry between Palamon and Arcite leads to "strife / . . . in the heaven above" (I, A, 2438–2439) between Venus and Mars. It would seem that the supreme god, Jupiter, should be able to restore peace. But Venus' father Saturn, incensed by the potential threat to his daughter's power, intercedes. The god of mishaps, Saturn has "more power than any man knows" (I, A, 2455). He controls such events as drowning, strangling, peasant rebellions, collapse of buildings, and plague. This threatening god promises that, even if Mars helps Arcite, Palamon "shall have his lady" as Venus promised (I, A, 2472). How this apparently contradictory set of events will work out—Palamon winning Emelye even though Arcite wins the battle—is the subject of the remainder of the "Knight's Tale."

The great tournament takes place on a May morning, that typical time of romance and adventure. Athens, imagined as a medieval town, is bustling with preparations. Sounds "of horse and harness noise and clattering" (I, A, 2492) fill the air; sights of the elegant trappings of chivalric life, the work of goldsmiths and harness-makers and embroiderers, lend excitement to the proceedings. Presiding over all is Theseus, "arrayed as if he were an enthroned god" (I, A, 2528). Speaking for Theseus, a herald sets forth the ground rules of the competition: lest "gentle blood" (I, A, 2539), the blood of members of the nobility, be shed, none may use lethal weapons; this is to be a manly contest, not a massacre. When the chieftain of either side falls (that is, either Lygurge on Palamon's side or Emetreus on Arcite's), the battle is over. This ducal decision, praised by all, lends further mystery: how can the rivalry for Emelye be resolved while one of the rivals lives?

The ensuing battle is described with relative briskness and brevity. Both Lygurge and Emetreus fall; the battle is done; Theseus, in his capacity as "true judge, and no partisan" (I, A, 2657), gives the decision to Arcite. All on earth rejoice that the matter is finally resolved; but in the heavens, discord prevails. Venus, Palamon's champion, "weeps so, for wanting of her will" (I, A, 2665) that her tears fall into the lists. But Saturn has already promised that even though "Mars shall help his knight," Arcite, neverthe-less Palamon, Venus' "own knight, / Shall have his lady" (I, A, 2471–2473). Now it is time for Saturn to make good on his promise.

To all appearances, Arcite is Fortune's darling. At the moment of his greatest triumph, he has taken off his helmet and is riding up to Emelye to present himself to her. Apparently swayed in her commitment to lifelong virginity by Arcite's manly deeds in the lists, Emelye looks upon him favorably:

> And she agayn hym caste a freendlich ye
> (For wommen, as to speken in comune,
> Thei folwen alle the favour of Fortune).

> And she cast a friendly eye upon him
> (For women, to speak in general,
> They all follow the favor of Fortune).

(I, A, 2680–2682)

Emelye's favor is a reward for prowess; the best man gets the pretty girl. How could life be better for Arcite? Rewarded for his years of love service, he is at last on top of Fortune's wheel.

But as all know, the top of Fortune's wheel is a precarious perch. At that precise moment, at the request of the malevolent Saturn, Pluto, the god of the underworld, sends an "infernal fury" (I, A, 2684) out of the ground. Arcite's horse leaps for fear; Arcite, unprepared for the sudden movement, is thrown from his horse, falls to the ground, and "lay as if he were dead," his "breast broken" by the force of the blow (I, A, 2690–2691). This literal fall from Fortune is tragedy indeed, happening as it does just at his highest point of accomplishment. All lament this *aventure*. Arcite is the victor in battle, as Mars promised. But it will be a cold triumph indeed if Arcite dies, as it appears he must.

The nature of Arcite's injuries, the ensuing complications, and the remedies attempted are described in precise detail. Chaucer was familiar with the limited medical knowledge of his day; here, his diagnosis and treatment of Arcite are based on a well-known medieval theory. Health in the human body was believed to be the result of a correct balance of the "humours," or bodily fluids; disease or injury was caused by an imbalance; and treatment involved righting the balance. Arcite was injured in the chest (appropriately enough, for this lovelorn knight's troubles began in the region of the heart). Complications include swelling of the chest and trunk. The "clotted blood" or excess of fluid is a source of inner corruption; so "leechcraft," medical treatment, involves attempts to release that blood, thus restoring the balance of fluids (I, A, 2745). "Leechcraft" is a good term here, because drawing blood by the application of leeches, bloodsucking insects, was an accepted medical treatment in the Middle Ages and long thereafter. To release the excess fluid, several remedies are attempted: bloodletting, "drink of herbs" (I, A, 2748), emetics, and laxatives. But Arcite just gets sicker and sicker:

> The pipes of his longes gonne to swelle,
> And every lacerte in his brest adoun
> Is shent with venym and corrupcioun.

> The pipes of his lungs began to swell,
> And every muscle from his chest downward
> Is destroyed with venom and corruption.
>
> (I, A, 2752–2754)

With a fatalism that seems appropriate, given the abysmal state of medieval medicine, the narrator gives Arcite up for dead. The battle for Arcite's life between "Nature," the body's own recuperative powers, and "physic," medicine, has ended in Nature's surrender (I, A, 2758, 2760). "All is broken" (I, A, 2757) in the region of Arcite's heart:

> Nature hath now no dominacioun.
> And certeinly, ther Nature wol nat wirche,
> Fare wel phisik! Go ber the man to chirche!

> Nature now has no domination
> And certainly, when Nature will not work,
> Farewell physic! Go bear the man to church!
>
> (I, A, 2758–2760)

On his deathbed, Arcite laments the turning of Fortune's wheel:

> "What is this world? What asketh men to have?
> Now with his love, now in his colde grave
> Allone, withouten any compaignye."

"What is this world? What do men ask to have?
Now with his love, now in his cold grave
Alone, without any company."

(I, A, 2777–2779)

The medieval definition of tragedy is based on this idea of the fall. Bad luck seems worse when it happens to a person at the top; the accidental death of a young knight, particularly at his moment of triumph, seems more tragic than the slow decline unto death of a decrepit old man. All Arcite's energies have been devoted to the winning of Emelye; now, having by rights won her, he is nevertheless doomed to a cold and solitary grave. Even at the bottom of Fortune's wheel, Arcite's nobility is such that he can find it in his (broken) heart to praise his worthy opponent and urge Emelye to marry him. With generous words on his lips, Arcite dies, to the great lamentation of all, especially Emelye and Palamon.

In the face of such tragedy, one can only find consolation in the philosophical reflections of Theseus' father Egeus. Egeus clearly has the image of Fortune's wheel in mind when he talks of "this world's transmutation" (I, A, 2839). The old, like Egeus, have experienced mutability, having seen the world "change both up and down, / Joy after woe, and woe after gladness" (I, A, 2840–2841). Given the impossibility of lasting joy, the inevitability of woe, all must accept their own transitoriness. No man ever died who did not once live; no man who lives will escape death. The world is a "thoroughfare," and the living merely "pilgrims, passing to and fro" on their way to death (I, A, 2847–2848). With allusions like these to the theme of pilgrimage, Chaucer firmly secures his "Knight's Tale" to the frame of the journey to Canterbury.

Arcite's last rites render a dignified conclusion to a worthy life. Since the characters in the "Knight's Tale" are pagan, not Christian, Arcite is cremated, not buried. Similarly, Theseus' speech resolving the situation between Palamon and Emelye is, like his father Egeus', an articulation of a philosophy that does not depend on Christian beliefs on the afterlife. Rather, Theseus encourages a Stoic acceptance of death as the inevitable end of all living things.

Stoicism, a school of philosophy flourishing in Greece circa 300 B.C., held as a central belief that, in the face of adversity, man's best stance was to face the hard facts and accept them courageously. Chaucer was much influenced by Boethius, a Roman philosopher (c. 480–524), whose masterwork, *The Consolation of Philosophy*, Chaucer translated. Boethius' title captures the idea that rational examination of the issues is indeed a source of consolation. The function of Theseus' speech is to present a philosophical world-view that allows Palamon and Emelye to accept closure of this period of upheaval. If they can understand and accept this particular manifestation of evil in the universe, Arcite's death, they can go on with their own lives.

According to Theseus, the cosmos was created by a First Mover, a philosophical principle of beginning at the source of all subsequent motion. Some modern astronomers postulate that the universe may have started with some sort of massive explosion, or "Big Bang," from which all later planetary motion resulted; some medieval philosophers postulated a similar source of all subsequent motion in an all-powerful force. A pagan, Theseus does not call this being by the name of the Christian God; but the philosophical idea of the First Mover does have much in common with the idea of God in the Judeo-Christian tradition.

In Theseus' philosophy, the Prime Mover is the first maker of all the elements of the universe: "the fire, the air, the water, and the land" (I, A, 2992). These disparate elements are held together by a cosmic organizing principle, "the fair chain of love" (I, A, 2988). As experience proves, all created things have their allocated life span, their "certain days and duration" (I, A, 2996). Although the First Mover is eternal, nothing else is. Oak trees, stones, rivers, towns, men and women: all are mortal.

Given the evanescence of all earthly things, it is, according to Theseus, "wisdom . . . / To make virtue of necessity" (I, A, 3041–3042) and accept death. Philosophy can render acceptable even the tragedy of Arcite's dying young at his moment of glory:

> *"And certeinly a man hath moost honour*
> *To dyen in his excellence and flour,*
> *Whan he is siker of his goode name."*

> "And certainly a man has most honor
> To die in his excellence and flower,
> When he is certain of his good name."

> (I, A, 3047–3049)

If life is a "foul prison" (I, A, 3061) in which no joy lasts, why lament Arcite's passing from it? Therefore, concludes Theseus, the proper resolution is as Arcite requested: to "make of sorrows two / One perfect joy" (I, A, 3071–3072). The marriage of Palamon to Emelye constitutes acceptance of the death of Arcite. So it happens, and so the words of all three gods are fulfilled: Arcite wins the battle but loses the lady as Mars prophesied; Palamon loses the battle but wins the lady as Venus predicted; and Emelye accepts marriage, as Diana foretold. All ends happily.

But the Canterbury pilgrims know that the joy and bliss that Palamon and Emelye experience is itself one of earth's transient joys. All order is temporary, all dependent on the same accidents of fate that brought Arcite to the top of the wheel and cast him low again. It is understandable that a knight, survivor of battles in which Fortune, apparently at random, decreed death to one and triumph to another, might look for a philosophical system that postulates an overriding and rational order. The noble tale of Palamon, Arcite, and Emelye gives the Canterbury pilgrims a chance to reflect on this popular medieval theme: the fall from Fortune.

Now the Host, Harry Bailly, wants the Monk to speak. Perhaps he expects this man of religion to add the perspective of Christian faith to this pagan tale of love and death—which would be a most orderly and logical link between the tales. But, after the long and woeful tale just heard or read, does the pilgrim audience—does the modern reader—want another somber story? Chaucer thinks not and lets his Miller, "drunken" (I, A, 3120), interrupt with another kind of tale. But this is a "churl's tale," so Geffrey issues a warning: if you are easily offended, "Turn over the leaf, and choose another tale" (I, A, 3169, 3177). What better guarantee that the audience will choose the "Miller's Tale"?

SUGGESTIONS FOR FURTHER READING

Bloom, Harold, ed. and intro. *Geoffrey Chaucer's "The Knight's Tale."* New York: Chelsea House, 1988. This collection of essays offers a variety of critical approaches.

Brown, Peter. "The Prison of Theseus and the Castle of Jealousy." *Chaucer Review* 26, no. 2 (1991): 147–162. Brown sees the prison as both a realistic setting and a symbol of "jealousy's imprisoning power."

Hallissy, Margaret. "Poison and Infection in Chaucer's Knight's and Canon's Yeoman's Tales." *Essays in Arts and Sciences* 10, no. 1 (1981): 31–40. Hallissy shows how poison is a metaphor for the contagious nature of moral evil in both tales.

Jensen, Emily. "Male Competition as a Unifying Motif in Fragment A of the *Canterbury Tales*." *Chaucer Review* 24, no. 4 (1990): 320–328. Jensen relates the tales of the Knight, the Miller, and the Reeve on the basis of the varying balance between two key factors: male competitiveness and female passivity.

Jones, Terry. *Chaucer's Knight: The Portrait of a Medieval Mercenary.* London: Weidenfeld and Nicolson, 1980. Jones examines the character in the context of mercenary warfare rather than in the chivalric tradition of medieval knighthood.

Kolve, V. A. *Chaucer and the Imagery of Narrative: The First Five Canterbury Tales*. Stanford, Calif.: Stanford University Press, 1984. 85–107. In Chapter 3, "The Prison/ Garden and the Tournament Amphitheatre," Kolve explicates the tale by means of symbolism from the visual arts.

Muscatine, Charles. "Form, Texture, and Meaning in Chaucer's *Knight's Tale*." *Chaucer: Modern Essays in Criticism*. Ed. Edward Wagenknecht. London: Oxford University Press, 1959. 60–82. Muscatine discusses character and structure as "expressing the nature of the noble life" and the "two noble activities, love and chivalry."

The Miller's Tale

Men sholde wedden after hire estaat,
For youthe and elde is often at debaat.

Men should marry according to their estate,
For youth and age are often at debate.

(I, A, 3229–3230)

Like the "Knight's Tale" which precedes it, the "Miller's Tale" is a story of the competition between men in love with the same woman—but with a difference. But where the "Knight's Tale" is a romance, the "Miller's Tale" belongs to an equally popular but different medieval genre, the *fabliau*. The audience has been warned in the linking passage that it should come as no surprise that the Miller, a "churl," or low, vulgar character, would tell a "churl's tale" (I, A, 3169). The *fabliau*, or churl's tale, is the medieval equivalent of the dirty joke. The characters, being of low *estat*, are motivated by the basest possible drives. Love for the *fabliau* character is a matter not of the heart, mind, and spirit as it is in the romance, but of the body only. Appropriately, then, the tale is told in the low style; vulgarity abounds, and the modern audience becomes well acquainted with the medieval version of common four-letter words for the most basic of human functions.

Parallel to the angelic Emelye in the "Knight's Tale" is the earthy Alisoun, no virgin like Emelye but the eighteen-year-old wife of the aged John, a carpenter of Oxford. To medieval people, the idea of an old man marrying a young girl was wildly funny. Such a man deceives himself, they thought, about his own ability to satisfy a young girl; it is a foregone conclusion that his frustrated wife will one day betray him with a younger and more virile man. (This situation arises again in the "Merchant's Tale.")

Immediately, the medieval audience would expect sexual complications simply from the fact that foolish John has taken in a "poor scholar" (I, A, 3190), a student at Oxford University, as a boarder in his house.

Oxford is now and was then a university town. The "town" or local residents often found itself at odds with the "gown," the university students (who wore as symbol of their calling the academic robes familiar today as graduation garb). Unlike Chaucer's Oxford Clerk, a dedicated scholar, many students saw university life as a prime opportunity to misbehave and considered the women of the town as fair game for seduction. Nicholas the poor scholar is typical of such students. His prime study is astrology, considered a science in the Middle Ages; in his room he keeps the *Almagest*, a famed astrological treatise, other "books great and small" (I, A, 3208), and assorted tools of the astrologer's art. But his main interest is nonacademic: "secret love and . . . pleasure" (I, A, 3200). How foolish John the carpenter is to rent a room to such a young man—especially since John has a voluptuous young wife.

The common literary motif of the old man in love with the young woman is called by a Latin name: the *senex amans*, the old man in love. John is a typical example of that stereotype:

> This carpenter hadde wedded newe a wyf,
> Which that he lovede moore than his lyf;
> Of eighteteene yeer she was of age.
> Jalous he was, and heeld hire narwe in cage,
> For she was wylde and yong, and he was old
> And demed hymself been lik a cokewold.

> This carpenter had newly wed a wife,
> Whom he loved more than his life;
> She was eighteen years of age.
> He was jealous, and held her tight in cage,
> For she was wild and young, and he was old
> And deemed himself likely to become a cuckold.

> (I, A, 3221–3226)

The cuckold, the husband whose wife had been unfaithful, was believed to wear on his head a set of horns visible to everyone but him. The betrayal of a jealous *senex amans* like John provided material for a stock *fabliau* plot, a plot so common that, even this early in the story, the medieval audience would gleefully anticipate the predictable outcome. Audience anticipation of the adultery to come is reinforced by the Miller's long and appreciative description of Alisoun's appealing features: her clothes, her face, her body, even the scent of her breath. Alisoun, in short, is adorable, like a little flower. She would be just right for a lord to bed or a yeoman to wed. Notice the distinctions of *estat*: an upper-class man would not have to marry her, but a lower-class man would.

Since John the carpenter has indeed married her, she should be faithful to him; but implicit in the *senex amans* motif is the assumption that Alisoun is sexually unsatisfied and thus easily seducible by a younger and more virile man—a man just like Nicholas. How foolish of John to leave the two at home alone while he goes to Osney! The husband out of the way, Nicholas quickly makes his move: he "held her hard by the haunchbones" (I, A, 3279) and begs her to satisfy him. The comedy of this situation increases when the audience remembers the extreme length and perfect purity of the courtship of Emelye by Palamon and Arcite—years passed with no lustful thoughts on the part of either noble knight. But such a man as Nicholas wants one thing only.

Alisoun is no Emelye either. She makes a perfunctory attempt at refusal:

> And with hir heed she wryed faste awey,
> And seyde, "I wol nat kisse thee, by my fey!
> Why, lat be!" quod she. "Lat be, Nicholas,
> Or I wol crie 'out, harrow' and 'allas'!
> Do wey youre handes, for youre curteisye!"

> And with her head she quickly twisted away,
> And said, "I will not kiss thee, by my faith!
> Why, let be," said she. "Let be, Nicholas!
> Or I will cry 'out, harrow, and alas!'
> Remove your hands, for your courtesy!"

                                                                    (I, A, 3283–3287)

Were she to cry out, her neighbors might think she was being raped, for "raising the hue and cry" was a key element in proving resistance under medieval English rape law. But it rapidly becomes clear that Alisoun consents to Nicholas's advances. So swift is this courtship that it is clear that Alisoun is a woman of exceedingly flexible moral standards—she is, in modern terms, easy. She promptly agrees to have sex with Nicholas as soon as it can be arranged. No problem, Nicholas assures her: students are smarter than carpenters any day. And so they agree to deceive Alisoun's jealous husband.

The rest of the *fabliau* involves an elaborate plot to get the couple together in the absence of John. To add complexity to the predictable situation, Chaucer adds yet another plot and introduces a new character, the parish clerk Absolon. Not a priest in holy orders but an unordained deacon (comparable to an altar server today), the parish clerk assists at liturgical ceremonies, for example, by wielding the censer, or incense burner, on the holidays. In the course of these clerical duties, he falls in lust with the carpenter's wife:

> I dar wel seyn, if she hadde been a mous,
> And he a cat, he wolde hire hente anon.

> I dare well say, if she had been a mouse,
> And he a cat, he would have pounced immediately.
>
> (I, A, 3346–3347)

Absolon has several other functions appropriate to his status as a learned, or at least literate, man; he does barbering and bloodletting; he draws up legal documents; he sings and plays musical instruments. His music and singing shape his self-image in that he sees himself as a courtly lover, serenading his lady in hopes to win her love.

But Alisoun is no lady, courtly or otherwise. Having just heard the "Knight's Tale," the Canterbury pilgrims know how foolish Absolon is for treating Alisoun as if she were Emelye. Standing beneath his lady's window, he plays his cithern (a stringed instrument) and sings love songs. Foolish also is John, who, deaf to events taking place right in his household, hears Absolon but doesn't understand what his singing means. Absolon's courtship goes on, with Absolon assuming all the poses of the courtly lover (more music, sleepless nights, gifts) and Alisoun ignoring him because "she loves so this pleasant Nicholas" (I, A, 3386).

Nicholas soon has an opportunity to prove how pleasant he is when John makes another trip to Osney. It would seem that this provides the lovers with the opportunity they need; but Osney is apparently too short a trip for Nicholas to have the desired full night of love. Besides, in accordance with the popular town-versus-gown motif, the whole business will be more fun if the student can "beguile" the carpenter (I, A, 3404). So Nicholas uses the Osney trip to plan an elaborate hoax.

As was mentioned at the beginning of the tale, Nicholas is a student of astrology. Since all university subjects look mysterious to the uneducated, Nicholas can easily use his alleged learning to beguile John. Nicholas begins by staying in his room for such an unnaturally long time that John knocks on his door to find out if anything is wrong. When Nicholas does not respond, John peeks in through a small aperture in the door made for the cat to come and go. He sees Nicholas sitting, "gaping upwards, / As if he had gazed upon the new moon" (I, A, 3444–3445), that is, as if he had gone mad. John is shocked and attributes Nicholas's deranged state to an excess of learning:

> "This man is falle, with his astromye,
> In some woodnesse or in som agonye.
> I thoghte ay wel how that it sholde be!
> Men sholde nat knowe of Goddes pryvetee.
> Ye, blessed be alwey a lewed man
> That noght but oonly his bileve kan!"

> "This man is fallen, with his astronomy,
> Into some madness or some agony.
> I always thought that it should be!
> Men should not know of God's privacy.
> Yes, blessed be always an unlearned man
> Who knows nothing but his belief!"

                                                                    (I, A, 3451–3456)

The anti-intellectual's credo is as John states it: the less known, the better; all knowledge is a violation of "God's privacy"; study leads to madness.

But as the audience knows, Nicholas is perfectly sane. He confides to John the alleged result of his astrological studies: a flood is coming, worse than Noah's, and the only way their little household can survive is for each to spend a night in three separate large buckets, "kneading-tubs" (I, A, 3564), tied to the roof-beams. When the floodwaters rise, they can cut the cords and float away, "as merry . . . / As does the white duck after her drake" (I, A, 3575–3576). This image of connubial bliss in the animal world is in comic contrast to the real purpose of the kneading-tub plot. While John is in his tub, obediently waiting for the deluge, Nicholas and Alisoun will climb down from their respective lofty perches and have the long-awaited night of love. To guarantee that John will not see this, Nicholas assures him that the whole plan's success rests on John's not being able to see his wife, lest he commit sin by gazing upon her with lust. Little does John know that Nicholas plans to keep all lust for himself and for Alisoun.

Alïsoun, clever liar that she is, proclaims her fidelity and begs her husband to rescue her from watery doom. Although John is truly in love with his faithless wife (he "weeps and wails" that the flood might "drown Alisoun, his honey dear" [I, A, 3617–3618]), and although he is a victim of deception by both Nicholas and Alisoun, the medieval audience would have little sympathy for a man so foolish as he. In the first place, a *senex* is mad to marry a beautiful, sexy eighteen year old. In the second place, jealous though he is, he does not take any appropriate measures to protect her from temptation: he takes in a young boarder and fails to prevent nightly serenades by Absolon. Now, in ignorance and fear, he unwittingly becomes involved in an absurd scheme to facilitate his wife's adultery. Priding himself on his ignorance, he is too stupid to know how stupid he is, how smart the student Nicholas, how wily his wife. To medieval people, John deserves what he gets.

It seems that Nicholas and Alisoun will finally get their undisturbed night of love. But since John the carpenter has not appeared in public lately, the third lover, Absolon, assumes that John has made yet another trip to Osney. He, too, sees this as his chance to woo the carpenter's wife.

> "To Alisoun now wol I tellen al
> My love-longynge, for yet I shal nat mysse
> That at the leeste wey I shal hire kisse."

> "To Alisoun now will I tell all
> My love-longing, for yet I shall not miss
> That, at least, I shall kiss her."

(I, A, 3678–3680)

In the courtly love tradition, the kiss is the culmination of a chaste courtship. By allowing herself to be kissed, the lady shows favor to her knight, who has long courted her and performed various deeds of valor in her honor. Absolon thinks of Alisoun in terms of this highly idealistic tradition. But like her husband John, Absolon has deceived himself about Alisoun: she is a fast and easy girl who does not require much courting; Nicholas got her to yield easily, just by grabbing her in inappropriate places and mouthing a few quick words of love. Like John, Absolon is blind to Alisoun's true character. So like John's, Absolon's comeuppance will be comic, not tragic.

John is in his kneading-tub, Alisoun and Nicholas are in bed. Having prepared himself for the anticipated kiss by "chewing grain and licorice, / To smell sweet" (I, A, 3690–3691)—using the medieval equivalent of breath-mints—Absolon goes to Alisoun's window and begins his serenade:

> "Awaketh, lemman myn, and speketh to me!
> Wel litel thynken ye upon my wo,
> That for youre love I swete ther I go. . . .
> Ywis, lemman, I have swich love-longynge
> That lik a turtel trewe is my moornynge.
> I may nat ete na moore than a mayde."

"Awake, my lover, and speak to me!
Little do you think upon my woe,
That for your love I sweat where'er I go. . . .
It's true, my love, I have such love-longing
That like a turtle-dove's is my mourning.
I cannot eat more than does a maid."

(I, A, 3700–3702, 3705–3707)

The high-style language is right out of the courtly love tradition. But
unladylike Alisoun is annoyed, and wants only to get rid of her pesty
courtier and get back into bed with Nicholas. So she chases him away in
low-style language:

"Go fro the wyndow, Jakke fool," she sayde;
As help me God, it wol nat be 'com pa me.' "

"Go from the window, Jack fool!
As help me God, it will not be 'come kiss me!' "

(I, A, 3708–3709)

Absolon refuses to leave without the kiss for which his heart longs. Alisoun
asks if he will go away once he gets his kiss. "Yes, certainly, my love,"
Absolon replies. "Then get ready," says she, "Here I come." And so occurs
the climactic event. In the darkness of the night, Absolon does not realize
that Alisoun has presented her posterior. The audience was warned that
this was a churl's tale, and so it is. But the low and bawdy humor traditional
in the *fabliau* requires that the basest instincts be exploited to the full; and
so the kiss is not the last of the tale's vulgarisms.

Earlier, when Absolon was introduced, the audience was informed that
he was "somewhat squeamish / Of farting" (I, A, 3337–3338). Apparently
an irrelevant detail then, Absolon's squeamishness is now essential to the
plot. Having kissed Alisoun's nether regions, an act still deemed insulting
today, Absolon's "hot love was cold and all quenched" (I, A, 3754). Now
he is intent only on revenge. So he concocts a plot of his own. He gets a
hot branding iron from a blacksmith and returns to the infamous window
to beg for another kiss.

This situation arouses Nicholas's competitiveness with Absolon. As was
obvious before, when Nicholas bypassed a simple opportunity in favor of
the more ambitious plot to "beguile" John the carpenter, much of Nicholas's
pleasure in Alisoun depends on outwitting other men also in love with her.
To him, she is the pawn in a contest between men. So now, Nicholas, awake
(he "was risen for to piss," we are told bluntly [I, A, 3798]), decides that

the next step should be that Absolon "should kiss his ass ere he escape" (I, A, 3800). When Absolon comes to the window for Alisoun's kiss, Nicholas places his naked posterior out that same very active window. Not contented with this expression of contempt, Nicholas further insults the squeamish Absolon:

> *This Nicholas anon leet fle a fart*
> *As greet as it had been a thonder-dent.*

> This Nicholas anon let fly a fart
> As great as if it were a thunderclap.

(I, A, 3806–3807)

Though revolted, Absolon is ready:

> *with his iren hoot,*
> *And Nicholas amydde the ers he smoot.*
> *Of gooth the skyn an hande-brede aboute,*
> *The hoote kultour brende so his toute,*
> *And for the smert he wende for to dye.*

> with his iron hot,
> And he smote Nicholas upon the ass.
> Off goes the skin a hand-breadth about!
> The hot branding-iron so burned his buttocks,
> That for the pain he thought that he would die.

(I, A, 3809–3813)

At this climactic moment, Chaucer's careful planning becomes apparent. Scalded, Nicholas screams: "Help! Water! Water!" (I, A, 3815). The sleeping John, hanging in his kneading-tub, hears the cry and, assuming that Noah's flood has come again, does as he was told. He cuts the cord which ties his tub to the rafters, and, with no deluge beneath him, down he falls to the floor, and "lay aswoon" (I, A, 3823). The neighbors, hearing all this commotion, come running. Although poor John has broken his arm, he gets no sympathy from the "folk," who "laugh at his fantasy" of Noah's flood (I, A, 3840). Since none of the other three have visible injuries (Nicholas having by now presumably covered up his scalded *toute*), John bears the brunt of the neighbors' mockery: "he was held mad in all the town" (I, A, 3846). Mad indeed John is for having selected so disloyal a wife as Alisoun; but Absolon and Nicholas do not escape punishment either. Nicholas's posterior and Absolon's sensitivities have been injured.

It seems that only Alisoun gets what she wants: a night with Nicholas, and her husband none the wiser.

Idealistic devotion, noble rivalry, and mutual respect, as demonstrated by Palamon and Arcite in the "Knight's Tale," are replaced in the "Miller's Tale" by lechery and vulgar competitiveness between Nicholas and Absolon, and the uxorious foolishness of John. Alisoun, readily available to her handy young boarder, is the more sluttish when compared to the virginal Emelye, reward for male valor but only within holy matrimony. Although all the characters in the "Miller's Tale" have sinned in their own way, no one has suffered severely, no one dies: the *fabliau* world is a light-hearted world in which sex without love has no serious consequences. As in the "Knight's Tale," characters fall from fortune (most noticeably John, from his foolish perch in the rafters); but since neither they nor their peccadilloes are really of cosmic importance, their misadventures are matter for comedy. Like the appreciative Canterbury pilgrims, the modern audience laughs at the foolishness of men governed by their appetites for a girl as sweet as apples, as pretty as a flower.

"This tale is done" (I, A, 3854), and all the pilgrims laugh except Oswald the Reeve, "of carpenter's craft" (I, A, 3861). Angry at the insult to his fellow tradesman in this tale of the cuckolding of a carpenter, the Reeve determines to requite the Miller, going him one better with an even more churlish tale of the beguiling of a miller.

SUGGESTIONS FOR FURTHER READING

Beidler, Peter G. "Art and Scatology in the Miller's Tale." *Chaucer Review* 12, no. 2 (1977): 90–102. Beidler explains why the vulgar language of the "kiss-and-burn story" is essential.

Hines, John. *The Fabliau in English.* London: Longman, 1993. 107–159. Hines argues that the *fabliau* form is appropriate for an argument between "two churls."

Howard, Donald R. *The Idea of the Canterbury Tales.* Berkeley: University of California Press, 1976. 237–247. Howard traces the interconnections between the "Miller's Tale" and the "Reeve's Tale," especially with regard to the rivalry between the two tale-tellers.

Jensen, Emily. "Male Competition as a Unifying Motif in Fragment A of the Canterbury Tales." *Chaucer Review* 24, no. 4 (1990): 320–328. Jensen relates the tales of the Knight, the Miller, and the Reeve on the basis of the varying balance between two key factors: male competitiveness and female passivity.

Kolve, V. A. *Chaucer and the Imagery of Narrative: The First Five Canterbury Tales.* Stanford, Calif.: Stanford University Press, 1984. 158–216. In Chapter 4, "Nature, Youth, and Nowell's Flood," Kolve explicates the tale by means of symbolism from the visual arts.

Schweitzer, Edward C. "The Misdirected Kiss and the Lover's Malady in Chaucer's *Miller's Tale*." *Chaucer in the Eighties.* Eds. Julian N. Wasserman and Robert J. Blanch. Syracuse, N.J.: Syracuse University Press, 1986. 223–233. Schweitzer shows how the climactic "misdirected kiss" is both a cure for Absolon's lovesickness and a burlesque of Arcite's devotion to Emelye.

Williams, David. "Radical Therapy in the Miller's Tale." *Chaucer Review* 15, no. 3 (1981): 227–235. Williams describes the tale's "amusing denouement" as a radical "cure by physical shock."

The Reeve's Tale

A gylour shal hymself bigyled be.
A beguiler shall himself be beguiled.

(I, A, 4321)

The Reeve requites the Miller by constructing a more vulgar tale of the gulling of a miller. Like the "Miller's Tale" it is a *fabliau*, or racy story; like the "Miller's Tale" it is a town-and-gown story pitting two clerks, this time from the other great English university, Cambridge, against a Trumpington miller. The humor of the story rests on a common medieval comic theme: the trickster tricked, the guiler beguiled. The miller, a dishonest tradesman, was "a thief . . . of corn and meal" (I, A, 3939). Therefore, it is only fitting that something belonging to him be stolen, and by the same people from whom he had himself stolen. What is it that the miller values that two young university students can steal?

The miller is described as an earthy man of the lower classes, a churl. He does not accept his *estat*, however, but harbors pretensions to a higher one. In the Middle Ages, as today, marriage can be a means of achieving upward social mobility. This miller has married above himself:

A wyf he hadde, ycomen of noble kyn;
The person of the toun hir fader was.
With hire he yaf ful many a panne of bras,
For that Symkyn sholde in his blood allye.
She was yfostred in a nonnerye;
For Symkyn wolde no wyf, as he sayde,
But she were wel ynorissed and a mayde,
To saven his estaat of yomanrye.

A wife he had, come of noble kin;
The parson of the town was her father.
He gave many a pan of brass with her,
So that Symkyn would ally with his blood.
She was raised in a nunnery;
For Symkyn would have no wife, as he said,
Unless she were well brought up, and a maid,
To preserve his estate of yeomanry.

                                                      (I, A, 3942–3949)

A tradesman by craft and a yeoman by birth, Symkyn is a free man with a
business of his own; this places him in the lower middle classes, which was
not a bad place to be, considering the increasing affluence of medieval
tradespeople. Nevertheless, it is pretentious of him to require that his wife
be an educated woman, raised well, and a virgin too. It is obvious that the
only way such a woman would marry a lower-class man like him is if *she*
had some disadvantage preventing *her* from marrying up. And she does:
Symkyn's wife, for all her "noble kin," is illegitimate. Her father is the
"parson of the town," the parish priest, and the church had forbidden
clerical marriage since the fourth century. This accounts for the parish
priest's giving his daughter a substantial dowry ("many a pan of brass") to
sweeten the deal. The miller's pride in his wife's social standing is specious:
a priest's bastard daughter is no great catch, except for a churl like him.
Between the two of them, they are, by medieval standards, absurdly
pretentious, parading around overdressed on holy days and insisting on a
degree of respect unmerited by their status. She is haughty and overbearing,
insisting on being called "dame," or lady (I, A, 3956), too conscious of what
she considers her exalted upbringing and family connections.

    This pompous pair has two children, a twenty-year-old girl and a
six-month-old boy. The baby boy's only role is as an important prop. The
girl, however, is crucial to the plot. At twenty, she is a bit old, by medieval
standards, to be unwed. Her physical attractiveness is that of a lower-class
girl. No ethereal courtly lady like Emelye in the "Knight's Tale," she is a
peasant girl, earthy like her father, with a pug nose like his, "thick" and
"well-grown . . . / With buttocks broad and breasts round and high" (I, A,
3973–3975). Such a girl, medieval people would have believed, is made for
sex and procreation; she is a "wench," not a lady, and the absurdity of her
family's delaying her marriage is only an invitation to trouble.

    But the miller's daughter is a priest's granddaughter, and the priest hopes
to make a socially advantageous marriage for her by making her his heir.
Therefore he is "strange . . . of her marriage," choosy about it (I, A, 3980):

His purpos was for to bistowe hire hye
Into som worthy blood of auncetrye.

His purpose was to bestow her high
Into some worthy blood of good ancestry.

(I, A, 3981–3982)

People with money, even if of low birth, could use that money to finance a marriage with the cash-poor members of the nobility, and this is what the priest wants for his granddaughter.

Where has this money come from? Chaucer is usually precise about the source of his characters' income (as befits a man who worked for a salary all his life). The money fueling the social pretensions of these characters comes from the church: the parson is using "holy church's good" for his own family, which he regards as "holy church's blood" (I, A, 3983–3984). Clerical celibacy, the prohibition against the marriage of clergy, was instituted to put an end to just such ecclesiastical abuses as are described here: the church's money going to clerics' families, who are "devouring" (I, A, 3986) the church in the process. This complex marital and financial situation is explained in such detail at the beginning of the tale as to establish the comic principle: that the prideful should be brought low.

This miller's mill is in Trumpington, not far from Cambridge, site of the great university. One of the reasons for the miller's affluence—and the social pretensions consequent upon it—is that he has a monopoly on milling in "all the land about" (I, A, 3988), including the university. Since the university's manciple (or purchaser) is sick, the miller can steal more than ever from the less experienced substitutes who bring the college's corn and meal to the mill. This continues to the point that the warden, the head of the college, protests to the miller, who, predictably, denies all wrongdoing.

As Nicholas in the "Miller's Tale" could not resist an opportunity to pit his educated wits against the lesser intelligence of John the carpenter, so "two poor young scholars" (I, A, 4002) at Cambridge, John and Aleyn, request the warden's permission to try to correct the wrong by gulling the dishonest miller. Arriving at the mill, they pretend interest in the unfamiliar process. One clerk stands at the point of the hopper where the corn goes in, the other where the corn comes out. In this way they hope to avoid any possibility of any part of the corn going to the miller, rather than back to them as it should. But Symkyn the miller, experienced in the ways of theft, considers himself more than a match for these two college boys. For all their "philosophy" (I, A, 4050), their love of learning, he will outwit them because, he reassures himself, "The greatest clerks are not the wisest men"

(I, A, 4054). The perennial rivalry between street-smarts and book-learning again pits town against gown, tradesman against clerks.

For the miller to skim off part of the ground corn, the clerks must be distracted from their observation posts at either end of the hopper. This Symkyn achieves by releasing their horse, forcing them to chase it. The miller then steals their corn and has "his wife go knead it in a cake" (I, A, 4094). The score at this point, John and Aleyn know, is: miller one, clerks zero.

To avoid becoming laughingstocks, the clerks need more time to get themselves to the top of Fortune's wheel again and knock the miller down. So they ask the miller if they can stay the night. Basking in his victory, the miller is generous but cannot resist a dig at the two students' learning: "My house is small, but you are learned," he says (I, A, 4122); so demonstrate by argument that my house is much larger than it is. Symkyn is mocking the art of argumentation as then taught in universities. Logic, to Symkyn, is useless; argument cannot change even the most trivial fact, like the size of a room. Thus the unlearned man justifies his own ignorance by reassuring himself that nothing useful is learned in college anyway.

Anti-intellectual though he is, Symkyn is right about one thing: his house is very small. Even a prosperous yeoman like him might live in a one-bedroom cottage, sharing the limited space among three adults and a baby. But although it was common for medieval people to share not only cramped quarters but even their own beds with houseguests, Symkyn has an extra bed, which he sets up "in his own chamber" (I, A, 4139) not more than 10 or 12 feet away from his own bed. This bed is for Aleyn and John; Symkyn and his wife have their own double bed; the "daughter had a bed, all by herself / Right in the same chamber" (I, A, 4142–4143); and the baby has a cradle at the foot of his parents' bed. These are the sleeping arrangements in Symkyn's house—at least when the night begins.

The reader will notice right away that both the "Miller's Tale" and the "Reeve's Tale" are not only actually shorter but move at a much faster pace than did the "Knight's Tale." The slow, stately pace of the romance lends dignity and high seriousness. In contrast, the *fabliau* plot moves along rapidly, as befits a joke. Characters and action are described in the low style, featuring not only common but even vulgar language. Geffrey the narrator has already warned the audience that a churl's tale will be told churlishly, and anyone who doesn't like it should turn the page and choose another tale.

After a big dinner, the family and their guests go to bed. The miller, like his counterpart on the Canterbury pilgrimage, is drunk; his sound (and noisy) sleep is crucial to the success of the plot. Not only does the miller snore, but he breaks wind in his sleep; and the combination of the two sounds in such close quarters keeps Aleyn and John awake. Aleyn, restless, concocts a plan to requite the miller for stealing their corn: he will have sex with (*swyve* [I, A, 4178]) the miller's daughter. Aleyn feels he has a legal right to this; because the miller has stolen something that belonged to them (the corn), he can steal something back (a father was believed to own his daughter's virginity). Promptly, Aleyn acts on this belief: he gets up, sneaks over to the daughter's bed,

> *And shortly for to seyn, they were aton.*
> *Now pley, Aleyn, for I wol speke of John.*

> And shortly for to say, they were at one.
> Now play, Aleyn, for I will speak of John.

> (I, A, 4197–4198)

While Aleyn "plays," John grows jealous: his fellow student is having a good time, getting something back from the miller, and he is getting nothing. A smart clerk, he too concocts a plot:

> *And up he roos, and softely he wente*
> *Unto the cradel, and in his hand it hente,*
> *And baar it softe unto his beddes feet.*

> And up he rose, and softly he went
> Unto the cradle, and took it in his hand,
> And bore it softly to the foot of his bed.

> (I, A, 4211–4213)

In an age before artificial lighting, the nights were dark indeed. So, when the miller's wife wakes up "and went out to piss" (I, A, 4215), she readily mistakes John's bed for that of her husband. John seizes his opportunity with the miller's wife. The success of this encounter—"she had not had so merry a fit in a long time" (I, A, 4230)—mocks the miller's own inferior sexual expertise.

Both students have a good night, and so do both women. So satisfied is the miller's daughter that she even tells Aleyn of the location of the cake made from the stolen corn. It appears that Aleyn will really be victorious now, having not only the girl's virginity but the cake too. But Aleyn has been so busy with his own nocturnal activities that he is not aware that John has been similarly engaged. Searching for John's bed in the pre-dawn darkness, he feels the cradle, assuming that it is still at the foot of the marital bed. So, looking for the other bed, he inadvertently goes into the miller's bed. Thinking the miller is his fellow John, he brags of having had sex with the miller's daughter "three times in this short night" (I, A, 4265). This news wakes the horrified miller:

> "Who dorste be so boold to disparage
> My doghter, that is come of swich lynage?"

> "Who dares to be so bold as to disparage
> My daughter, who is come of such lineage?"

(I, A, 4271–4272)

On the medieval marriage market, a virgin is worth more than a nonvirgin. So Aleyn's action now had "disparaged" or reduced the marriageability of the miller's daughter, for whom both he and his clerical father-in-law had such high ambitions. The miller looks like a fool for not having been able to protect his daughter's valuable virtue.

In an attempt to take revenge for the loss, the miller grabs Aleyn by the throat and punches him in the nose. The ensuing fistfight awakens Symkyn's wife, sound asleep after her night of love. She thinks it is the two clerks fighting. In an attempt to separate them, she grabs a stout stick. Having only the light of a moonbeam, she mistakes the gleaming bald pate of her husband for the head of one of the clerks, "and smote the miller on the piled skull" (I, A, 4306). Meanwhile, the two clerks grab their cake, mount their horse, and flee, leaving the miller with a daughter and wife sullied and a sore skull besides. Thus gown triumphs over town with the scholars triumphant and the guileful miller beguiled. The Reeve is satisfied with his own revenge: "Thus have I requited the Miller in my tale" (I, A, 4324).

Intricately interlaced between and within each of the first three of *The Canterbury Tales*, the theme of requital constitutes a strong unifying principle. The Miller wants to *quyte* the Knight, asserting his right to tell a tale out of order. He uses contrasting characters to debunk and mock the high idealism of the love relationship in the "Knight's Tale." The Miller's character Nicholas wants to get the better of both John the carpenter and Absolon. Offended by the insult to his fellow carpenter John, the Reeve tells another *fabliau* with an even lower moral tone in which two students (parallel to Nicholas) pay back a dishonest miller with trickery of their own. In all three tales, the idea of giving as good or better than one gets motivates the behavior of characters within the tale as well as between the tale-tellers. Thus are the three tales carefully linked, while at the same time variety is provided by following up a long, serious, slow-moving romance with two short, funny, fast-paced *fabliaux*. In the most clearly unified set of tales in the collection, Chaucer has also provided considerable variety.

Yet another principle of unity in the three tales is the key image that informed the "Knight's Tale": Fortune and her wheel. In each of the three tales, the competition between men is so intense that no one man can stay at the top for long. Palamon wins Emelye at last despite Arcite's best efforts; John the carpenter loses the fidelity of his pretty young wife owing to the strenuous efforts of the lusty Nicholas; the miller is cuckolded and his daughter disparaged. The top of Fortune's wheel is a precarious position because the less fortunate below, striving to be more fortunate, are always pushing. The competitive relationship between men extends to the narrators too; each is striving to be the best, to win the prize. Fortune favors now one, now another. The motif of *quyting* and the image of Fortune's wheel reminds the audience that the tale-telling on this pilgrimage is a contest, with winners and losers.

SUGGESTIONS FOR FURTHER READING

Hines, John. *The Fabliau in English.* London: Longman, 1993. 107–159. Hines argues that the *fabliau* is appropriate for an argument between "two churls."

Howard, Donald R. *The Idea of the Canterbury Tales.* Berkeley: University of California Press, 1976. 237–247. Howard traces the interconnections between the "Miller's Tale" and the "Reeve's Tale," especially with regard to the rivalry between the two tale-tellers.

Jensen, Emily. "Male Competition as a Unifying Motif in Fragment A of the Canterbury Tales." *Chaucer Review* 24, no. 4 (1990): 320–328. Jensen relates the tales of the Knight, the Miller, and the Reeve on the basis of the varying balance between two key factors: male competitiveness and female passivity.

Kolve, V. A. *Chaucer and the Imagery of Narrative: The First Five Canterbury Tales.* Stanford, Calif.: Stanford University Press, 1984. 217–256. In Chapter 5, "Death as Tapster and the Horse Unbridled," Kolve explicates the tales by means of symbolism from the visual arts.

Muscatine, Charles. *Chaucer and the French Tradition.* Berkeley: University of California Press, 1957. 198–204. Muscatine shows how Chaucer uses the French *fabliau* tradition.

The Man of Law's Tale

Now Jhesu Crist, that of his myght may sende
Joye after wo, governe us in his grace.

Now Jesus Christ, who of his might may send
Joy after woe, govern us in his grace.

(II, B[1], 1160–1161)

A favorite didactic image in the visual arts of the Middle Ages is that of a ship adrift in a storm-tossed sea. The human soul often felt itself unable to control its own fate, bereft of protection by a higher power. The storm-tossed ship, then, is an image of human vulnerability. Women, especially when they lacked a strong male protector, must have felt themselves as powerless as that ship. For such women, faith in a strong fatherly God was encouraged. Only He could protect a weak woman. The Man of Law's Custance, or Constance, constant in her faith despite a multitude of hardships, teaches a lesson to the medieval audience. If so frail a woman could endure so much, all the more must the medieval Christian endure life's difficulties and be constant in faith in God, the ultimate port in a storm.

At the beginning of Custance's story, her life is stable and secure; she is a beloved virgin daughter in the house of her father, the emperor of Rome. Custance enjoys "excellent renown" (II, B[1], 150) for her womanly virtues:

"In hire is heigh beautee, withoute pride,
Yowthe, withoute grenehede or folye;
To alle hire werkes vertu is hir gyde;
Humblesse hath slayn in hire al tirannye.
She is mirour of alle curteisye."

"In her is high beauty, without pride,
Youth, without childishness or folly;
To all her works, virtue is her guide;
Humility has slain all tyranny in her.
She is the mirror of all courtesy."

(II, B[1], 162–166)

Beauty balanced by humility; youth without immaturity; courtesy, holiness and generosity: this is a catalogue of the virtues expected of women in the Middle Ages. Custance is thus a "mirror," a perfect example, of positive feminine qualities.

So famous for perfection is she that a group of merchants carry news of her to the court of the sultan of Surry, who promptly falls in love with her by reputation alone and determines to marry her. Their religious disparity—he is a Mohammedan and she is a Christian—would ordinarily be an impediment to the marriage. But so determined is the sultan to marry Custance that he is also determined to become a Christian. So the marriage negotiations are completed, and this high-born woman is dispatched to an unpredictable fate.

As befits an emperor's daughter, Custance travels with a great retinue consisting of "bishops . . . / Lords, ladies, knights of renown, / And other folk enough," (II, B[1], 253–255). Nevertheless, her departure from her father's house is sad:

Allas, what wonder is it thogh she wepte,
That shal be sent to strange nacioun
Fro freendes that so tendrely hire kepte,
And to be bounden under subjeccioun
Of oon, she knoweth nat his condicioun?

Alas, what wonder is it that she wept
On being sent to a strange nation
Away from friends that kept her so tenderly
And to be bound in subjection
To someone of whom she knows not his condition?

(II, B[1], 267–271)

An emperor's daughter will still be her husband's subordinate in marriage; worse, she does not know what kind of man he is (his "condition"). The storyteller, a Man of Law, knows well that not all men make good husbands; his comment about husbands all being good is meant ironically, to suggest the opposite. Despite the risks involved in leaving her father and her home, Custance resigns herself to women's lot in life:

> *"Wommen are born to thraldom and penance,*
> *And to been under mannes governance."*

> "Women are born to thralldom and penance,
> And to be under man's governance."

(II, B[1], 286–287)

When God ejected Adam and Eve from the Garden of Eden, Eve, and all women ever after, were punished by "thralldom," subjection to their husbands. Because they are subordinate creatures, women's happiness is contingent on the character of the men who "govern" them. So Custance has good reason to weep in fear of her unknown fate.

And ill-fated this marriage is, as the narrator predicts in an extended lament on the baleful influence of the stars, the gods, and the emperor's own poor judgment in not consulting an astrologer on the matter of Custance's marriage. The astrological references would have reminded the medieval audience that all men and women are as helpless with respect to the planetary influences on their fate as is the unfortunate heroine.

No sooner does Custance arrive at the kingdom of her betrothed than his mother takes an instant dislike to her. The sultaness is determined to take revenge on her son for his decision to "abandon his old sacrifices" (II, B[1], 325) for his new bride. Medieval Christians took religion so seriously that many were willing to die (or to kill) rather than abandon their faith, but this did not mean that they were any more understanding of those of other faiths who felt equally strongly about their own religions. Quite the contrary: to the medieval Christian, a non-Christian was simply an evil-doer, a "well of vices" (II, B[1], 323) like the sultaness. So when the sultan's mother feigns conversion to Christianity and stages a huge feast for Custance and her retinue, the medieval audience would have seen it as only typical of faithless unbelievers that the "cursed crone" (II, B[1], 432) causes not only all the Christians at the dinner table but even her own son to be chopped into pieces. Only Custance survives.

The narrator reflects on the meaning of Custance's survival:

> *Men myghten asken why she was nat slayn*
> *Eek at the feeste? Who myghte hir body save? . . .*
> *No wight but God.*

Men might ask why she too was not slain
At the feast? Who might save her body? . . .
No one but God.

(II, B[1], 470–471, 476)

Oddly, given the violence of the sultaness's hatred, Custance is not killed.
Her punishment is to be placed aboard a rudderless ship and set adrift.
Despite her misfortunes, Custance retains her faith in God and prays
constantly throughout all the "years and days" (II, B[1], 463) of her
turbulent voyage. A lone woman like Custance can turn for protection only
to her Father in heaven.

By this point, it would have been clear to the medieval audience that
Custance's improbable story of relentless misfortune is an allegory of the
Christian soul's relationship with God. Allegory, a popular genre in the
Middle Ages, fulfilled what many saw as the ultimate purpose of literature:
to teach religious and moral values. Characters in an allegory represent
qualities of the human spirit (in this case, constancy); their behavior
models proper response to life events (in this case, patience in adversity).
If it is virtuous to endure misfortune, then, by that same logic, the greater
the misfortune endured, the greater the virtue. Things will get much worse
for the heroine before they get better, so that she might demonstrate her
virtue (and instruct members of the audience on endurance of their own
petty misfortunes).

Totally vulnerable to human depravity, Custance, a "weary woman full
of care" (II, B[1], 514), tosses about at sea, until at last she is shipwrecked
on the seacoast of Northumberland. There a constable takes her home to
his wife Hermengyld. Although both the constable and his wife are pagans,
as are all their countrymen, the wife is so impressed by Custance's virtue
that she converts to Christianity. When her husband, hitherto a staunch
pagan, finds out about this (through the miracle performed by the newly
saintly Hermengyld), he is so impressed by the virtue of both his wife and
Custance that he, too, converts to Christianity.

These conversion stories show that the "Man of Law's Tale" is influenced
by another popular medieval genre, the *legenda*, or saint's life. A saint in
the Roman Catholic church, then as now, is one whose perfection is such
that the church officially declares that he or she is in heaven with God and
worthy of veneration by the faithful on earth. But whereas the Catholic
church in the modern period has established strict procedures for evaluat-
ing saintliness, in the Middle Ages believers were ready to deem any
unusual event miraculous and to attribute it to the power of a saint. So the

legendae are full of improbable events. Conversion of non-Christians, sometimes by the thousands, was often attributed to a saint's influence. Custance's convert count is only three (the sultan, Hermengyld, and the constable); this is relatively modest compared to the heroic achievements recounted in other medieval *legendae*.

In the *legendae*, virtue must be tested to prove itself heroic. Thus a "young knight," prompted by Satan, develops a "foul affection" for Custance (II, B[1], 585–586), but she rejects his advances:

> *And for despit he compassed in his thoght*
> *To maken hire on shameful deeth to deye.*

> And for spite he plotted in his thought
> To make her a shameful death to die.

(II, B[1], 591–592)

All his love turns to hate, and he vows revenge. He murders Hermengyld and frames Custance for the crime by laying the murder weapon beside the body.

But if, as is said in the "Prioress's Tale," "murder will out" (VII, 576), so will innocence. Custance is brought before the king, Alla, as one presumed guilty. Alla's heart fills with pity at the sight of this "innocent," this "lamb" (II, B[1], 617–618). An accused murderer in a foreign land, Custance is in an unusually vulnerable situation: she "stands alone" (II, B[1], 655), deprived of the customary protection afforded to a high-ranking woman. Without her father the emperor, or a husband, Custance is vulnerable to evil men like the lustful knight. But a good man, a man of "compassion" whose "gentle heart is filled with pity" (II, B[1], 660), a man like Alla, responds to Custance's weakness by becoming her protector.

In addition to this earthly protector, she prays for Christ to be her "strong champion this day" (II, B[1], 635). Christ responds with a miracle. When the evil knight swears that Custance is guilty, a hand "smote [him] upon the neck-bone" (II, B[1], 669), killing him, and a marvelous voice from on high proclaims the knight's guilt and Custance's innocence (II, B[1], 669–677). As is typical in the *legendae*, these miracles so impress the pagans that they are converted in droves, including Alla. Alla's conversion means that he, like the sultan of Surry before him, can marry Custance without the impediment of religious differences. They are married, and all seems well.

But the trials of the holy never cease in this imperfect world. Again, as in the previous betrothal to the sultan of Surry, it is the mother—in this

case Donegild, Alla's mother—who is the agent of evil. Unlike her predecessor, however, she does not prevent the marriage but bides her time.
Custance is not one of those saints who die for the privilege of retaining
their virginity. Instead, she is a good wife; she accepts the physical aspect
of marriage, mindful of her duty in her *estat*:

> *They goon to bedde, as it was skile and right;*
> *For thogh that wyves be ful hooly thynges,*
> *They moste take in pacience at nyght*
> *Swiche manere necessaries as been plesynges*
> *To folk that han ywedded hem with rynges,*
> *And leye a lite hir hoolynesse aside.*

> They went to bed, as was reasonable and right;
> For, though wives are very holy things,
> They must take in patience at night
> Such necessary acts as are pleasing
> To the folk who have wedded them with rings
> And leave a little holiness aside.

(II, B[1], 708–713)

Custance's "patience" in the "necessary acts" of marriage results in the birth
of the all-important "knave-child," the son and heir (II, B[1], 715).

But in the interval between conception and birth, Alla must go off to
battle in Scotland. This gives his wicked mother her chance to undo all
Custance's good fortune. In place of the joyous birth announcement, Alla's
mother counterfeits a message that Custance had been "delivered . . . / Of
so horrible a fiendish creature" (II, B[1], 750–751) that no one in the castle
could remain there. In the Middle Ages physical deformities were thought
to be either a punishment for sin or a product of witchcraft, or both; so
Custance can only be an "elf," a malign otherworldly creature operating by
means of "charms" or "sorcery" (II, B[1], 754–755).

But Alla responds to the misfortune with charity and hope, as a good
medieval Christian should. He sends a letter accepting the child and his
mother:

> *"Kepeth this child, al be it foul or feir,*
> *And eek my wyf, unto myn hoom-comynge.*
> *Crist, whan hym list, may sende me an heir*
> *Moore agreable than this to my likynge."*

> "Keep this child, be it foul or fair
> And also my wife, until my homecoming.

Christ, when he will, may send me an heir
More agreeable, more to my liking than this."

(II, B[1], 764–768)

Again, however, Donegild subverts the message. New forgeries command that Custance and the child be once again set adrift upon the sea.

The repetitious woes of Custance cause lamentations among the people of Alla. The constable, charged with carrying out what was thought to be the king's cruel punishment, raises the age-old unanswerable question: How can a just God permit such evil in the universe?

> "O myghty God, if that it be thy wille,
> Sith thou art rightful juge, how may it be
> That thou wolt suffren innocentz to spille,
> And wikked folk regne in prosperitee?"

> "O mighty God, if it be your will,
> Since you are rightful judge, how may it be
> That you will allow innocents to die
> And wicked folk to reign in prosperity?"

(II, B[1], 813–816)

In the face of these imponderables, medieval people believed that the only proper spiritual response for a Christian was the constant faith in Christ articulated by the heroine:

> "He that me kepte fro the false blame
> While I was on the lond amonges yow,
> He kan me kepe from harm and eek fro shame
> In salte see, althogh I se noght how.
> As strong as evere he was, he is yet now.
> In hym triste I, and in his mooder deere,
> That is to me my seyl and eek my steere."

> "He who kept me from false blame
> While I was on the land among you,
> He can keep me from harm and also from shame
> In the salt sea, although I do not see how.
> As strong as ever he was, he is yet now;
> In him I trust, and in his mother dear.
> He is to me my sail and also my rudder."

(II, B[1], 827–833)

The human condition is subject to fate, chance, and the malice of others, in the face of which man is as helpless as a lone woman with a newborn child. Only Christ and his mother Mary can help and guide the Christian soul in this situation. If the little boat is the soul, Christ is its sail and its *steere*, or rudder; Christ moves and guides the soul, and the soul must place itself trustfully in his care, with faith and hope that he will "bring her home" at last (II, B[1], 874).

The image of the ship at sea must be seen in conjunction with another important medieval mental image, Fortune's wheel. Alone at sea, Custance is at its bottom. Positive forces are mobilizing to help her: Alla returns home, learns the truth, mourns the loss of his wife and child, and kills his wicked mother. But Custance, ignorant of these events, is again "fallen . . . into heathen hand" (II, B[1], 909). Her ship nears land, which should presage renewed good fortune. But in another cyclical pattern, a villainous man, a steward, casts lustful eyes upon her as did the knight, and climbs aboard the ship with intent to rape her. Custance fights back "well and mightily" (II, B[1], 921); the villain falls overboard and drowns. This threat removed, it is replaced by another: Custance is adrift again. The narrator laments the fate of "this weak woman" (II, B[1], 932). But biblical examples show that God aids the weak: David slew Goliath, and Judith slew Holofernes. While Custance appears to have neither the ingenuity of David nor the assertiveness of Judith, God's help arrives in the form of good men who protect Custance against depraved men who would take advantage of her powerlessness.

After a long time, Custance's father finally learns of his daughter's mistreatment by the mother of her first betrothed. He sends his delegate to wreak vengeance on the people of Surry. On his way (as Fortune would have it), the delegate meets Custance's ship. Although her poor *array* does not indicate her *estat* as emperor's daughter, he is moved by pity and, taking her under his protection, brings her and her child to live with him and his wife (who is actually Custance's aunt). In addition to this improvement in her circumstances (her movement upward on Fortune's wheel), her husband Alla, having come to Rome on pilgrimage to do penance for the killing of his mother, meets the worthy senator and through him is reunited with his wife and child. The final swift turn of Fortune's wheel restores Custance to her rightful position, to "bliss" and "joy" as great as is possible on this earth (II, B[1], 1075–1076). Now all that remains is to be reunited with her father; and Custance plans this great occasion as that most common of medieval rituals, a ceremonial meal. The emperor has accepted an invitation to come to Alla's house for a feast. This feast will be in joyful contrast to the feast at which the treacherous sultaness destroyed Custance's happiness. At this meal, Custance reveals her identity to her father. But it is this same beloved father who set Custance adrift in the first place by sending her into a strange land for her first marriage; she begs him to do it no more. Happiness for Custance is being at a family dinner, surrounded by beloved protectors, safe from ever being "alone . . . in the salt sea" again (II, B[1], 1109–1110).

Turmoil ends, then, with an image of earthly happiness: a family reunited at a celebratory feast. Alla and Custance resume married life. Eventually, the child inherits his grandfather's position as emperor of Rome. Since this is a religious allegory, not a fairy tale, Alla and Custance live happily, but not forever after:

> *Joye of this world, for tyme wol nat abyde;*
> *Fro day to nyght it changeth as the tyde.*
>
> Joy of this world will not last for all time;
> From day to night it changes as the tide.
>
> (II, B[1], 1133–1134)

In this unstable world, no "joy" or "quiet" lasts forever (II, B[1], 1131). In only a year, Alla dies. With the death of her husband, Custance's world is again destabilized. She must journey once more, this time to Rome, capital of Christendom. When she finds her father there, she is finally secure from the vicissitudes of *aventure* (II, B[1], 1151). In her earthly father's house, she lives as a proper widow, "in virtue and in holy alms-deed" (II, B[1], 1156).

At death, Custance goes to the home of her heavenly Father, receiving the reward for patient endurance. Heaven is a place of peace, security and stability, of "joy that lasts forever more" (II, B[1], 1076). Only there does Custance's soul find a safe harbor and an end to the turning of Fortune's wheel. Custance's sea voyage mirrors the pilgrimage to Canterbury, which in turn mirrors the journey of the Christian soul to its Father's house. Even as the Canterbury pilgrims seek to reach Becket's shrine, they know that even this beautiful edifice is only a foretaste of the City of God, the Heavenly Jerusalem.

Many of *The Canterbury Tales* end with a little prayer for the audience. Sometimes these are tongue-in-cheek, even satirical, capping off a bawdy tale hardly conducive to salvation. But here the prayer is entirely appropriate. Just as Custance achieves the ultimate success, eternal salvation, so the Man of Law prays that his audience will be rewarded by Christ with a permanent turn of Fortune's wheel, with "joy after woe" (II, B[1], 1161), heavenly reward after earthly suffering. Nowhere is the didactic message of a tale clearer. A combination of an allegory and a saint's life, the tale of Custance is a pattern for the Christian life as it was imagined in the Middle Ages.

SUGGESTIONS FOR FURTHER READING

Braswell, Laurel. "Chaucer and the Art of Hagiography." *Chaucer in the Eighties*. Eds. Julian N. Wasserman and Robert J. Blanch. Syracuse, N.Y.: Syracuse University Press, 1986. 209–221. Braswell sees the "Clerk's Tale," the "Second Nun's Tale," the "Man of Law's Tale," and the "Prioress's Tale" as operating according to the conventions of the popular medieval story type, the *legenda*.

Delany, Sheila. "Womanliness in the Man of Law's Tale." *Chaucer Review* 9, no. 1 (1974): 63–72. Delany sees Custance as an "emblematic model for men and women alike."

Dinshaw, Carolyn. *Chaucer's Sexual Poetics*. Madison: University of Wisconsin Press, 1989. 88–112. In Chapter 3, "The Law of Man and Its 'Abhomynaciouns,' " Dinshaw offers an interpretation of Custance as victim of the legal system in a patriarchal society.

Hallissy, Margaret. *Clean Maids, True Wives, Steadfast Widows: Chaucer's Women and Medieval Codes of Conduct*. Westport, Conn.: Greenwood Press, 1993. 89–112. In Chapter 7, "The Good, the Bad, and the Wavering: Women and Architectural Space," Custance's wanderings are seen as images of the helplessness of the unprotected woman.

Kolve, V. A. *Chaucer and the Imagery of Narrative: The First Five Canterbury Tales*. Stanford, Calif.: Stanford University Press, 1984. 297–358. In Chapter 7, "The Rudderless Ship and the Sea," Kolve explicates the tale by means of symbolism from the visual arts.

Manning, Stephen. "Chaucer's Constance, Pale and Passive." *Chaucerian Problems and Perspectives*. Eds. Edward Vasta and Zacharias P. Thundy. Notre Dame, Ind.: University of Notre Dame Press, 1979. 13–23. Custance, though on first reading apparently a "somewhat pallid creature," is, in Manning's view, "not [a] passive ninny" but a strong feminine "presence."

Martin, Priscilla. *Chaucer's Women: Nuns, Wives, and Amazons*. Iowa City: University of Iowa Press, 1990. 131–155. In Chapter 8, "The Saints," Martin analyzes the character of Custance along with that of Grisilde in the "Clerk's Tale" and Cecilea in the "Second Nun's Tale" as examples of perfect womanly virtue.

The Wife of Bath's Prologue and Tale

"*Experience, though noon auctoritee*
Were in this world, is right ynogh for me
To speke of wo that is in mariage."

"Experience, though no authority
Existed in this world, is quite enough for me
To speak of woe that is in marriage."

(III, D, 1–3)

Experience versus authority: the first line of the "Wife of Bath's Prologue" sounds a key note that will inform both prologue and tale. According to Chaucer's description of her in the "General Prologue," Alisoun of Bath violates authority in the matter of *array*. At the time of the Canterbury pilgrimage, she is a widow. One important requirement of the *estat* of widowhood is to wear widow's garb, attire prescribed by unwritten tradition as well as by the writings of advisors to women. A widow, they believed, should wear modest attire in a somber hue. A wimple should cover her forehead, a short, straight veil her hair. The lines of her dress should be simple. Most significantly, her demeanor should match her clothing. The proper widow should cast her eyes downward and wear a sorrowful facial expression. Observance of all these "shoulds," these rules of proper behavior, would constitute an outward demonstration of an inner attitude of mourning. However, as is obvious in her portrait in the "General Prologue," the Wife of Bath's *array* is flamboyant for a woman past forty, much less a widow. Her red stockings alone mark her off as improper. Her hat, as big as a shield, her five coverchiefs, her foot mantle about her hips, and her spurs on her feet indicate not only that she is ready for travel but also that she

3. *A woman jousting with a friar.* Yale MS. 229 fol. 100v. By permission of the Beinecke Rare Book and Manuscript Library, Yale University.

ready for a new love. Extroverted in manner, assertive in speech, she defies authority by her appearance alone.

To medieval people, the term *auctoritee* was loaded with significance. The term carried the weight of the important thoughts of the past as embodied in books. Reading books, much less writing them, was the privilege of a small minority. Literacy rates were low among medieval people in general, both men and women. Even among men, only the clergy (an even smaller minority) were educated in the ancient languages of scholarship: Greek and Latin. Only clerics, then, were able to read the books of the great *auctours*. While not all would complete the course of study and actually become ordained priests, the system operated as if this was their intention. Clerical education involved learning the old books: the scriptures, the writings of the early interpreters of the scriptures known as the Fathers of the Church, and the works of classical authors such as Homer and Virgil. To medieval people, this body of writing constituted all knowledge, and it was accessible to them only through the classical languages Greek and Latin. Students learned these languages specifically to read the old books.

Having done that, however, the medieval learner was not encouraged to question those authors. Here is a major difference between the medieval educational system and our own. The students were not trained to extend their own knowledge through innovation or to think for themselves, much less claim *auctoritee* for themselves. Instead, education meant memorizing authoritative statements from the past to use in argumentation. Formal education in the Middle Ages, then, was a matter of men teaching the thoughts of men to other men in languages known only to men. The ideas, and the books that contained them, constituted what the Wife of Bath calls *auctoritee*: a body of knowledge considered certain, complete, and unquestionable.

In contrast to the male-dominated system of formal education, women's education was informal, practical, and home-based. A typical medieval woman would learn domestic skills appropriate to her *estat*. While upper-class women might learn art, music, or embroidery to supplement these basic skills, it was not assumed that even they had to be literate in their native languages, much less in the languages of scholarship. Some writers of conduct books (manuals of instruction in manners) believed that a woman should know how to read so that she could better help her husband. Others thought that only girls destined for the convent needed to learn how to read at all, since married women could consult their own personal authorities: their husbands. A wife's ability to read might work against a husband's best interest; a married woman might gain an edge over her husband in argument, a situation that medieval people thought disruptive of proper order within the family.

Education, then, was a matter of learning what the authors of the past had to say. Those authors, and most medieval readers, were men. So to the Wife of Bath *auctoritee* equals male domination. Authority allows men to control women through books, books that, ironically, cannot contain truth precisely because they were written by men. The Wife opposes to the concept of authority her own concept of *experience*. Experience allows the individual to respond to questions discussed by the authorities. Experience is personal and subjective. It does not require special learning, access to formal education, or study of archaic languages. What it does require is the living of a life. In the context of the Wife of Bath's discussion, authority equals men, whereas experience equals women. The opinions about women recorded in the old books are wrong, she believes, because the authorities who wrote them, being men, had no experience of women. Women, who naturally have experience of themselves, were not considered authorities, even on themselves. The "Wife of Bath's Prologue and Tale" can be read as her attempt to correct through speech the distortions and omissions in written language about women. In the process of correcting, she is also redefining the nature of authority.

In speaking at all, especially so assertively and at such great length, the Wife of Bath is taking over a role that medieval people considered appropriate only to men. In courtesy books and sermons, the virtue of feminine silence is stressed. The ideal woman is a quiet woman. Women's private speech is described in many medieval sources as "clattering" or "jangling," an unpleasant and discordant sound. Public speaking before an audience, as done by teachers and preachers, is a strong way to claim authority. The subject on which the Wife of Bath claims authority, the subject at which she is an expert through her experience, is marriage.

As the "General Prologue" tells us, the Wife of Bath has been married five times. She was twelve at the time of her first marriage, young for a woman of her social position (the urban middle class) but not shockingly so. It was more unusual for a woman to outlive five husbands. Because of the risks of childbearing in the primitive medical conditions of the Middle Ages, women often died young. The Wife's relative longevity may be Chaucer's way of suggesting that the Wife has had no children, although that matter is never settled definitely. Children or no, the Wife of Bath knows that the church frowned on marrying so many times. The church, that most serious of authorities, had rules for every aspect of life. One area that was most specifically restricted by church law was marriage.

Marriage, though permitted, was considered to be an *estat* inferior to perpetual virginity; if one wished to be perfect, one would join a celibate religious order. If one could not be perfect, if one found that a lifelong commitment to abstinence from sexual intercourse was too difficult, then marriage was a second-best choice. But the virtuous Christian, especially the Christian woman, was advised to marry only once, probably in youth when the fires of lust were most difficult to control. Following the death of a husband, the ideal was for the widow to give up remarriage for the sake of devoting her thoughts to God. To marry a second time was seen as an indication that a woman was not committed to her own spiritual development. To marry five times, and to be eager for a sixth marriage, shows that the Wife of Bath is sensual and consequently mired forever in spiritual inferiority. She does not apologize for this, but accepts her sexuality, saying that she was born under the sign of Venus and is therefore fated to be fleshly.

But more important than what the Wife does on this matter of remarriage is the way in which she justifies her actions. Her intellectual stance is that of a person who looks at the evidence and decides for herself. This independence of mind is commonly valued in modern times but was decidedly not in Chaucer's day—certainly not for women. The image shown in the photo at the beginning of this chapter, a woman jousting with a friar, would to the medieval eye have represented a comical but still threatening disruption of the social order. Horsemanship and swordplay were for men only in the Middle Ages, and combativeness of any sort in women was strongly discouraged. For a woman to assume a male stance— mounted and armed—and to take issue not just with any man but with a man who represented the church's teaching authority was an act of cosmic rebellion against the natural order of things. The believing Christian, male or female, was expected to obey the teaching authority of the church unquestioningly. The Wife of Bath fights this. Instead, she violates hierarchical order by jousting with a friar, that is, by challenging the *auctours*, the authoritative sources, and interpreting them herself, without what she regards as interference from the clergy.

The way she handles the biblical evidence on the morality of remarriage is an example of her method. In the story of the Samaritan woman in the Bible, Christ appears to criticize the woman for having been married five times. The Wife recounts the episode:

"Herkne eek, lo, which a sharp word for the nones,
Biside a welle, Jhesus, God and man,
Spak in repreeve of the Samaritan:
'Thou hast yhad fyve housbondes,' quod he,
'And that ilke man that now hath thee
Is noght thyn housbonde,' thus seyde he certeyn.
What that he mente therby, I kan nat seyn."

"Listen, too, what a sharp word indeed,
Beside a well, Jesus, God and man,
Spoke in reproof of the Samaritan:
'You have had five husbands,' he said,
'And that man that has you now
Is not your husband,' thus he said surely.
What he meant by that, I cannot say."

(III, D, 14–20)

Although this story was commonly interpreted by church authorities as a prohibition against remarriage, the Wife claims not to be sure what Christ meant. In other words, she calls into question the accepted church teaching on the story and decides to interpret it for herself. In doing, so she defies ecclesiastical authority.

The proper path of knowledge was considered to be from God to scripture, from scripture through the teachings of the early church theologians, down the church hierarchy, finally arriving at the common believer. For any individual, especially a woman, to decide for herself how to interpret the Bible was a defiance of proper chains of command in the church. The Wife's position, then, is a declaration of intellectual independence. Although "men may divine and gloss, up and down" (III, D, 26), official interpreters (all men) may "gloss," explain, and interpret a text as they will, the Wife will ignore their interpretations and decide for herself. She will joust with a friar and win.

It is clear from her many references that the Wife of Bath is familiar with the Bible, the early church theologians, and a great variety of Greek and Latin classics; in other words, she knows all the great *auctours*. It is never made clear how a woman of her time and social class would have access to this kind of information. In our own day, it is common to see women in authoritative positions, and we are used to thinking of women as having access to the same form and content of education as men do. But for a medieval woman to know these kinds of things is in itself a defiance of the medieval idea of order. To use her knowledge to engage in theological disputation is an exceedingly unladylike, even a subversive, activity.

No matter what the church may say, the Wife of Bath sets her own experience against it. If the church frowns on remarriage, the Wife of Bath advocates it on the grounds that she is not interested in becoming a perfect Christian, but only in being an adequate one. She explains her position on the matter of moral mediocrity by citing the theological distinction between a counsel and a commandment. A commandment is an order to avoid sin, like "Thou shalt not commit adultery." Such an order binds everyone in all circumstances. A counsel, on the other hand, is a suggestion, a piece of advice on how to increase in virtue. For example, the counsel to take vows of perpetual virginity applies only to those who wish to be perfect. So, argues the Wife, "counseling is no commandment" (III, D, 67). One can legitimately choose the less virtuous path.

The Wife illustrates the difference between counsel and commandment by analogy to two everyday household objects: dishes and bread. Everyone knows, she says, that

> *"a lord in his houshold,*
> *He nath nat every vessel al of gold;*
> *Somme been of tree, and doon hir lord servyse."*

> "a lord in his household
> Has not every vessel all of gold;
> Some are of wood, and do their lord service."

(III, D, 99–101)

Virgins are like the gold vessels in God's household, like the good dishes in a modern household saved for special occasions: precious but untouched. Wives are like the inexpensive everyday plates made of wood in the Middle Ages: of less value but used every day.

Similarly, virgins are like "pure wheat-seed" (III, D, 143), the flour from which white bread was made. White bread was considered a delicacy in the Middle Ages, suitable for an aristocrat's table; peasants would eat dark bread. Wives are not as special as white bread; they are ordinary like "barley-bread" (III, D, 144), cheap and common, but nutritious. Everyone has his or her own "proper gift" (III, D, 103), personal talent, or role to play, even if it is an imperfect and inferior one. Because the Wife is not interested in being perfect, she need not obey all the recommendations set forth for those who would be. As a married woman rather than a consecrated virgin, she can be the everyday dishes and the brown bread in the household of the Lord.

In the process of marrying, she gains another kind of perfection, as an authority on the institution of marriage and a scholar on the subject of men:

> *"Diverse scoles maken parfyt clerkes,*
> *And diverse practyk in many sondry werkes*
> *Maketh the werkman parfyt sekirly;*
> *Of fyve husbondes scoleiyng am I."*

> "Diverse schools make perfect students;
> And diverse practice in many sundry works
> Makes the workman perfect, certainly;
> I am a scholar of five husbands."

(III, D, 44c-44f)

Like a carpenter who studies under a master, who then becomes a master carpenter himself and can teach others, the Wife is now a master of the art and science of marriage and can teach the Canterbury pilgrims.

Finding a sixth husband would give her an opportunity to hone her already substantial skills even further. But by wanting to remarry, the Wife defies the long tradition of the steadfast widow. Ideally, the widow is supposed to be in lifelong mourning; in the conduct books she is advised that she should pray for her husband, fast, and give alms to the poor, weeping all the while. Certain activities were clearly unsuitable to widows; one of these is traveling, or "wandering" as medieval people would call it, just as the Wife of Bath is doing now on the pilgrimage. We have already noticed how the Wife violates clothing customs. By speaking at such length and so assertively, the Wife misuses speech, that most troublesome of women's talents. Medieval widows were advised that the use of speech must be confined to prayer, and prayer must be confined to the home or the church. That way they could preserve themselves from the very kind of temptation that the Wife of Bath seeks so enthusiastically, sexual temptation.

Her explicit sexuality is the trait for which the Wife of Bath is most often remembered. Her beliefs and behaviors are in flagrant opposition to what medieval people saw as appropriate sexual expression within marriage. The Wife knows that she is attractive to men. Although she is not coy or reluctant, but enthusiastic about sex, she is also capable of sufficient control over her impulses to use sex in marriage as a weapon. She controls her husbands, particularly the three old ones, in two ways: by demanding sex and by withholding it.

The Wife of Bath sees marriage as basically about the use of what she calls the "member . . . of generation" (III, D, 116), the sex organ. Why, she asks, would God have made people with male and female sex organs if He did not intend them to use these organs? Sex organs are not, she reasons, merely for purgation of urine or for distinguishing a female from a male; they are also designed to pay what medieval people thought of as the *marital debt*. This concept in medieval canon law (church regulations) obliges husbands and wives to have sex with each other on demand. On the other hand, medieval canon law also restricted the number of times a married couple might have intercourse, so that they would not be excessive in their demands on each other.

Canon law limitations on marital sex sought to prevent just such a situation as the Wife of Bath describes:

> *"In wyfhod I wol use myn instrument*
> *As frely as my Makere hath it sent.*
> *If I be daungerous, God yeve me sorwe!*
> *Myn housbonde shal it have bothe eve and morwe,*
> *Whan that hym list come forth and paye his dette.*
> *An housbonde I wol have—I wol nat lette—*
> *Which shal be bothe my dettour and my thral,*
> *And have his tribulacion withal*
> *Upon his flessh, whil that I am his wyf.*
> *I have the power durynge al my lyf*
> *Upon his propre body, and noght he."*

> "In wifehood I will use my instrument
> As freely as my Maker has sent it.
> If I am reluctant, God give me sorrow!
> My husband shall have it evening and morning
> Whenever he wants to come forth and pay his debt.
> I will have a husband—I will not cease—
> Who shall be both my debtor and my slave,
> And have his tribulation too
> Upon his flesh, while I am his wife.
> I have the power during all my life
> Over his own body, and not he."

> (III, D, 149–159)

In marriage, the Wife intends to use her "instrument," her sexual organ, as generously as God gave it to her. If she is coy or plays hard to get, she asks that God punish her as if for a sin. Her husband can pay his marital debt any time he wants to; but she will also require him to have sex whenever she wants to. She reasons that she has a right to make these demands, and, by medieval standards, she does. But to exercise marital rights in this frame of mind is morally wrong even in marriage because it is excessive, selfish, and unloving. The Wife's language—debtor, slave, retribution, power—is not the language of love; her terminology connotes dominance, not reciprocity.

If marriage is about sex, it is about money too. The Wife's first three husbands were rich and old. To marry a rich old man was one way for a woman to make money quickly in the Middle Ages (and probably still is today). If a young girl like the twelve-year-old Alisoun married an old man, it is likely that she would be left a widow. In English law, the widow inherited at least a third of her husband's possessions by right and more if the husband chose to will it to her. If the Wife of Bath was the widow successively of three rich men, she has inherited at least one-third, and probably more, of each estate. This means that, by the time she is widowed the third time, she is a wealthy woman.

Now because the first three husbands were old, and because male potency generally declines with age, these men were hard pressed to have sex with the Wife of Bath as often as she wanted them to.

> *"The thre were goode men, and riche, and olde;*
> *Unnethe myghte they the statut holde*
> *In which that they were bounden unto me.*
> *Ye woot wel what I meene of this, pardee!*
> *As help me God, I laughe whan I thynke*
> *How pitously a-nyght I made hem swynke!"*

> "The three were good men, and rich, and old;
> They could hardly hold the statute
> By which they were bound to me.
> You know well what I mean by this, by God!
> So help me God, I laugh when I think
> How pitifully I made them work at night!"

> (III, D, 197–202)

The three good, rich old men could hardly "hold the statute," that is, meet the canon law requirements of paying the marital debt. You know what I mean by this, the Wife jokes (and so we do). She laughs when she thinks how piteously she made them work at night. Although the Wife thinks the old men's senile efforts humorous, the medieval audience would see a more sinister aspect.

In the Middle Ages, people believed that sexual activity shortened the lives of men. They did not know that the seminal fluid lost in sex was replenished every day, but rather regarded it as part of a limited lifetime supply of life-sustaining fluids. Logically, it would follow from this assumption that an old man would have even less of these vital spirits than he did when younger. According to their erroneous science, then, sex was risky for all men and particularly for old men. This is an element of the humor of the *senex amans* motif, seen also in the "Miller's Tale" and the "Merchant's Tale." But having made the mistake of marrying a young woman, Alisoun of Bath's old husbands had no choice but to try to render the marital debt whenever she demanded it, as well as they could, even at the risk of hastening death.

Even if they live, married life is bleak. Once Alisoun has married the rich old men "at church door" (III, D, 6), they hand over "their land and their treasure" (III, D, 204). Then she has them in her hand; she has power over them and has no need to please them anymore. In fact, she can choose to withhold sex on the occasions when they desire it:

> "I wolde no lenger in the bed abyde,
> If that I felte his arm over my syde,
> Til he had maad his raunson unto me;
> Thanne wolde I suffre hym do his nycetee."

> "I would no longer in the bed abide,
> If I felt his arm over my side
> Till he had made his ransom unto me.
> Then would I allow him to do his silliness."

(III, D, 409–412)

To Alisoun, the act of marital sex is reduced to a monetary transaction: husbands paying for sex with their own wives. Whether demanding sex or denying it, the Wife of Bath's only goal is to achieve dominance over her husbands.

All of this behavior is counter to the advice given to medieval women on how to behave in marriage. The medieval wife is supposed to be selfless, devoted to her husband, loving, concerned about his health and well-being, and devastated when he dies. But to the Wife of Bath marriage is not about love; it is about sex, money, and power. The marital argument is a vehicle for her to maintain and increase her power.

Just as she challenges the authorities in intellectual battle (jousts with a friar), so she engages in battle on the home front. The Wife demonstrates through a simulated marital argument how she gets power over her husbands through speech. Having mastered the art of the marital argument, she will now teach her techniques to her audience. First, a wife must disregard all advice given to women to be humble, to placate their husbands, to be peaceful and nonargumentative. Instead of being passive, the Wife is aggressive, a warlike woman. She brags of how she "complained first" and started a "war" (III, D, 390). To be successful in such a battle, a woman must know how men think. Men's thoughts on women are recorded in the books of the ancient *auctours*, many of which are filled with misogynistic (woman-hating) commonplaces: old sayings, old beliefs about women. The Wife of Bath knows these old books thoroughly. She knows that in the misogynistic lore all women are considered alike, and all dreadful. The Wife's fifth husband, Jankyn, has just such a book, which he reads in the evening by the fireside. But even before she met Jankyn, the Wife of Bath knew how to use this kind of information to her own advantage.

In a long monologue, the Wife of Bath shows how one can turn accusations against women into arguments against men. If men can generalize about women in their old books, so a husband can be accused of any fault of which men in general are typically guilty. Since no one can ever prove that he has *not* committed a certain offense, the argumentative power of an accusation, whether true or false, is never wasted.

But the main and most effective technique is to keep up a rapid fire of accusations, a series of blows so closely spaced that her husband cannot respond. See, for example, the long passage that begins at III, D, 235. "Why," said the Wife of Bath, "don't I have better clothes? Why are you spending time at my neighbor's house? Is she so beautiful? Are you so amorous? And why are you chatting with our maid? You old lecher, stop this foolishness! But if I have a friend that I want to talk to innocently, you chide like the Fiend if I walk or play at his house, while you yourself come home as drunk as a mouse and sit on your bench preaching to me. You say to me, it is a piece of bad fortune if you wed a poor woman, because she costs you so much. But if she's rich and of high lineage, it's a torment to keep her, too: she's proud and melancholy. If she's good-looking, then every man wants her; she will never maintain her chastity if it's assailed on every side. But if she's ugly, she'll leap on any man like a spaniel does, until she finds someone to take her." The monologue continues with the litany "You say . . . you say. . . ." What the Wife is doing is throwing her husband's possible arguments back at him, before he has a chance to articulate them himself.

Like most marital arguments, the Wife's simulated one-sided debate focuses on trivia. But on a significant issue, marital fidelity, the Wife's attitude is casual. The official teaching of the medieval church was that fidelity to one's wife or husband was absolute; no excuse justified adultery. The Wife, however, is much more permissive in her attitude toward sexuality than was common in her age. In the Middle Ages, the virginity of the virgin, the chastity of the wife, or the fidelity of the widow was considered the most important thing about them. The Wife, on the other hand, believes in total sexual freedom. Again she illustrates her belief by referring to another set of common domestic objects, the candle and the lantern:

> *"He is to greet a nygard that wolde werne*
> *A man to lighte a candle at his lanterne;*
> *He shal have never the lasse light, pardee.*
> *Have thou ynogh, thee thar nat pleyne thee."*

> "He is too stingy who would refuse to let
> A man light a candle at his lantern;
> He shall have no light the less, by God.
> If you have enough yourself, there's no cause to complain."

> (III, D, 333–336)

Women's sexual organs are compared to a lantern; men's to a candle. If a man can light his own candle at his own lantern (if a married man can have sex with his own wife), he will have light enough; he will not have the less light if other men light their candles at that same lantern. The husband will not get less sex because other men have had sex with his wife also. What, then, does he have to complain of?

With this flawed reasoning (humans cannot really be reduced to candles and lanterns), the Wife mocks the high ideal of marital fidelity just to win a point in an argument. Like sex, like money, argumentation is a way of gaining power. At a time when women did not have much authority in the larger world outside the home, the Wife's behavior shows how a woman's power drives could lead to problems in the little world of the family.

The Wife of Bath's first three husbands, then, are summarized as if they are one composite husband: old rich men who, worn out by nagging and sex, died and left their money to her. After these inheritances, she is in a financial position to marry her two younger husbands. A younger, poorer, but more attractive husband would be a luxury that only a well-heeled widow could afford. Much as today a financially successful middle-aged man can afford to discard his middle-aged wife and acquire a new young "trophy" wife, medieval widows were in a better financial position to snare an attractive young man than they were as penniless young girls. So with her two latter husbands, her fourth and fifth, the Wife of Bath has used her money to satisfy what she calls her "colt's tooth" (III, D, 602), her sexual attraction to young men.

But the Wife of Bath is aging. By the time of the Canterbury pilgrimage, she is over forty. With lifespans shorter than they are today owing to poor health care, a medieval woman of forty was considered old and termed a "hag" or a "crone." At a time of her life when medieval people believed that she should be preparing for death, the Wife is indulging in her sexual attraction to young men. The Wife knows that many would see her behavior as undignified, even grotesque. She interrupts the story of her marriages with a nostalgic reflection on her advancing age:

> "But—Lord Crist!—whan that it remembreth me
> Upon my yowthe, and on my jolitee,
> It tikleth me aboute myn herte roote.
> Unto this day it dooth myn herte boote
> That I have had my world as in my tyme.
> But age, allas, that al wole envenyme,
> Hath me biraft my beautee and my pith.
> Lat go. Farewel! The devel go therwith!
> The flour is goon; ther is namoore to telle;
> The bren, as I best kan, now moste I selle."

> "But—Lord Christ!—when I remember
> My youth, and my jollity,
> It tickles me about my heart's root.
> Until this day it does my heart good
> That I have had my world as in my time.
> But age, alas, that will poison all,
> Has bereft me of my beauty and my pith.
> Let go. Farewell! The devil go with it!
> The flour is gone; there is no more to tell;
> The bran, as best I can, I now must sell."

                                                                (III, D, 469–478)

Age has stolen Alisoun's beauty and her "pith," her very essence as a person. Most of her life had been built on her attractiveness to men; so it is painful to arrive at that time of life at which beauty wanes. Let it go, say farewell, says the Wife (in terms reminiscent of modern psychology). One must accept aging. Another domestic metaphor describes her image of herself as a woman past forty: the flour, the good part of the wheat, is gone. All that is left to sell is the bran, the shell, the part that is usually thrown away.

After her sad reflection on aging, she returns to her story. When she was younger, the Wife's wealth got her what she wanted: the two young husbands. The fourth husband has little individuality; the marriage seems to have been brief and, except for his infidelity, followed the usual wife-dominant pattern. Because he is "a reveler," a partygoer, and by implication also a flirt (III, D, 453), she makes him jealous in revenge. Now she regrets making him suffer, but she has no worries about his soul: he must be in heaven now because she was his purgatory on earth. The most interesting thing about the fourth husband is that the Wife was able to arrange a fifth marriage while the fourth husband was still alive. During the marriage she met an Oxford clerk who, having left school, was living with the Wife's *gossib* (III, D, 529), her gossip, also named Alisoun. The Wife pauses once more in her narrative to describe the characteristic features of the gossip relationship.

The term *gossib*, or god-sister, describes a relationship between two close women friends. In acknowledgment of the importance of their chosen relationship, such women might choose each other for godmothers of their children; thus they are god-sisters, related to each other through the child. A confidential relationship between two women, then as now, is characterized by confidential speech: gossip. Women today gossip with their friends in the same way that Chaucer describes in the "Wife of Bath's Prologue."

> "God have hir soule! Hir name was Alisoun.
> She knew myn herte, and eek my privetee,
> Bet than oure parisshe preest, so moot I thee!
> To hire biwreyed I my conseil al.
> For hadde myn housbonde pissed on a wal,
> Or doon a thyng that sholde han cost his lyf,
> To hire, and to another worthy wyf,
> And to my nece, which that I loved weel,
> I wolde han toold his conseil every deel.
> And so I dide ful often, God it woot,
> That made his face often reed and hoot
> For verray shame, and blamed hymself for he
> Had toold to me so greet a pryvetee."

"May God have her soul! Her name was Alisoun.
She knew my heart, and also my secrets
Better than our parish priest, I can tell you!
To her I told all my confidences.
For if my husband pissed upon a wall
Or did something that should have cost him his life,

> To her, and to another worthy wife,
> And to my niece, whom I loved well,
> I would have told his confidences, all of them.
> And so I did quite often, God knows it,
> Which often made his face red and hot
> For very shame, and he blamed himself
> For having told me such a private thing.
>
> (III, D, 530–542)

A gossip knows everything about her friend. To her, all thoughts would be confided, whether trivial (one's husband pissing on a wall) or serious (one's husband committing a capital offense). Women love to confide in their women friends, so not only the individual gossip but others (another worthy wife, a niece) would know the Wife's *conseil*, her confidential business. She laughs at the thought of how men would blush if they knew that intimate details of their private lives were confided to the gossip. In this description, Chaucer has the gossip relationship between women down pat. He acknowledges how important this relationship is to women by giving Alisoun of Bath and her gossip the same name. The two women are so close that they are virtually identical.

The Wife's husband was away in London all that Lent. During the penitential season, the Wife is supposed to be occupied with spiritual duties. Instead, she uses it as a better opportunity to play, to see and be seen. In Lent, liturgical ceremonies abound: visitations, vigils, processions, preachings, pilgrimages, miracle plays, and weddings. The Wife has a good time going to all these religious events for their social value. With her husband away, Alisoun has plenty of opportunity to go back and forth to her gossip's house and there spend time with Alisoun's boarder Jankyn.

Alisoun and Jankyn have "such daliance," such a flirtation (III, D, 565), that they agree to marry when the Wife next becomes a widow. The Wife of Bath justifies this breach of fidelity to her living husband with another of her typical domestic metaphors:

> "*I holde a mouses herte nat worth a leek*
> *That hath but oon hole for to sterte to,*
> *And if that faille, thanne is al ydo.*"

> "I hold a mouse's heart not worth a leek
> If he has only one hole to run to,
> And if that fails, all is lost."
>
> (III, D, 572–574)

According to the analogy of the mouse and the hole, a woman should plan for the future by providing herself with a new husband during the lifetime of her current one, just in case.

Despite the fact that the Wife is older than either her fourth or her fifth husbands, the fourth husband does indeed die before she does, and his funeral is one of Chaucer's funniest scenes. By this time, having had three occasions to practice before, the Wife knows proper behavior for a widow at her husband's funeral. She cries all the time and displays a sad countenance, "as wives must, for it is custom"; but she covers her face with her veil to disguise the fact that she really "wept but little," being already provided with a new husband (III, D, 588–589, 592). The Wife is following her husband's body as it is borne in procession to church, and her intended, Jankyn, is one of the pallbearers.

> "As help me God, whan that I saugh hym go
> After the beere, me thoughte he hadde a paire
> Of legges and of feet so clene and faire
> That al myn herte I yaf unto his hoold.
> He was, I trowe, twenty wynter oold,
> And I was fourty, if I shal seye sooth;
> But yet I hadde alwey a coltes tooth."

> "So help me God, when I saw him go
> After the bier, I thought he had a pair
> Of legs and feet so clean and fair
> That I gave all my heart unto his hold.
> He was, I think, twenty winters old,
> And I was forty, to tell the truth;
> But yet I always had a colt's tooth."

> (III, D, 596–602)

The Wife has acknowledged her lustful attraction to young men. As medieval people would have expected, Lust, one of the Seven Deadly Sins, has serious consequences. The Wife's lust causes her to make a big mistake when, only a month after the death of the fourth husband, she marries Jankyn,

> "And to hym yaf I al the lond and fee
> That evere was me yeven therbifoore."

> "And to him I gave all the land and property
> That ever was given to me before that time."

> (III, D, 630–631)

On their wedding day, she gives Jankyn all the money and property inherited from the three rich old husbands. It was customary in the Middle Ages for men thus to endower their wives, but it was not customary for women to do this for their husbands. Alisoun had an absolute right to her money and had more economic experience than Jankin. In thus handing over money and property to Jankyn against the common practice in medieval marriage, she gives up her authority over him as well.

This is a good deal for a twenty year old like Jankyn. He is marrying a woman twice his age, who is therefore likely to die first. Even if she lives, he still benefits, for she has given him all her inheritances. If money is power, as the Wife has alleged throughout her prologue, then she has lost power and Jankyn has gained it. With this one mistake, the Wife of Bath loses the authority built up over a lifetime.

Perhaps emboldened by his new financial power, Jankyn sees himself as a traditional dominant husband. To symbolize and reinforce his authority, he is a man with a book. The conflict between the Wife of Bath and Jankyn focuses on this book. For the medieval person, books were repositories of absolute truth. So expensive and scarce in the Middle Ages were books that it would not be uncommon for even a literate person to own no books at all. The fact that Jankyn has only one book means that he reads it over and over. Constant repetition and exclusive use lend this book even more authority. Jankyn's book is a "book of wicked wives," a compendium of misogynistic lore (III, D, 685). Such anthologies of separate works, sometimes on a single subject like this one, sometimes on unrelated topics, were common in the Middle Ages. This book collects a chorus of voices affirming a single proposition: women are evil.

Who would have written such a book? Certainly not a woman. The writer or compiler would be a clerk: a priest or a man in training to become one. The Wife questions the authority of such texts which, according to her, have a built-in bias:

> "For trusteth wel, it is an impossible
> That any clerk wol speke good of wyves,
> But if it be of hooly seintes lyves,
> Ne of noon oother womman never the mo.
> Who peyntede the leon, tel me who?
> By God, if wommen hadde writen stories,
> As clerkes han withinne hire oratories,
> They wolde han writen of men moore wikkednesse
> Than al the mark of Adam may redresse."

"For you can believe it, it is impossible
For any clerk to speak well of wives,
Unless it is of holy saints' lives,
But of no other women.
Who painted the lion, tell me, who?
By God, if women had written stories
As clerks have within their oratories,
They would have written of men more wickedness
Than all the sons of Adam may redress."

(III, D, 688–696)

Just as a painting depicting the killing of a lion would look different if depicted from the lion's viewpoint, if women had the authority to write, they would testify to the evil deeds of men. The Wife of Bath clearly sees that the type of authority available through books is male authority. Jankyn is using the power of the book to supplement his domestic power. The written word, he thinks, will keep his unruly wife in check.

The stories to which Chaucer refers in this passage were repeated over and over in medieval writings. The parallel stories of Livia and of Lucia are typical examples.

"Lyvia hir housbonde, on an even late,
Empoysoned hath, for that she was his fo;
Lucia, likerous, loved hire housbonde so
That, for he sholde alwey upon hire thynke,
She yaf hym swich a manere love-drynke
That he was deed er it were by the morwe;
And thus algates housbondes han sorwe."

"Late one evening, Livia
Poisoned her husband, because she was his foe;
Lucia, lecherous, loved her husband so
That, so he would always think of her,
She gave him such a kind of love-drink
That he was dead before morning;
And therefore husbands always have sorrow."

(III, D, 750–756)

Both killed their husbands: one for hate and one for love. Livia poisoned her husband because she hated him. Lucia loved her husband so much that to ensure his devotion she gave him a love potion so powerful that it killed him. The stories show that, whether they hate their husbands or love them, women are destructive. This no-win situation shows that, as the Wife of

Bath says, it is impossible for a clerk to speak well of wives. The Wife of Bath's frustration, disgust, and anger at Jankyn, who would "never stop / Reading this cursed book all night" (III, D, 788–789), triggers the culminating argument.

The Wife's war throughout her prologue has been with the authority of the book. On the subject of women, the *auctours*, the makers of books, have no experience. Women, who have experience of themselves, have no authority. Jankyn's claim to the authority of a husband, reinforced by the authority of his book, drives his wife not only to rage but also to physical violence:

> "Al sodeynly thre leves have I plyght
> Out of his book, right as he radde, and eke
> I with my fest so took hym on the cheke
> That in oure fyr he fil bakward adoun.
> And he up stirte as dooth a wood leoun,
> And with his fest he smoot me on the heed
> That in the floor I lay as I were deed."

> "All suddenly I ripped three leaves
> Out of his book, right while he was reading, and also
> With my fist I hit him on the cheek
> So that he fell backwards into our fire.
> And up he started like a mad lion,
> And with his fist he struck me on the head
> So that I lay on the floor as if dead."

                                                    (III, D, 790–796)

The Wife's attack on Jankyn's book is a strong image of the real source of the couple's problems: the authority attributed to old ideas. The resulting marital fistfight acts out the intellectual battle that has been raging in this household all along.

The modern reader must realize that by medieval standards husbands were considered to be acting within their rights when they beat their wives. To medieval people, superiors in a hierarchy were allowed to discipline their inferiors, much as it was considered appropriate, until very recently, to spank children. For the Wife of Bath to hit her husband at all, much less first, is a violation of medieval norms for proper wifely behavior because she is a subordinate. Therefore, he has a right, when she initiates violence, to retaliate. But when he thinks he has killed her, he is horrified. Medieval people did not believe that the right to marital discipline included murder.

At this point, the Wife has Jankyn at a serious disadvantage. He will do anything to save her life and incidentally save himself from a charge of murder. Pathetically, she cries out to him,

> " 'O! hastow slayn me, false theef?' " I seyde,
> " 'And for my land thus hastow mordred me?
> Er I be deed, yet wol I kisse thee.' "

> " 'Oh! have you slain me, false thief?' I said,
> 'And for my land have you murdered me?
> Yet before I die, I will kiss you.' "

(III, D, 800–802)

Remorseful, Jankyn promises never to hit her again; he begs the forgiveness of what he thinks is a dying woman. Knowing she has the upper hand now, she leaps up and hits him again. She gets the last blow as well as the last word in the argument.

This crisis allows her to triumph over Jankyn and to restore her position as the ultimate marital authority:

> "But atte laste, with muchel care and wo,
> We fille acorded by us selven two.
> He yaf me al the bridel in myn hond,
> To han the governance of hous and lond,
> And of his tonge, and of his hond also;
> And made hym brenne his book anon right tho."

> "But finally, with much care and woe,
> We came to an agreement between the two of us.
> He gave me all the bridle in my hand,
> To have the governance of house and land,
> And of his tongue, and of his hand also;
> And I made him burn his book right away."

(III, D, 811–816)

The image of a bridled horse is appropriate here because the Wife of Bath is now the rider and Jankyn the horse; she controls the relationship. In recognition of this reversal, he returns to her the governance of house and land, the possessions that she so unwisely made over to him on their wedding day. He also cedes power over his tongue and hand; he will not speak against her or beat her any more. To make sure that Jankyn doesn't get out of control again, the Wife immediately makes him burn that book of wicked wives. The authority of the book has made Jankyn into too assertive a husband. To restore what she sees as the correct power balance, the book, the receptacle of male authority, has to be destroyed.

When the Wife gets back all the mastery, all the sovereignty in the marriage, she is happy. After that day they never have any more arguments, and she is as kind to him as any wife from Denmark to India. The Wife concludes her prologue by presenting the proper marital relationship as one in which the wife has the upper hand. The power issues in the prologue will recur in the tale as the Wife explores the issue of what women most desire. The Wife knows what she desires: she wants the kind of authority that in her culture is traditionally given only to men.

The Wife's prologue and her tale are connected by this key idea of *auctoritee*. Chaucer sees that a woman wants the freedom to choose and govern as she wishes, to have power, at minimum over herself, but even more, over her husband. So it is fitting that the tale the Wife tells begins with a rape, a woman's ultimate loss of control, and ends with a complete reversal, a female-dominant marriage.

The Wife's tale is a romance, a story of adventure set in an Arthurian fairyland. The domestic society headed by King Arthur is organized as a typical medieval feudal household. At its center is a married couple, a king and his queen, surrounded by bachelors, unmarried young men, the king's retainers. These young men must prove themselves as men in the courtly world in order to earn rights to marry. In the meantime, bachelors must uphold the chivalric ideal by being chaste themselves and by being prepared to defend, even at the cost of their own lives, the dignity of chaste womanhood. Thus, the more grievous the violent crime perpetrated by one of these youths:

> And so bifel that this kyng Arthour
> Hadde in his hous a lusty bacheler,
> That on a day cam ridynge fro ryver,
> And happed that, allone as he was born,
> He saugh a mayde walkynge hym biforn,
> Of which mayde anon, maugree hir heed,
> By verray force, he rafte hir maydenhed.

> And so it happened that this king, Arthur,
> Had in his house a lusty young knight,
> Who, one day, came riding from a river,
> And it happened that, alone as he was born,
> He saw a maid walking in front of him,

> From which maid, soon, against her will,
> By very force, he seized her maidenhead.
>
> (III, D, 882–888)

Against her will, by force he seized her maidenhead; he raped her. *Maugree hir heed*: this critical phrase links the tale to its prologue and calls attention to a key theme in the tale. The Wife has argued for the importance of will in women. Rape ignores that will. Rape constitutes a radical failure to consider what a woman wants. This particular rape is all the more serious by medieval standards because the young woman has been robbed of an irreplaceable treasure: her virginity.

For this reason there is great clamor in the kingdom. Rape, in this land of Faery, is a capital offense, and the knight is accordingly condemned to die. Before carrying out the death penalty, King Arthur, at the request of the queen and her ladies, turns the decision of whether to spare or to execute the knight over to this company of women. Their will shall prevail. They are capable of authorizing that the death penalty be carried out. Their decision, however, is to delay the punishment on one condition: that the knight undergo a journey to learn "what thing it is that women most desire" (III, D, 905).

The motif of a knight setting forth on a journey during which he changes, sometimes physically but always psychologically, is a common one in the romance tradition. Such a journey is difficult, requiring a large commitment of time, the typical twelvemonth and a day. The requirement of the psychological journey as a punishment for the crime of rape recognizes that a rapist shows a radical lack of understanding of women. In order for such a man to be released, he must change radically, to the point where he can learn to respect will in women. The knight can live only if he no longer presents a threat to the community of women.

The knight sets forth on a pilgrimage into the world of women. To find out the answer to the question that will save his life, he must listen respectfully to women, that is, regard them as authorities on themselves. Some of the suggestions made to him on what women most desire simply repeat the misogynistic commonplaces found in those old books written by clerks:

> *Somme seyde wommen loven best richesse,*
> *Somme seyde honour, somme seyde jolynesse,*
> *Somme riche array, somme seyden lust abedde,*
> *And oftetyme to be wydwe and wedde.*

Some said women love riches best,
Some said honor, some said jolliness,
Some rich array, some said pleasure in bed,
And often to be widowed and wed.

(III, D, 925–928)

One of the commonplace opinions on what women most desire is based on
the idea that women cannot keep a secret. This idea is so interesting to the
talkative Wife of Bath that she engages in a long digression about King
Midas' wife, who betrayed her husband's secrets to a brook. Digression,
however, was not considered a flaw in medieval literature, but merely an
amplification of the story. The Wife returns to her main story line when
the young knight meets an old wife.

The term *wyf* in Middle English meant women in general as well as
married women in particular. (Alisoun herself is the "woman" of Bath.)
This old wife is unmarried. The knight notices immediately that she is ugly.
The old woman, the hag or the crone, is often seen in medieval sources as
a wise woman or a witch who intuitively, as if by magic, has knowledge of
things unknown to others. This old wife claims to have the answer that
the knight seeks. She will tell him the secret only if he will make a promise
to do whatever she wants in return. Twice she uses the loaded medieval
term *trouthe* (III, D, 1009, 1013). This term not only has the connotation
of the modern term *truth*, which it so closely resembles, but it also means
a binding verbal commitment. In days before written contracts, lawyers,
and courts, a man's spoken word was his bond; a man who broke his word
lost his reputation. No matter how circumstances changed, no matter how
difficult the task, even in the face of death, a man must keep his pledged
word, his troth. Commonly, troth is pledged between and man and man,
and only in the marriage ceremony between man and woman. But here,
the old wife insists on a commitment, a troth-plight, before she reveals her
secret. If the young knight doesn't learn what she knows, he will die. She
will teach him, but only at a price; he must "requite" her (III, D, 1008), pay
her back for her efforts. He plights his troth; she tells her secret.

Confident, the knight returns to the court to the gathering of women
who will judge him. All the women of the court are there, women from
each of the three *estats* of women's lives: virgins, wives, widows. All wait
for the knight's answer:

"Wommen desiren to have sovereynetee
As wel over hir housbond as hir love,

And for to been in maistrie hym above.
This is youre mooste desir."

"Women desire to have sovereignty
As much over their husbands as over their lovers,
And to be in mastery above them.
This is your greatest desire."

(III, D, 1038–1041)

This, then, is what women want: the same position of power in marriage that they once had in courtship. Before marriage, a man defers to the wishes of his love; he honors her, he places her not only above all other women but above himself too. Then, in the hierarchical system prevalent in the Middle Ages and not unknown today, once a woman is married, she becomes subordinate to her husband. Chaucer knows that women don't like this. They want to be in mastery or sovereignty above their husbands; they want to have the kind of power that they had before marriage.

Having said this, the knight knows that his fate now depends on the will of the women of the court. But the old wife has given him the correct answer; no virgin, wife, or widow contradicts him. He has completed his task; he has learned to think the way women do. He now understands that his crime was a crime precisely because, in violation of her will, it deprived a woman of her right to mastery or sovereignty over her own body. Knowing what he knows now, he could never rape again; so his life is spared.

But he must keep his troth to the old wife. It had never occurred to the knight that what the old wife would want was him. He is horrified at the idea that he must either violate his troth or marry one who, even she admits, is "foul, and old, and poor" (III, D, 1063). He is ashamed of a marriage in which he is "disparaged" (III, D, 1069), reduced in prestige and social status. Marry her he must, and so he does. He marries reluctantly, "with no joy, nor feast at all," but with "heaviness and much sorrow," and "privily," not in public as is customary but in private, showing that he is ashamed of this relationship (III, D, 1078–1080).

Private ceremony or not, once married it is his responsibility to have sex with his wife. The knight's reluctance is comical, especially contrasted with his old wife's enthusiasm. All day the knight has been hiding, like an owl, who never appears except at night. It is conventional in marriage poetry of the Middle Ages that the new husband's enthusiasm for sex is so great that he can hardly wait for the day to pass. This knight's attitude is quite the opposite: he wishes bedtime would never come. But it does, and husband and wife are brought to bed. It was part of the traditional medieval marriage ceremony that the couple were accompanied to the marriage bed by representative members of the wedding party. They would then discreetly leave, and it was assumed that the marriage would be consummated. But it is not clear that this marriage will be.

The woebegone groom is tossing and turning back and forth, extremely reluctant to do his duty. His old wife teases him for his sexual reticence:

> "Fareth every knyght thus with his wyf as ye?
> Is this the lawe of kyng Arthures hous?
> Is every knyght of his so dangerous?"

> "Does every knight behave like this with his wife?
> Is this the law of King Arthur's house?
> Is every knight so careful of his virtue?"

(III, D, 1088–1090)

The old wife's use of the term *daungerous* is calculated here. *Daunger*, in the courtly love tradition, describes the virtuous reticence of a young maiden— just such a maid as the knight deprived of her maidenhead. The reluctant bridegroom is the same lusty bachelor who got into all this trouble for being too sexually aggressive, for being a rapist. While he cannot actually be raped by his old wife, he now knows what it is like to act against *his* will.

The old wife reminds him that he owes her the consummation of their marriage, not only because she is his wife but also because she has saved his life. Why, since she has never treated him unjustly, is he so reluctant to give her her due? The knight replies truthfully, if not tactfully,

> "Thou art so loothly, and so oold also,
> And therto comen of so lough a kynde,
> That litel wonder is thogh I walwe and wynde."

> "You are so loathsome, and so old too,
> And come of such low kindred,
> That it is little wonder that I toss and turn."

(III, D, 1100–1102)

Old, ugly, and low-born: these are the knight's objections to his new wife. She accepts these terms as fact and proceeds to demonstrate to the knight how unimportant they are to the success of the marriage.

Like her fictional creator, the Wife of Bath, this old wife is skilled at logical argumentation. Despite the fact that these subjects form the matter of men's education, not women's, the old wife can reply to each of the knight's objections in detail. She sets out to prove, through logic and argument, that the three reasons why the young knight objects to her are all superficial and therefore wrong. The old wife uses the traditional elements of an argument: she defines terms, she cites examples, she quotes authority, and finally she drives her point home.

Rearranging the order of her husband's objections to suit herself, the old wife begins by addressing herself to the issue of low birth. The term *gentil* in the Middle Ages referred primarily to the upper classes, those of high birth. It was believed that character traits were transmitted through blood-lines and that therefore lineage counts: the son of an earl would by nature be morally superior to the son of a churl. However, medieval people could not help but notice that this general principle did not always apply. Nobility of character, the second and more important type of *gentilesse*, was often found in people of low *degree*. The old wife reminds her husband that he is "most virtuous" who does "gentle deeds"; it is the gentle deeds, not the accident of birth, that makes the "greatest gentleman" (III, D, 1113–1116). Conversely, a "villain's sinful deeds make a churl" (III, D, 1158), not his lower class ancestry. In her own case, this is, of course, all the more true:

> "And therfore, leeve housbonde, I thus conclude:
> Al were it that myne auncestres were rude,
> Yet may the hye God, and so hope I,
> Grante me grace to lyven vertuously.
> Thanne I am gentil, whan that I bigynne
> To lyven vertuously and weyve synne."

> "And therefore, dear husband, I conclude thus:
> Even if my ancestors were rude,
> Yet may the high God, so I hope,
> Grant me grace to live virtuously.
> Then I am gentle, when I begin
> To live virtuously and avoid sin."

(III, D, 1171–1176)

Having disposed of her low birth, she moves on to a related issue that her husband did not mention, her poverty. She cites the example of Christ, who chose to live as a poor man. Certainly, no one can believe that Jesus, the king of heaven, would choose a "vicious living," a life of vice (III, D, 1182). Not only Christian theologians but also classical philosophers believed that poverty indicated detachment from material things. With the right attitude, a man can be rich even if he doesn't have a shirt. Thus the proper attitude toward poverty also reverses common values.

> "He that coveiteth is a povre wight,
> For he wolde han that is nat in his myght;
> But he that noght hath, ne coveiteth have,
> Is riche, although ye holde hym but a knave."

> "He who covets is a poor person,
> For he wants what is not in his power to obtain;
> But he who has nothing, but covets nothing,
> Is rich, even if other people think him a knave."

(III, D, 1187–1190)

The old wife cites other virtues of poverty before she moves to her conclusion: the second character trait to which her husband objects is in reality an indicator of virtuous living.

Finally, his third and most serious objection is that she is old and therefore ugly. Here Chaucer wants his audience to remember the passage in the "Wife of Bath's Prologue" in which the Wife complains about her lost youth. At the time of the pilgrimage to Canterbury, the Wife is over forty and feels old. Her discouragement about losing her attractiveness to men is reflected in her characterization of the old wife in her tale. The old Wife of Bath would like to believe what the old wife in her tale is saying: that age is a virtue, not a defect; and more, that an old woman can still be loved by a young man. So she gives her old wife the argument that old age should be respected. Old women can be desirable as wives because of, not in spite of, age and ugliness:

> "Now ther ye seye that I am foul and old,
> Than drede you noght to been a cokewold;
> For filthe and eelde, also moot I thee,
> Been grete wardeyns upon chastitee."

> "Now though you say that I am foul and old,
> Then you need not dread being a cuckold,
> For filth and age, I must remind you,
> Are great protectors of chastity."

(III, D, 1213–1216)

Thus she wraps up her argument that low birth, poverty, old age, and ugliness, despite common beliefs to the contrary, are actually assets in a woman and make her more desirable as a wife.

The reader notices that, like the audience of Canterbury pilgrims listening to Alisoun of Bath, the knight has listened carefully and without interruption to everything his old wife has to say. At this point, it is important to remember the words with which the Wife began her prologue and tale: authority and experience. *Auctoritee* involves being not only an author, but also a master or a teacher. This state, seldom achieved by women in the Middle Ages, is the one to which both the Wife of Bath and her old wife aspire. Alisoun of Bath has been a student of marriage through five marriages; now she wishes to be considered an expert. Her character, the old wife, is similar: she lectures her husband as one with *auctoritee*, the right to be listened to. Old and loathsome as she is, she cannot use the seductive techniques available to young, attractive women but must rely on her intellectual abilities. The old wife's long monologue, like the Wife of Bath's own, argues the point that women should be valued not only for youth and beauty but also for maturity and intelligence. In modern times, it is is common for women to act as teachers from the earliest elementary years through the university, but at that time the function of teaching belonged only to men. In creating the character of the old wife in her tale, the Wife creates a teacher figure who gives the knight the last stage of his education. As she demolishes his erroneous beliefs one by one, he learns from her, finally, to reject his culture's false expectations of women.

Now he is ready for a test. She gives him a multiple choice:

> "Chese now," quod she, "oon of thise thynges tweye:
> To han me foul and old til that I deye,
> And be to yow a trewe, humble wyf,
> And nevere yow displese in al my lyf,
> Or elles ye wol han me yong and fair,
> And take youre aventure of the repair
> That shal be to youre hous by cause of me. . . .
> Now chese yourselven, wheither that yow liketh."

> "Choose now," she says, "one of these two things:
> To have me foul and old until I die,
> And be a true humble wife to you
> And never displease you in all my life;
> Or else have me young and fair,
> And take your chances on the visitors
> Who shall come to your house because of me. . . .
> Now choose yourself, whichever one you like."
>
> (III, D, 1219–1225, 1227)

The knight's response shows that at last he is ready to accept the idea of female sovereignty in practice as well as in theory:

"My lady and my love, and wyf so deere,
I put me in youre wise governance;
Cheseth youreself which may be moost plesance
And moost honour to yow and me also.
I do no fors the wheither of the two,
For as yow liketh, it suffiseth me."

"My lady and my love, my dear wife:
I put myself in your wise governance.
Choose yourself what might be most pleasing
And most honorable to both you and me.
I don't care which of the two you pick,
For what you want satisfies me."

(III, D, 1230–1235)

This complete surrender of his thought processes to his wife's authority is so sudden that the old wife apparently must check her hearing. She asks him again and specifically whether she has obtained mastery over him:

"Thanne have I gete of yow maistrie," quod she,
"Syn I may chese and governe as me lest?"
"Ye, certes, wyf," quod he, "I holde it best."

"Then, have I gotten mastery from you?" she said.
"Since I may choose and govern as I wish?"
"Yes, certainly, wife," he says, "I think it best."

(III, D, 1236–1238)

Now this old wife has achieved what women most desire: *maistrye*, the authority to teach. The young husband, having learned so well, deserves a reward and gets one. Since this is, after all, a tale of fairyland, the old wife is miraculously transformed into what men most desire: an attractive young woman. After this metamorphosis both husband and wife are happy, which expands the old wife's point: there is no need for men to fear women's power because if women get authority they will use it to a good end. In the tale, Queen Guinevere and her ladies use their power over the knight not to decapitate him at once, as they could, but rather to give him a chance to learn from his error. The consequence is the miraculous transformation of a man from a rapist into a good husband. The young knight has truly completed his journey to male maturity.

The conclusion of the tale reinforces the key concepts with which the Wife began her prologue. What the knight learns is not written in books; he learns by listening to his wife's speech. Book-learning conveyed authority in the Middle Ages, but in creating the Wife of Bath, and in turn *her* character, the old wife, Chaucer makes the point that experience, knowledge gained from life, is also important. Particularly on the subject of women, words written in books are flawed because men wrote the books. Women know themselves, but their teaching or writing carries no *auctoritee*. This leads to the great contradiction built into the clerkly texts: the people with authority have no experience, and the people with experience have no authority. The speaking voice of a woman is identified with experience but was seen as less true than the words written in books. What is more true, then: books or life?

The "Wife of Bath's Prologue and Tale" is one possible answer to this question. In order to study women, the knight must stop reading, and must go on a journey through the world observing real women and listening to their words. The ladies of King Arthur's court did not send the knight to the library to find out what women most desire. He must disregard what the books say and listen to the speech of women. This is why the "Wife of Bath's Prologue and Tale" are among the longest pieces in *The Canterbury Tales*. This is also why both are full of references to the great *auctours* of the past, as if to prove that while the Wife can master them and thus become a master herself, she needs the additional knowledge gained by her own experience to give her true *auctoritee*.

Having proved her thesis to her satisfaction, the Wife winds up her tale with a prayer for all the other women in her audience, from the listeners of the Middle Ages to the readers of the present day:

> and Jhesu Crist us sende
> *Housbondes meeke, yonge, and fressh abedde,*
> *And grace t'overbyde hem that we wedde;*
> *And eek I praye Jhesu shorte hir lyves*
> *That noght wol be governed by hir wyves;*
> *And olde and angry nygardes of dispence,*
> *God sende hem soone verray pestilence!*

> and Jesus Christ send us
> Husbands meek, young, and fresh in bed,
> And grace to outlive the men we wed;
> And also I pray that Jesus shorten the lives
> Of all who will not be governed by their wives;
> And old, angry misers, stingy of expense,
> God send them soon a true pestilence!

(III, D, 1258–1264)

The Wife of Bath would not be in her independent position were it not for her *estat*, widowhood. She prays that Jesus will give other women the same *estat* privileges by shortening the lives of insubordinate husbands and misers. "God send them pestilence," she prays, at a time when *pestilence* meant plague, a catastrophic disease that modern demographers suggest might have halved the population of Europe during the fourteenth century. This prayer is the culmination of Chaucer's comic characterization of the Wife of Bath: she invokes the power of the Almighty to supplement her own powerful will, and cursed be any mere mortal man who dares try to thwart that will.

Throughout her prologue and tale, the Wife of Bath takes an uncommon intellectual stance for a medieval woman. She asserts her own authority, based on her own experience. She believes that she has the ability to choose for herself against the dictates of authority. In a hierarchical system she refuses obedience. She approaches theology, both scripture and the writings of the Fathers of the Church, with a skeptical eye, interpreting sacred texts for herself. Her mode of thought is similar to, and therefore congenial to, that of many modern readers. We like to think of ourselves as questioning authority; to say that a person has a mind of his or her own is to us a compliment. Therefore it is easy to miss the fact that the Wife of Bath is in utter violation of the norms for medieval womanhood. In the little kingdom of the home, husbands are supposed to rule supreme, and wives to accept their position as contented subjects. Alisoun of Bath reverses that arrangement. The idea of the woman on top, the woman who claims authority over her husband, was to medieval people a symbol of the total disruption of cosmic order. But Chaucer makes his character so likeable that her controversial position wins the audience's approval.

The Wife of Bath's theories on marriage contribute to the ongoing discourse on this subject among the Canterbury pilgrims. When it is time to discuss the "Clerk's Tale" and the "Merchant's Tale," the reader will be expected to remember this feisty, aggressive, assertive woman: Alisoun, the Woman of Bath.

SUGGESTIONS FOR FURTHER READING

Carruthers, Mary J. "The Wife of Bath and the Painting of Lions." *PMLA* 94 (1979): 209–222. Carruthers contends that the root of the Wife's strength lies in her "economic experience as a wealthy west-country clothier"; this position of power allows her to "create . . . a mutually nourishing marital bond truer than any envisioned by the traditionalists."

Dinshaw, Carolyn. *Chaucer's Sexual Poetics*. Madison: University of Wisconsin Press, 1989. 113–131. In Chapter 4, " 'Glose / Bele Chose': The Wife of Bath and Her Glossators," Dinshaw sees the Wife of Bath's speech as rebellion against the authority of written texts.

Hallissy, Margaret. *Clean Maids, True Wives, Steadfast Widows: Chaucer's Women and Medieval Codes of Conduct*. Westport, Conn.: Greenwood Press, 1993. 163–184. In Chapter 10, "*Summa Feminarum*: The Archwife," Alisoun is presented as a misogynist's worst nightmare: a compendium of all the faults of women.

Hanning, Robert W. "From *Eva* and *Ave* to Eglentyne and Alisoun: Chaucer's Insight into the Roles Women Play." *Signs* 2 (1977): 580–599. Hanning sees the Wife of Bath and the Prioress as representing "two apparently irreconcilable contraries" in medieval men's view of women: the "emblem of all men's striving" as represented by the Prioress, and the "cause of his loss of self-control, freedom, and happiness" as represented by the Wife of Bath.

Kittredge, George Lyman. "Chaucer's Discussion of Marriage." *Chaucer: Modern Essays in Criticism*. Ed. Edward Wagenknecht. New York: Oxford University Press, 1959. 188–215. In his classic discussion of the running debate on marriage in the "Franklin's Tale," the "Clerk's Tale," the "Wife of Bath's Tale," and the "Merchant's Tale," Kittredge sees the tales as dramatizing interactions between the tale-tellers.

Margulies, Cecile Stoller. "The Marriages and the Wealth of the Wife of Bath." *Medieval Studies (Toronto)* 24 (1962): 210–216. Margulies shows how Alisoun "used to best advantage all her marital rights," especially legal and economic.

Martin, Priscilla. *Chaucer's Women: Nuns, Wives, and Amazons*. Iowa City: University of Iowa Press, 1990. 84–105. In Chapter 6, "The Merchandise of Love: Wives and Merchants," Martin examines the correlation between sex and money in the "Wife of Bath's Tale," the "Merchant's Tale," and the "Shipman's Tale."

Oberembt, Kenneth J. "Chaucer's Anti-Misogynist Wife of Bath." *Chaucer Review* 10 (1976): 287–302. Oberembt contends that the Wife of Bath is Chaucer's response to misogynistic literature.

Rowland, Beryl. "Chaucer's Working Wyf: The Unraveling of a Yarn-Spinner." *Chaucer in the Eighties*. Eds. Julian N. Wasserman and Robert J. Blanch. Syracuse, N.Y.: Syracuse University Press, 1986. 137–149. Rowland explicates the significance of the Wife's trade: weaving.

The Friar's Prologue and Tale

"Thou shalt with me to helle yet tonyght,
Where thou shalt knowen of oure privetee
Moore than a maister of dyvynytee."

"You shall go with me to hell tonight,
Where you shall know more about our secrets
Than a master of divinity does."

(III, D, 1636–1638)

Although Chaucer does not allow the Wife of Bath the last word on marriage, he wisely follows her tale with a complete change of subject. The Friar chides her for dealing with substantive issues, with "school-matter" of "great difficulty," which, he says, should be left to "preaching and to schools of clergy," that is, to men (III, D, 1272–1277). Now the Friar wants to turn from these weighty issues to *game*, comedy. Chaucer has often juxtaposed the term *game* to its opposite, *ernest*, seriousness. The two polarities, *ernest* and *game*, are not, however, mutually exclusive. Comedy in literature can be a vehicle of social criticism by means of which real problems are examined. So it is with the linked tales of the Friar and the Summoner, both of which depict a church in moral disarray.

A friar is a member of a religious community dedicated to the service of God. Friars take vows of poverty, chastity, and obedience; some also take vows of stability, meaning that they promise not to leave their abbey. Chaucer's Friar is a limiter, a preacher licensed to raise funds for his community within a specific geographical area. His "General Prologue" portrait describes how, in the course of his wanderings, he manages to break all his vows, especially his vow of poverty. Collecting money for his order gives him an opportunity to skim off the top for himself. Thus when he criticizes the Summoner, he does so despite his own guilt.

Summoners in Chaucer's day were employees of church courts whose task it was to "summon" alleged evildoers to those courts. Their modern analogues would be process-servers who deliver subpoenas to people involved in civil or criminal litigation. Because in the Middle Ages there were two separate court systems—civil and ecclesiastical—a system arose whereby moral offenses could be punished in ecclesiastical court. The Summoner, then, is defined by the Friar as a "runner up and down / With summonses for fornication," for premarital sex (III, D, 1283–1284). But, as the "General Prologue" says, this Summoner takes bribes to suppress the summonses. Like a police officer who accepts a bribe to lose a traffic ticket, the Summoner abuses the prerogatives of his office for his own profit. But so does his critic the Friar.

The behavior of both Friar and Summoner indicates the seriousness of the problems affecting the church in the fourteenth century. At its origin a persecuted minority sect, by the Middle Ages the Christian church had become a vast bureaucracy. As the largest nongovernment organization of its time, the church offered the institutional affiliation so prized by medieval people, as well as a career path for men without land and women without dowries. Religious orders, then as now, did attract members committed to a life in God's service. But the scarcity of secular alternatives guaranteed that at least some would join the religious life for less than ideal reasons. Abuses arose, such as those perpetrated by the Friar and the Summoner, both of whom use their ecclesiastical positions for their own profit. Each of these two malefactors uses his tale to *quyte* or pay each other back insult for insult. While their mutual rivalry is funny, their tales are *game* only on the surface. The Friar and Summoner are *ernest* in their hatred for each other, and Chaucer is *ernest* also in his criticism of the abuses that infected the medieval church.

The "Friar's Tale" begins with a summary of the kind of offenses for which a sinner might be summoned to ecclesiastical court: premarital sex, witchcraft, pimping, slander, adultery, robbing churches, violating wills and marriage contracts, failing to take the sacraments, taking interest on loans, and buying church offices. The Friar's list includes practices that, in modern law, belong to the separate sphere of civil offenses. While in the United States today, debate rages over whether acts regarded as immoral by some should be illegal for everyone, medieval people, being all of the same religion, saw no problem with overlap between church and state law. The church court system was under the control of a high official, "an archdeacon, a man of high degree," who "did execution" or enforced church law (III, D, 1301–1302). The summoner was his agent. Though not to be confused with the Canterbury pilgrim, this summoner of the "Friar's Tale" has a similar job, and, the Friar suggests, a similar racket to supplement the income from his legitimate function. The Friar's summoner had a network of acquaintances among medieval low-lifes, "bawds" (pimps), and "wenches" (prostitutes [III, D, 1339, 1355]). These would reveal the names of their customers to the summoner, who "would fetch a feigned mande-ment" or summons (III, D, 1360), pretending to summon both prostitute and customer. Then he would "let the wench go" (III, D, 1362) while accepting a bribe from the customer in exchange for destroying the forged summons. This procedure provided most of his rent or income, and none of it had to be returned to his supervisor the archdeacon.

But the summoner did not confine himself to extorting money from the guilty. He was also not above seeking a bribe from a poor, pathetic old widow. On his way to do that, he meets a fellow-traveler, a man all dressed in green (a color indicating the supernatural, the other world). The man in green identifies himself as a bailiff or estate manager. Embarrassed to identify himself as a summoner because of the bad reputation of his occupation, the summoner lies and says he is a bailiff too. The two travelers hit it off so well that they pledge their "troth . . . / To be sworn brethren till they die" (III, D, 1404–1405). Trade loyalties were an important part of medieval life, leading to the formation of such associations as those to which the five Guildsmen described in the "General Prologue" belong. Now that these two have pledged brotherhood, their relationship moves to a more confidential plane.

Like the church office of summoner, the secular office of bailiff was ripe for abuse. Knowing this, the summoner regards the bailiff as a master of the art of maximizing profits, with no regard to "conscience" or "sin" (III, D, 1422). This, the bailiff admits, he is. This summoner, as rivalrous with the bailiff as his fictional creator the Friar is with the Summoner, tries to one-up the man in green by claiming that he is even more of an extortioner: he has no conscience at all, no "stomach" or pity for his victims, and, moreover, he intends to persevere in sin: he "will not be shriven" (III, D, 1440–1441). Having so revealed himself to the man in green, the sum-moner feels entitled to similar confidences on his sworn brother's part, and so he asks him to reveal his true identity.

Brotherhood implies honesty, but these two con-men have been deceiv-ing each other. The summoner is no bailiff, but neither is the man in green, who is actually "a fiend" whose "dwelling is in hell" (III, D, 1448). Like the summoner, who "rides about" as the archdeacon's representative looking for victims, the fiend represents his boss, Satan, and he "rides for the same intent," looking for souls to damn (III, D, 1449, 1452). He has apparently found one in the summoner, as the summoner has already revealed his sins and declared his intention of remaining unshriven.

Instead of focusing on the implications of having taken a vow of brotherhood to a fiend, the summoner fixates on the mechanics of the man in green's deceptive appearance. The summoner's curiosity stops the narrative and diverts it into a discussion of demonology. Devils do not have a fixed shape but can assume various appearances: man, ape, or angel. This shapeshifting facilitates recruitment to the devil's company. But theological inaccuracy must be avoided, even in *game*; so the fiend explains how the devil's machinations do not mean that he is more powerful than God, but rather that God allows the devil to tempt man. In the cosmic hierarchy, fiends are subordinate to God, merely

> "Goddes instrumentz
> And meenes to doon his comandementz,
> Whan that hym list, upon his creatures."

> "God's instruments
> And means to do his commandments,
> When he wishes, upon his creatures."

> (III, D, 1483–1485)

Although the fiend's intention is to lure souls to damnation, when their intended victim "withstands . . . temptation" (III, B, 1497), he is all the more virtuous for having been tempted. Paradoxically, the temptation becomes "a cause of his salvation" despite the fiend's wicked "intent" (III, D, 1498–1499).

This theological concept, intent, will become crucial to the outcome of the tale. Medieval theologians taught that one could only sin deliberately, not through error or accident. While the summoner has pledged brotherhood to the fiend, he did so believing that the man in green was a bailiff. That is, it was not his intent to commit himself to the devil. Since the essence of sin lies in the will, one cannot sin unless one has truly intended the sinful act; nor is a commitment binding if made in error. In other words, the summoner's first pledge of troth was not binding. At this point, he has a second chance to repent and be saved.

But in folklore the pact with the devil is always presented as having irresistible appeal because it offers the promise of special secret knowledge not otherwise available. So the summoner, now with full knowledge and intent, re-commits himself:

> "My trouthe wol I holde, as in this cas.
> For though thou were the devel Sathanas,
> My trouthe wol I holde to my brother,
> As I am sworn."

> "I will keep my pledge, in this case,
> For even if you were the devil Satan,
> I will keep my pledge to my brother,
> As I am sworn."
>
> (III, D, 1525–1528)

The summoner seems damned; but, as the fiend himself said, resistance to the devil can be a cause of growth in virtue, and consequently of salvation. Paradoxically acting as "God's instrument" (III, D, 1483), the man in green gives the summoner one more chance to reverse himself and gain salvation. The new chance is again based on the concept of intent.

Riding toward a town, they meet a man driving a cart loaded with hay. The carter, angry at his horses, curses them: "The devil have all, both horse and cart and hay!" (III, D, 1547). Take it all, the summoner urges his demonic companion; the carter has given it to the devil. But the fiend refuses on the grounds that the carter did not really mean to send horse, cart, and hay to the devil: "It is not his intent" (III, D, 1556), and so his words are not binding. Sure enough, when the horses behave, the carter reverses himself and begs Jesus to bless them. This proves the fiend's point: "The churl spoke one thing, but he thought another" (III, D, 1568). Without true intent, his verbal formula was not binding. Like a modern person who angrily tells another to go to hell, perhaps not believing in hell at all or not genuinely wishing to consign his source of annoyance to eternal damnation, the formula of words is only an expression of anger, not a serious moral act.

But sometimes a person says "Go to hell," and means it. At this point in the tale, the summoner has correct understanding of the theological role of intention, and he has a chance to repent. He does not. Instead he reverts to his usual occupation: extorting money from innocent victims. This was the goal of his journey before he met the man in green, and now he intends to carry out his original plan. The widow is feisty, however; so getting the bribe out of her will be a professional challenge. The summoner invites the bailiff to watch his technique, as if to suggest that, in the matter of evildoing, a summoner could educate the very fiend.

The summoner begins by accusing the ancient dame of having "some friar or priest" with her; for her sexual transgressions, he has a summons for her to appear in church court or else risk the "pain of cursing," penalty of excommunication (III, D, 1583, 1587). The old lady protests: not only is she no fornicator, but she is too sick even to get to court. May she have a copy of the summons, that she may respond by "procurator," send a representative? For a mere twelve pence, says the summoner, he will "acquit" her of the whole matter (III, D, 1599)—a matter which, of course, he has invented in the first place. The old lady protests that she does not have twelve pence in the world:

> "Ye knowen wel that I am povre and oold;
> Kithe your almesse on me, povre wrecche."

> "You know well that I am poor and old;
> Show charity to me, a poor wretch."

>   (III, D, 1608–1609)

Generosity toward the poor is a biblical criterion for the good man; conversely, exploitation is a cause of damnation. But the fiend has just demonstrated to the summoner that all morality is a function of intent. Words spoken without intention are without force, but words spoken with intention are powerful. So if the summoner's soul is to be damned, it will be in consequence not merely of his deeds or words but of his intent.

At the old widow's request for charity, the summoner swears thus: "The foul fiend fetch me / If I excuse" her from paying twelve pence (III, D, 1610–1611). Now the summoner is damned if he collects the money from the old widow, because that is a sin; and damned also, by his own words, if he excuses her from payment. He complicates the moral situation further by alleging that she owes him her pan for the fine he once paid for her when she committed adultery. This accusation is too much for the old widow, who protests vociferously:

> "Thou lixt!" quod she, "by my savacioun,
> Ne was I nevere er now, wydwe ne wyf,
> Somoned unto youre court in al my lyf;
> Ne nevere I nas but of my body trewe!
> Unto the devel blak and rough of hewe
> Yeve I thy body and my panne also!"

"You lie!" said she, "by my salvation,
I was never before now, as widow or wife,
Summoned to your court in all my life;
Nor was I ever anything but faithful!
Unto the devil, black and rough of hue,
I give your body and my pan too!"

(III, D, 1618–1623)

Now both the summoner himself and the old widow have uttered words consigning the summoner's soul to hell. What remains is to determine whether these words were spoken with full intent and therefore have binding force. The fiend is the arbiter of intent. He asks the widow: Do you will what you said, do you speak "in *ernest*" (III, D, 1627)? She certainly does, and she strengthens the curse by repeating it yet again, but with the proviso that she will withdraw her curse if the summoner will repent. But the summoner will not. Offered the opportunity to repent, the hardened sinner rejects it.

Full knowledge and intention constitute serious sin worthy of eternal hellfire. The summoner is triply damned: first, by his own words; second, by the widow's words; and third, by his own rejection of repentance. Thus he has chosen his fate. The fiend claims his own:

"Thy body and this panne been myne by right,
Thou shalt with me to helle yet tonyght,
Where thou shalt knowen of oure privetee
Moore than a maister of dyvynytee."
And with that word this foule feend hym hente;
Body and soule he with the devel wente
Where as that somonours han hir heritage.

"Thy body and thy pan be mine by right,
You shall go with me to hell tonight,
Where you shall know more about our secrets
Than a master of divinity does."
And with that word the foul fiend seized him;
Body and soul he went with the devil
Where all summoners have their heritage.

(III, D, 1635–1641)

Going to hell is no joke to the medieval reader. The *game* of the tale has its *ernest* element in reminding the medieval audience of the reality of evil, of the devil and of hell, and of the role of human choice in damnation. The summoner was curious about hell's secrets. Now, says the fiend, he will have first-hand experience. Not only that summoner but all summoners are hell-bound, unless they repent. Repentance breaks fealty with the devil and rejoins the penitent to God. Even though the summoner had sworn blood brotherhood with the devil, he, like all sinners, could have repented. Because he did not, he damned himself.

Damnation is not God's will for His creatures. The Friar reminds the audience that the "pains of this cursed house of hell" (III, D, 1652) can be avoided by prayer and avoidance of temptation. The Friar, inadequate instrument of God's grace though he is, ends his tale with sound spiritual advice to the audience:

> *Disposeth ay youre hertes to withstonde*
> *The feend, that yow wolde make thral and bonde.*
> *He may nat tempte yow over youre myght,*
> *For Crist wol be youre champion and knyght.*
> *And prayeth that thise somonours hem repente*
> *Of hir mysdedes, er that the feend hem hente!*

> Always dispose your hearts to withstand
> The fiend, who would make you thrall and bond.
> He may not tempt you beyond your might,
> For Christ will be your champion and knight.
> And pray that these summoners repent
> Of their misdeeds, before the fiend takes them!

> (III, D, 1659–1664)

The Friar's ending is a perfect combination of *ernest* and *game*. He cannot resist a final jape at his rival; but his theology of hell is accurate—and deadly serious.

SUGGESTIONS FOR FURTHER READING

Huppé, Bernard F. *A Reading of the Canterbury Tales*. Albany: State University of New York Press, 1964. 194–209. Huppé regards the "Friar's Tale" and the "Summoner's Tale" as "muckraking" in their "exposure of the corruption of the secular clergy."

Lumiansky, R. M. *Of Sondry Folk: The Dramatic Principle in the Canterbury Tales*. Austin: University of Texas Press, 1955. 129–140. In support of his famous thesis, that the tales are developments of the characters of the tellers, Lumiansky analyzes the "Friar's Tale" and the "Summoner's Tale" as motivated by the "clash of their professional interests."

Richardson, Janette. "Friar and Summoner, the Art of Balance." *Chaucer Review* 9, no. 3 (1975): 227–236. Richardson explains why the "devastation-by-insult" match between the two "results in a draw."

Whittock, Trevor. *A Reading of the Canterbury Tales.* Cambridge: Cambridge University Press, 1968. 129–142. Whittock argues that the two tales are critiques of abuses in the church.

The Summoner's Prologue and Tale

"And certeinly he hath it weel disserved."
"And certainly he has well deserved it."

(III, D, 2280)

The "Summoner's Tale" follows the "Friar's Tale" and is linked to it by the principle of requital: the Summoner must insult the Friar more effectively than the Friar has insulted him. Because narrator Geffrey has warned the audience that a churl will tell a churl's tale, the Summoner—an earthy, ugly man—can be expected to offer this crude narrative featuring images of the digestive tract. At the same time, the "Summoner's Tale" supplements the "Friar's Tale" by stressing the financial abuses consuming God's church, eating it away from within. Such poisons as are represented by the friar in the "Summoner's Tale" (and, by implication, the pilgrim Friar also) need to be expelled as harmful to the body of the church. The odd conjunction of the grossest bodily functions with the need for spiritual purgation links *ernest* and *game* in the "Summoner's Prologue and Tale."

The Summoner is furious about the Friar's story of the damnation of a typical summoner. Well might the Friar claim to know all about hell, says he, as "friars and fiends are but little apart" (III, D, 1674). Not only does the Summoner place friars in hell, but he places them in the most degrading places in hell. He recounts a tale of a friar who, in a vision of hell, saw twenty thousand of his colleagues nested in the anus of Satan. Like a young child, the Summoner finds the excretory functions fascinating; so it is no surprise that the central image of his tale will be that abrupt expulsion of digestive gases called in the Middle Ages, as now, a fart.

But the tale also establishes that friars themselves are disgusting elements of the church, needing to be expelled from its body. The orders of friars were originally intended to provide a communal way of life for religious men dedicated to poverty. A typical medieval religious order was the Franciscans, established by St. Francis of Assisi (1182–1226). Francis, son of a wealthy nobleman, rejected his father's way of life and embraced "Lady Poverty." The members of his order eschewed worldly possessions and supported themselves by begging; thus they were termed the medicant orders, from the Latin *mendicare*, "to beg." Their other functions included preaching and hearing confessions. Ideally, the mendicants could draw other souls to God by encouraging repentance and generosity to the poor. By Chaucer's day, however, many religious orders were attracting men and women who were not committed to the ideals of the order's founder, but instead used their ecclesiastical role for their own profit. Violating their own vows of poverty, the orders became prosperous. The preaching skills for which their members had originally become famous were misused for gain rather than for service. The Summoner's friar is a composite of all these abuses. Thus when he is insulted, he deserves it, as he is himself akin to the noxious gases let fly by the justifiably angry Thomas.

The friar's behavior is contrary to all the ideals espoused by the mendicant orders. Like Chaucer's Friar, the Summoner's friar is a limiter, a wandering preacher responsible for begging for his order within a designated geographical area. His duty to his fellow friars back at the convent is to bring home contributions and distribute them fairly among his brethren—a duty that will contribute to the humor of the conclusion. His duty to the larger Christian community is to exhort them to virtuous behavior; generosity to a friar helps the giver to save his soul. But when he encourages parishioners to make "trentals," to contribute to the friars for thirty masses to be said for the souls of contributors after their deaths, his purpose is less to save the donors' souls than to line the friars' pockets.

Even more ripe for abuse is the propensity of limiters to exploit their relative freedom from supervision. This friar appears to be the image of his calling, going from house to house with his bag and his staff, much like the Parson. But the friar collects so much that he needs a sturdy servant to help him carry it; and though he pretends to commit himself to pray for his contributors, in fact he promptly erases the tables on which he had with great flourish inscribed their names. This elaborate scam, similar to the Pardoner's, grew up around the custom of making financial contributions in return for spiritual benefits.

The friar's next intended contributor is one Thomas, whose house the friar had visited before. This suggests that Thomas has already been scammed by the friar, a situation that motivates Thomas's anger at the friar now. Because Thomas is sick, the friar has a prime opening for trying to get Thomas's money on the pretext of a deathbed attempt to save his soul. The friar begins his sales pitch by reassuring Thomas (falsely, of course) how diligent he has been in praying for Thomas.

Now he offers Thomas his own personal sermon,

> "Nat al after the text of hooly writ,
> For it is hard to yow, as I suppose,
> And therfore wol I teche yow al the glose."

> "Not completely according to the text of holy writ,
> For it is hard for you, I suppose,
> And therefore will I teach you all the gloss."

(III, D, 1790–1792)

Text and gloss: these two key terms occur at other points in *The Canterbury Tales*. The Pardoner uses the scriptural text, *"Radix malorum est Cupiditas"* (VI, C, 334), the love of money is the root of all evil, as the basis for his gloss or interpretation. The Wife of Bath glosses any text, interprets any scriptural passage, just as she pleases, without regard to accepted channels of authority. Preachers such as the friar were supposed to base their teachings on the text of scripture, which they were expected to interpret accurately. The friar's abandonment of the text (on the specious grounds that it is "hard" for simple Thomas [III, D, 1791]) and substitution of gloss detaches his interpretation from all scriptural validity; a gloss is true only insofar as it explains its text. So when the friar says that the purpose of his preaching is to teach men to be "charitable" and to "spend their goods where it is reasonable" (III, D, 1795–1796), it is not surprising that the friar will manipulate his gloss to designate himself as a worthy object of charity.

Thomas, sick and bedridden, should indeed be attending to the health of his soul, in case he is going to die. The friar presents himself as a worthier confessor than the curate—the local parish priest charged with the *cura*, or care of souls. He praises his own ability to "grope tenderly the conscience" of a sinner (III, D, 1817). The term *grope*, which will be used to comic effect at the climactic moment of the tale, means, in theological terms, the process by which the confessor prods the penitent to acknowledge and confess his sins. According to Thomas's wife, Thomas's besetting sin is anger—one of the Seven Deadly Sins. But curing Thomas of anger has little advantage for the friar; it is more to his advantage to preach against gluttony, so that Thomas might give him the cost of the food from which he abstains himself. The theme of gluttony, the excessive consumption of food and drink, introduces the imagery of the digestive system. Combined with the theme of groping and Thomas's anger, that digestive imagery will erupt in Thomas's fitting revenge.

Typical medieval sermons used illustrative examples and anecdotes as this one does—piling examples of abstinence one upon another. Moses, Elijah, Aaron, and Jesus, according to the friar, are forerunners of him and his brethren in being "wedded" to a whole series of Christian virtues:

> *"poverte and continence,*
> *To charite, humblesse, and abstinence,*
> *To persecucioun for rightwisnesse,*
> *To wepynge, misericorde, and clennesse."*

> "poverty and continence,
> To charity, humility, and abstinence,
> To persecution for righteousness,
> To weeping, mercy, and purity."

(III, D, 1907–1910)

Because of their superior virtue, friars are "more acceptable to God" than people like Thomas, with their "feasts at the table" (III, D, 1913–1914). This is especially true since the primal sin, for which man lost Paradise, was, according to the friar, gluttony. This dubious gloss of the text of the Eden story is supplemented by the friar's equally specious interpretation of Jesus' phrase "poor in spirit" (Matt. 5:3) as describing friars specifically.

The friar goes on some more about gluttony and abstinence, getting in a few words about generosity as well, before returning to Thomas's primary flaw (at least according to his wife): anger. More long anecdotes illustrate the consequences of the deadly sin of anger, to stimulate repentance, which in turn, the friar hopes, will stimulate generosity. But Thomas only gets angrier. Chaucer as well as all his original audience must have had the experience, familiar to modern churchgoers as well, of being driven to sins of wrath by overlong sermons.

When the friar comes to the point of offering Thomas the opportunity to confess his sins and be shriven, Thomas refuses, on the grounds that he has already been "shriven this day by my curate" (III, D, 2095). The rivalry between the wandering mendicants and the local parish clergy for the allegiance of the faithful is here revealed as having primarily a monetary basis. Getting desperate, the friar makes a direct request for a contribution to the building of a new cloister for his religious order. Irate Thomas promises a contribution of "such thing as is in [his] possession" (III, D, 2124) at that moment, but with a binding condition:

> *"That thou departe it so, my deere brother,*
> *That every frere have also muche as oother.*
> *This shaltou swere on thy professioun."*

> "That you divide it so, my dear brother,
> That every friar shall have as much as the other.
> You shall swear to this on your vows of religion."

(III, D, 2133–2135)

If a gift can be divisible by thirteen, it must be a generous gift; so the friar readily agrees.

In medieval literature, oaths and binding promises are often the crux on which a plot turns; so it is here. Thomas tells the friar to put his hand down Thomas's pants, and "grope well behind" to find something hidden in that *privetee*, private place (III, D, 2141, 2143). The action here burlesques the confessor's "groping" of the penitent's soul to cause him to confess his secret sins. The friar promptly gropes about in Thomas's nether regions (friars will do anything for money). Then, the friar's hand in place, Thomas has his revenge: "he let the friar a fart" (III, D, 2149). Now the friar is as angry as Thomas. His rash promise binds him absolutely to the task of distributing this contribution equally among his twelve brethren. What to do?

The friar complains of his dilemma to a friend, "a man of great honor" (III, D, 2163). Despite the sympathy of the lord and lady ("A churl has done a churl's deed," observes the lady philosophically [III, D, 2206]), all are baffled. The lord is in awe of the "churl['s] imagination" in concocting so difficult a problem in "ars-metric" (III, D, 2218, 2222)—arithmetic with an anal pun. Measuring the fart's intensity both of sound and smell is crucial to the solution. How can each man have an equal share "of the sound and savor of a fart" (III, D, 2226)? They cannot stand in a line, reasons the lord; the sound and savor will diminish, being "only a reverbation of air" which "wastes little by little away" (III, D, 2234–2235). How then could it be determined if the fart were "divided equally" (III, D, 2237)? No solution seems at hand. The puzzle is solved not by lord or lady or friar but by a squire—one of those young men being raised in household service to a lord in preparation for assuming their own knighthood at maturity. The purpose of these three inessential characters is to add to the humor of the friar's not being able to solve the puzzle himself. Not only are friars venal, but they are also stupid.

The squire's ingenious solution ensures even distribution of Thomas's gift. Each of the twelve friars positions himself by a spoke of a cartwheel, "and to every spoke's end . . . / Each friar shall very firmly lay his nose" (III, D, 2263–2264). Then Thomas, "with belly stiff and taut," shall position himself at the center of the cartwheel, there to repeat his original "churl's deed" (III, D, 2267, 2206). The geometry of the plan guarantees that "the sound of it will travel, / And also the stink, unto the spoke's end" (III, D, 2273–2274). The only exception to the equal distribution is that the friar

> "Shal have the firste fruyt, as resoun is.
> The noble usage of freres yet is this,
> The worthy men of hem shul first be served;
> And certeinly he hath it weel disserved."

> "Shall have the first fruit, as is reasonable.
> The noble custom of friars still is this,
> The worthy men are first served by them;
> And certainly he has well deserved it."

> (III, D, 2277–2280)

The squire gets a reward for ingenuity rivaling the churl's own. But the friar—in fact, all his convent—also deserve what they get. As the squire notes, friars, pledged to serve the poor and embrace poverty themselves, are motivated by desire for personal gain just as surely as are the laity.

A great principle of medieval humor is repayment in kind. The Summoner has repaid the Friar; the friar in the "Summoner's Tale" has gotten what he deserved, as have all his equally corrupt brethren. Thus the gaming purpose of the tale has been satisfied. The *ernest* criticism of clerical abuses is based on the well-known organic metaphor of the church as a living organism, within which members perform their proper function as do the parts of the human body. A laborer on church property might thus be seen as the church's hands. Following this analogy, the corrupt ecclesiastic is equivalent to bodily waste: utterly contemptible, deserving only of expulsion. Humor at the expense of such malefactors represents poetic justice. It is suitable that, when friars have sunk so low, they become matter for a bathroom joke.

SUGGESTIONS FOR FURTHER READING

Hines, John. *The Fabliau in English*. London: Longman, 1993. 162–176. Employing the method of source study, Hines shows how Chaucer uses the details of other well-known tales to construct his own tale.

Huppé, Bernard F. *A Reading of the Canterbury Tales*. Albany: State University of New York Press, 1964. 194–209. Huppé regards the "Friar's Tale" and the "Summoner's Tale" as "muckraking" in their "exposure of the corruption of the secular clergy."

Lumiansky, R. M. *Of Sondry Folk: The Dramatic Principle in the Canterbury Tales*. Austin: University of Texas Press, 1955. 129–140. In support of his famous thesis, that the tales are developments of the characters of the tellers, Lumiansky analyzes the "Friar's Tale" and the "Summoner's Tale" as motivated by the "clash of their professional interests."

Richardson, Janette. "Friar and Summoner, the Art of Balance." *Chaucer Review* 9, no. 3 (1975): 227–236. Richardson explains why the "devastation-by-insult" match between the two "results in a draw."

Whittock, Trevor. *A Reading of the Canterbury Tales*. Cambridge: Cambridge University Press, 1968. 129–142. Whittock argues that the two tales are critiques of abuses in the church.

The Clerk's Tale;
Lenvoy de Chaucer

"But as ye wole youreself, right so wol I."

"But as you will yourself, just so will I."

(IV, E, 361)

Until the late twentieth century, the traditional Christian marriage ceremony required a woman to promise to obey her husband. Six centuries
earlier, medieval people, acting in accordance with their understanding of
the teachings of St. Paul, believed that women should obey their husbands
as they would obey God. But the subjection of women, even if seen as a
deserved punishment for Eve's sin, did not give husbands total license over
their wives. St. Paul placed husbands under a reciprocal obligation to love
their wives "as Christ loved the church" (Eph. 5:25). Such infinite love as
Christ had for the church would preclude such behavior as is exhibited by
Walter in the "Clerk's Tale": abuse of authority for the sake of making one's
own will prevail. The term *will* is used over and over in this tale. To will is
to choose. If wives are absolutely subject to their husbands, saying "I will"
in the marriage ceremony precludes all future independent choices, all
future "I will not's." Abrogation of a wife's will would be safe only if her
husband was in turn conforming *his* will to Christ's.

In the "Clerk's Tale," Chaucer shows how drastic power imbalances in
marriage can lead to suffering for women and sinfulness for men. Like many
authors of his day, he sees the popular story of the patient Grisilde as a
cautionary tale. While all good Christians were instructed to behave with
humility and patience in the face of life's inevitable trials, sent by God for
His own unfathomable purposes, nevertheless no human is justified in
inflicting suffering on another, just to see how well she will endure it. Both
Walter and Grisilde represent extremes of behavior which teach a moral

lesson in literature but which, Chaucer apparently believes, should be avoided in real life.

Grisilde's life intersects with that of Walter, the marquis of Saluces, when his liegemen insist that Walter marry. Walter is a man of high "lineage," the "gentlest," or most nobly born, man in Lombardy, known for his "honor" and "courtesy" (IV, E, 71–74). But as the story begins he has neglected his responsibility as a political leader to marry and procreate. His liegemen are anxious that he conform his will to this duty, lest for lack of an heir the land fall at Walter's death to a successor not of the lineage that had always ruled it.

So his liegemen urge Walter:

> "*Boweth youre nekke under that blisful yok*
> *Of soveraynetee, noght of servyse,*
> *Which that men clepe spousaille or wedlok.*"

> "Bow your neck under that blissful yoke
> Of sovereignty, not of service,
> Which men call spousal or wedlock."

(IV, E, 113–115)

The liegemen describe marriage in words connoting hierarchical relationships. They suggest that Walter will be subjugated or placed in bondage like a beast of burden. But on the other hand, the yoke is one of "sovereignty, not of service"; although Walter will be bound, he will also retain power. In the arena of politics, Walter, as a marquis, has the habit of command. In marriage, he will retain power. As the Canterbury pilgrims already know from listening to the "Wife of Bath's Prologue and Tale," sovereignty is a key issue in marriage. While the Wife of Bath described in detail the tactics she used to obtain and maintain domestic sovereignty, the Clerk describes the opposite situation: a marriage in which a husband dominates his wife to the point that she has no will of her own.

Walter's liegemen, then, have reminded him of his responsibility to marry and secure the lineage. They offer to choose a wife for him, "born of the greatest and of the highest / Of all this land" (IV, E, 130–132). Medieval people considered it most appropriate that like should marry like. High nobility should marry within its own ranks; so, the liegemen believe, Walter should choose a woman of gentle birth. Walter accepts their plea that he should marry, but with the proviso that he will choose a wife without their advice. His liegemen in turn must pledge themselves "to worship her . . . / As if she were an emperor's daughter" (IV, E, 166, 168). All parties agree; and the only question as Part One ends is this: whom will Walter marry?

Near the marquis' palace, in a little village, live "poor folk" who "took their sustenance" by working on the land (IV, E, 200, 202). Poorest of these is Janicula, whose daughter, Grisilde, is a model of womanly virtue. Because she was raised in poverty, she is self-disciplined, free of "lecherous lust" (IV, E, 214). She drinks only water, not wine (since alcohol was believed to stimulate sexual desire, and abstinence, to indicate purity). She is hardworking, young, and a virgin; she is serious and wise; she is good to her poor old father; she even sleeps on a hard bed, indicating that she is not overly fond of comfort and luxury. In short, Grisilde has all the proper characteristics of a perfectly submissive wife, which is exactly what Walter wants.

Without Grisilde's knowledge, Walter has picked her out as his bride. The wedding is all planned; all wonder who the lucky girl will be. By modern standards Walter's behavior is unbelievably presumptuous, as if there is no doubt in his mind that he will be accepted. But to medieval people, Walter's high position alone makes him an amazing catch. He even has a new wardrobe made for Grisilde, using a model of similar build. The new clothing, with all the accessorizing "adornments" (IV, E, 258), reminds the audience that, if he chooses a woman of lower *estat*, she will experience an elevation in social rank so extreme that her old *array* must be left behind with her old life.

All dressed for the wedding, Walter goes to the little village in which Grisilde lives. As is appropriate for a woman of her *estat*, Grisilde has just returned to her humble abode after doing a humble task: fetching water from a well. Being humble herself, she has no idea that Walter is coming for her. She merely decides to stand at the threshold of her house to see who the bride might be. When Walter arrives at the threshold, she puts down her water bucket and falls upon her knees, as is proper, given that Walter is the ruler and she the subject. In that role, she "kneels still, / Till she had heard what was the lord's will" (IV, E, 293–294).

Walter quickly makes his will clear, not first to Grisilde but rather to her father Janicula. It was customary even until the recent past for a suitor to ask a woman's father for his daughter's hand in marriage. In the Middle Ages, this custom acknowledged the common belief that marriage was a matter of transmitting a woman from the care and protection of her father to that of her husband. Once the two men agreed, the woman's consent was assumed. This custom was to change gradually. In the time span encompassing Chaucer's life, the process was beginning; but it would still be in progress in Shakespeare's day, two centuries later, as is seen in the conflict between a young couple's wishes and parental prohibitions in *Romeo and Juliet*.

When Walter asks Janicula for Grisilde's hand in marriage, the request is only a formality. Because Janicula is Walter's feudal subordinate, his "faithful liegeman" (IV, E, 310), Janicula must respond with the humility suitable to one of low *estat*:

> "Lord," quod he, "my willynge
> Is as ye wole, ne ayeynes youre likynge
> I wol no thyng."

> "Lord," quoth he, "my willing
> Is as you will, and against your liking
> I will nothing."

(IV, E, 319–321)

Will can be defined as a mind of one's own. But a peasant like Janicula must be will-less with respect to his lord. The Middle Ages was a time when everyone thought of the world in terms of superior/inferior. Except for the king, everyone in secular life was subordinate to someone of higher degree; except for the pope, everyone in religious life was subordinate to a superior. Women were in general subordinate to men of similar *estat*, but those same men were subordinate to those of higher *estats* than they. So, in context of the thinking of the age, Janicula is not the spineless wretch he would seem if he were a character in a modern work. Similarly, Grisilde is not unusual in accepting Walter's conditions:

> "For I wol axe if it hire wille be
> To be my wyf and reule hire after me."

> "For I will ask her if it be her will
> To be my wife and rule herself according to my will."

(IV, E, 326–327)

According to the terms of the medieval marriage vows, all wives promise to obey, to rule their own wills after the wills of their husbands. Sovereignty is important to Walter, so he takes great pains to assure himself that Grisilde intends to be obedient:

> "I seye this: be ye redy with good herte
> To al my lust, and that I frely may,
> As me best thynketh, do yow laughe or smerte,
> And nevere ye to grucche it, nyght ne day?

And eek whan I sey 'ye,' ne sey nat 'nay,'
Neither by word ne frownyng contenance?
Swere this, and heere I swere oure alliance."

"I say this: are you ready, with a good heart,
To do everything I want, and I may freely act
As I think best, whether it makes you laugh, or hurts you;
And will you never begrudge it, night or day?
And when I say 'yes,' do not say 'no,'
Neither by word nor frowning countenance?
Swear this, and here I swear our alliance."

(IV, E, 351–357)

What Walter wants is to do anything he pleases, whether it pleases Grisilde or hurts her. No matter what he does, she may never show any signs of disapproval or disagreement, verbal or otherwise. Why does Grisilde accept what seem to be unbearably harsh conditions?

For one thing, Walter is asking no more than is implied in the conventional promise of wifely obedience; he is merely clarifying, not expanding, the marriage vows. For another thing, Grisilde, as a peasant, has to obey Walter anyway; she is his feudal subordinate before she becomes his wife. The lowly cultivate habits of obedience, a virtue that the highborn do not need. Perhaps this is why Walter, with his obsession with sovereignty, chooses a woman of lower *estat*. He wants a woman already well-practiced in will-lessness.

Grisilde, aware of the great honor bestowed on her by Walter's offer of marriage, accepts his conditions:

She seyde, "Lord, undigne and unworthy
Am I to thilke honour that ye me beede,
But as ye wole youreself, right so wol I."

She said, "Lord, unfitting and unworthy
Am I of this honor that you offer me.
But as you will yourself, just so will I."

(IV, E, 359–361)

As Walter wills, so wills Grisilde. She enters the marriage understanding its terms. Since he has raised her, all unworthy, from a low *estat*, everything she has comes from him.

To stress Grisilde's utter dependence, she changes her clothes. Medieval people saw *array* as a precise signifier of *estat*. Fabric, cut, color, trim, and design of garments reflected the wearer's social status. Peasants were

expected to wear simple, unadorned clothing of coarse, cheap cloth in basic
earth tones, to indicate their humble *estat* and their connection with the
land. The higher up the social ladder, the more elaborate garments could
be. Nobility could wear yards of expensive, brightly colored fabric trimmed
with jewels.

It would not be common, given the medieval belief in the suitability of
like marrying like, for a woman to make such a drastic shift from low *estat*
to high. But if one did, new *array* was needed. Not only can Grisilde not
be a marquise in her old clothes, but she cannot even bring them into the
palace. Walter has her ladies-in-waiting undress her (a noble lady never
did this for herself) and leave her old garments behind, so that she brings
"nothing of her old gear / . . . into his house" (IV, E, 372–373). In place of
her "old gear," she receives new clothes. The clothing change is described
as a "translation" (IV, E, 385), a reversal or metamorphosis. Nothing of the
old Grisilde can come with her to her husband's house; her old self, like
her clothing, must be abandoned.

And so they are married. To the wonderment of all, Grisilde adjusts
immediately to her new life. She is

> *so discreet and fair of eloquence,*
> *So benigne and so digne of reverence,*
> *And koude so the peples herte embrace,*
> *That ech hire lovede that looked on hir face.*

> so discreet and fair of eloquence,
> So benign and so worthy of reverence,
> And could so embrace the people's heart,
> That all who looked upon her face loved her.
>
> (IV, E, 410–413)

Grisilde becomes the perfect wife, performing all the duties of her new *estat*
to perfection. She knows how to attend to domestic matters ("wifely
homeliness" [IV, E, 429]), and she can also act in the diplomatic capacity
expected of the wife of a ruler:

> *whan that the cas required it,*
> *The commune profit koude she redresse.*
> *Ther nas discord, rancour, ne hevynesse*
> *In al that land that she ne koude apese,*
> *And wisely brynge hem alle in reste and ese.*

> when the situation required it,
> She could advance the common good.

> There was no discord, rancor, nor heaviness
> In all that land that she could not appease,
> And wisely bring them all to rest and ease.

(IV, E, 430–434)

The role of mediator or peacemaker comes naturally to Grisilde. In her husband's absence, she serves as diplomatic negotiator, so that

> *If gentil men or othere of hire contree*
> *Were wrothe, she wolde bryngen hem aton.*

> If gentle men or others of her country
> Were angry, she would bring them together.

(IV, E, 436–437)

Not only is she competent in her private and public roles, but she also meets her responsibilities to the lineage. Even though "all would rather that she had borne a knave child," a boy, at least the birth of her daughter proves that she is "not barren" and might bear a son soon (IV, E, 444, 448). As Part II ends, all seems well with Walter and Grisilde.

But soon thereafter, for no apparent reason, Walter experiences a strange desire to "tempt" or "assay" his wife (IV, E, 452, 456), to test this paragon to see how virtuous she can be. Medieval interpreters of scripture would have seen the book of Job in the Old Testament as a record of God's testing of His servant; and medieval theologians would have agreed that God does inflict suffering on the virtuous, for His own unfathomable reasons. But Walter is not God, and although medieval custom gave a husband authority over his wife, the deliberate attempt to cause Grisilde to suffer would not have been seen as within Walter's husbandly rights. The Clerk knows this and condemns Walter's behavior right away:

> *He hadde assayed hire ynogh bifore,*
> *And foond hire evere good; what neded it*
> *Hire for to tempte, and alwey moore and moore,*
> *Though som men preise it for a subtil wit?*
> *But as for me, I seye that yvele it sit*
> *To assaye a wyf whan that it is no nede,*
> *And putten hire in angwyssh and in drede.*

> He had tested her enough before,
> And found her ever good; why did he need
> To tempt her, and always more and more,
> Though some men praise it for a clever deed?

But as for me, I say that it is evil
To test a wife when there is no need,
And put her in anguish and in dread.

(IV, E, 456–462)

"Some men praise" Walter for his clever schemes to tempt his wife, but not Chaucer's Clerk. In testing the worth of a woman who is already his moral superior, Walter becomes increasingly evil himself.

Walter's first test is to tell Grisilde that, because of her own low birth, the populace will not accept her daughter as his heir. Therefore, he tells Grisilde, he is going to put the child to death. Mindful of her promise to accept Walter's will as her own and disagree with nothing, Grisilde accepts his decision calmly:

> "*Lord, al lyth in youre plesaunce.*
> *My child and I, with hertely obeisaunce,*
> *Been youres al, and ye mowe save or spille*
> *Youre owene thyng; werketh after youre wille.*"

> "Lord, all lies in your pleasure.
> My child and I, with heartfelt obedience,
> Are all yours, and you may save or kill
> Your own thing; work after your will."

(IV, E, 501–504)

This attitude, unmotherly by modern standards, nevertheless is a logical consequence of Grisilde's social inferiority. As Walter has reminded Grisilde, he raised her from low *estat*:

> "*I yow took out of youre povere array,*
> *And putte yow in estaat of heigh noblesse.*"

> "I took you out of your poor array,
> And put you into the estate of high nobility."

(IV, E, 467–468)

The specific reference to her clothing foreshadows later events; but his purpose now is to remind Grisilde that everything she has, including the child, was given her by her husband. What Walter has given, Walter can take away.

Although he is secretly pleased with her perfectly subservient response, he continues testing her. He sends an officer for the child, deceiving Grisilde into believing that the child will be killed. In a pathetic scene,

Grisilde begs the officer to give the child proper burial—except, of course, if Walter forbids it. The reader knows, as Grisilde does not, that Walter has sent the child to be raised by his sister. This practice, called "fostering out," was common among members of the medieval nobility. Although moderns believe that it is psychologically damaging to separate a young child from its parents, medieval people believed that the fostered-out child benefited from the social and educational experience of living with another noble family. The situation here, however, is unlike fostering-out arrangements in that Grisilde believes her child dead, slain by her own father. Despite this, and true to her promise, Grisilde resumes life as the perfect wife:

> As glad, as humble, as bisy in servyse,
> And eek in love, as she was wont to be,
> Was she to hym in every maner wyse;
> Ne of hir doghter noght a word spak she.

> As glad, as humble, as busy in service,
> And also in love, as she was accustomed to be,
> Was she to him in every kind of way;
> And of her daughter she spoke not a word.

(IV, E, 603–606)

Thus ends Part III, with a resolution that, one would think, should satisfy even Walter.

But perfection is not good enough to satisfy the insatiable Walter. After about four years, Grisilde gives birth to the desired son and heir. Despite the fact that producing this child to secure the heritage to his lineage is the point of Walter's marrying at all, Walter decides to test her further by feigning the boy's death as he had the girl's. The Clerk laments his cruelty:

> O nedelees was she tempted in assay!
> But wedded men ne knowe no mesure,
> Whan that they fynde a pacient creature.

> O she was tested needlessly!
> But wedded men know no moderation,
> When they find a patient creature.

(IV, E, 621–623)

Mesure, measure or moderation, was a highly valued virtue to medieval people; such excess as Walter displays here is the opposite of mesure, and therefore evil. Ironically, Grisilde's immoderate virtue tempts her husband in turn to immoderate vice. A more assertive wife might have been able to encourage *mesure* in Walter.

Patiently, Grisilde accepts the apparent murder of the boy child. Again, she accepts her suffering as she had promised:

> "Ye been oure lord; dooth with youre owene thyng
> Right as yow list; axeth no reed at me.
> For as I lefte at hoom al my clothyng,
> Whan I first cam to yow, right so," quod she,
> "Lefte I my wyl and al my libertee,
> And took youre clothyng."

> "You are our lord; do with your own thing
> Just as you wish; ask no advice of me.
> For as I left at home all my clothing,
> When I first came to you, just so," she said,
> "I left my will and all my liberty,
> And took your clothing."

(IV, E, 652–657)

Again the clothing imagery reinforces the idea of subjection and will-less-ness. Retainers of a great lord in the Middle Ages wore his livery or uniform; it seems that Grisilde regards the elegant wardrobe of a marquise as no more than the uniform of an underling. Her will, like her clothing, like her children, all belong to her lord, Walter. Again, Grisilde begs the execu-tioner to bury her "little son" properly; again, she returns to her previous perfect-wife behavior, without any sign of disapproval or unhappiness.

The repetition of key elements now has the effect of reinforcing the extremism of Walter's behavior. Rhetorically, the Clerk asks, of women in the audience in particular, should this now not be enough testing? Of course, it should; but in Walter Chaucer is portraying the psychological aberration that moderns call obsession:

> But ther been folk of swich condicion
> That whan they have a certein purpos take
> They kan nat stynte.

> But there be folk of such condition
> That when they have taken a certain purpose
> They cannot stop.

(IV, E, 701–703)

It is becoming apparent to everyone around him that Walter has gone too far.

But he "cannot stop," and he need not. Walter can torment Grisilde all he pleases because Grisilde is a poor man's daughter. Had Grisilde been a woman of noble family, Walter would have risked that family's retaliation if he mistreated his wife. But the powerless Janicula's reaction to his daughter's suffering is never even mentioned, because to medieval readers it would have been obvious that Janicula, a lowly peasant and Walter's subject, could not avenge any wrongs done to his daughter. Walter wanted sovereignty and got it by marrying a woman of an *estat* far below his own. So he can indulge his obsession without fear of human retribution.

Walter asks the pope for an annulment of his marriage to Grisilde, on the fictitious grounds of "rancor and dissension / Between his people and him" caused by his wife's low birth (IV, E, 747–748). Meanwhile, he sends for his children, directing that they return to their birthplace incognito. His daughter, now of marriageable age (about twelve), returns to Saluces dressed elegantly as befits a bride. The age of the daughter reminds the audience that Walter had been testing his wife, and Grisilde patiently enduring, for twelve years. What greater injury can Walter plan that will surpass the lengthy separation of mother and children?

As Part V begins, Walter announces to his wife that he is setting aside his marriage to her (as if she were a common concubine) in favor of this new marriage. Again, Walter reminds her that she brought nothing with her to the marriage—the very clothes she wears belong to him—and therefore she must not only "void . . . her place" in his house and "return to [her] father's house" (IV, E, 806, 809), but do so completely naked.

The seriousness of this insult cannot be exaggerated. To be a rejected wife is bad enough; to be returned to her father's house naked is far worse. Grisilde's reply, her longest so far, elaborates on the significance not only of the clothing—a major issue in their marriage—but also of the transition from her father's house to her husband's house. Both images, clothing and house, stand as metaphor for the fatal inequality in their relationship which has poisoned it from the start.

Grisilde acknowledges that between Walter's "magnificence" and her "poverty" there has never been any "comparison," or equality (IV, E, 815–817). She has never been "worthy . . . / To be [his] wife, no, not even [his] chambermaid" (IV, E, 818–819). Therefore, Walter's house was never truly her home:

> "And in this hous, ther ye me lady maade— . . .
> I nevere heeld me lady ne mistresse,
> But humble servant to youre worthynesse."

"And in this house, of which you made me lady, . . .
I never held myself lady or mistress,
But humble servant to your worthiness."

(IV, E, 820, 823–824)

Now, in all humility, she is ready to return to her father's house and "gladly
yield [her] place" to a woman more worthy of Walter's love (IV, E, 843–844).

As for her *array*, she reminds Walter that her old clothes were the only
dowry or marriage portion that she could have brought, and he chose to
reject them:

> "My lord, ye woot that in my fadres place
> Ye dide me streepe out of my povre weede,
> And richely me cladden."

> "My lord, you know that in my father's place
> You stripped me out of my poor garments,
> And richly clothed me."

(IV, E, 862–864)

She acknowledges that she owes him all her clothes back again:

> "Naked out of my fadres hous," quod she,
> "I cam, and naked moot I turne agayn."

> "Naked out of my father's house," she said,
> "I came, and naked must I return again."

(IV, E, 871–872)

Nevertheless, it is not fitting that

> "thilke wombe in which youre children leye
> Sholde biforn the peple, in my walkyng,
> Be seyn al bare."

> "this womb in which your children lay
> Should before the people, in my walking,
> Be seen all bare."

(IV, E, 877–879)

Therefore, in return for her virginity, a gift that he did accept and cannot
return, he should, if only to save himself from disgrace, give her a gift: a
"smock" (IV, E, 886) to cover her nakedness in the public streets. The
smock, a flimsy slip or shift, was the layer of women's clothing worn closest

to the body; it is thus the minimal garment, the closest possible thing to being naked. Although Walter grants this request, Grisilde's shame is still pathetic:

> *Biforn the folk hirselven strepeth she,*
> *And in hir smok, with heed and foot al bare,*
> *Toward hir fadre hous forth is she fare.*

> Before the folk she stripped herself,
> And in her smock, with head and foot all bare,
> She goes forth toward her father's house.

(IV, E, 894–896)

Her rich *array* and her stately home depended on Walter's continuing approval. Of herself, a poor man's daughter without political power or social standing, she is nothing.

Fortune's wheel has come full circle for Grisilde. She has returned to her father's house, to the low *estat* from which she was raised by Walter. Dressed in her old clothes, she resumes her old life as dutiful daughter. But the ever-inventive Walter has yet one more test. He summons Grisilde back to the palace to prepare the wedding feast for him and his new bride, on the grounds that she "knows . . . of old all my pleasure," knows what he likes (IV, E, 964). And Grisilde accepts, proclaiming her undying love and desire to serve. All wonder who this woman is, in her "poor *array*" (IV, E, 1020); Grisilde is no longer recognizable as the marquise that she once was.

At this point, many modern readers are disgusted not only with Walter for his gratuitous cruelty but also with Grisilde. From the perspective of modern psychology, her character traits are defects, not virtues. In fact, there are few Chaucerian tales about which medieval and modern values clash so much as in this tale of husbandly sadism and wifely masochism. But finally, Grisilde expresses an opinion of her own. Walter asks his ex-wife how she likes his new wife "and her beauty" (IV, E, 1031). Modern women readers often regard this question alone as an offense worthy of capital punishment. Grisilde replies that his bride is indeed the fairest of them all, and wishes them luck and happiness. But she offers an oblique criticism of her husband's behavior:

> *"O thyng biseke I yow, and warne also,*
> *That he ne prikke with no tormentynge*
> *This tendre mayden, as ye han doon mo;*
> *For she is fostred in hire norissynge*
> *Moore tendrely, and, to my supposynge,*

She koude nat adversitee endure
As koude a povre fostred creature."

"One thing I beseech you, and warn also,
That you do not prick and torment
This tender maiden, as you have done before,
For she is fostered in her nurturing
More tenderly, and, I suppose,
She could not endure adversity
As a poorly fostered creature could."

(IV, E, 1037–1043)

Because the marquis' new wife is a woman of high position, not a peasant like Grisilde, she has been tenderly raised and cannot endure harsh treatment.

Grisilde's warning to Walter has several dimensions of meaning. In it she exhibits once more her extraordinary virtue, concerning herself only with the well-being of the woman who is apparently displacing her. While she is indeed finally criticizing Walter, she does it in the gentlest possible way, as an expression of concern for another. The comment also calls attention to the class basis of her persecution. Had she and Walter been social equals, Walter would never have tormented her so. He has taken advantage of her "poor fostering" (IV, E, 1043), her humble upbringing, which has trained her in passive suffering; he could not have behaved so badly if his wife were a gentlewoman.

After this, even Walter is convinced that Grisilde has proved herself "constant as a wall," a paragon of "wifely steadfastness" (IV, E, 1047, 1050). Walter reveals all, produces the children, and restores all her former emblems of *estat*. In her fine clothes and jewels, she is brought into the main assembly room of the palace, the hall, and there honored as marquise. Once again, she is on top of Fortune's wheel. Incredibly, Grisilde does not hold any of this against Walter. They live out their lives "in high prosperity / . . . in concord and in rest" (IV, E, 1128–1129)—happily ever after.

The tale of Grisilde is repeated over and over in conduct books or behavior manuals directed toward medieval women. Chaucer's Clerk, a well-read man, knows this. But he also knows that this is a tale that can easily be misinterpreted. Both Chaucer's Clerk, then Chaucer in his own voice, append interpretations that make clear where they stand on the issues:

> *This storie is seyd nat for that wyves sholde*
> *Folwen Grisilde as in humylitee,*
> *For it were inportable, though they wolde.*

This story is not told that wives should
Imitate Grisilde in humility,
For that would be impossible, even if they would.

(IV, E, 1142–1144)

Grisilde is an impossible role model; her behavior is presented for admiration, not for emulation. Like the extravagant sufferings of saints, Grisilde's trials are meant to encourage both men and women to have patience in the lesser difficulties of their ordinary lives:

> *that every wight, in his degree,*
> *Sholde be constant in adversitee*
> *As was Grisilde.*

that every person, in his degree,
Should be constant in adversity
As was Grisilde.

(IV, E, 1145–1147)

Every *degree* or *estat*, from king to serf, has its problems, and Grisilde's story tells both men and women how best to endure them.

> *For sith a womman was so pacient*
> *Unto a mortal man, wel moore us oghte*
> *Receyven al in gree that God us sent.*

For since a woman was so patient
To a mortal man, all the more should we
Receive all that God sends us with grace.

(IV, E, 1149–1151)

As Grisilde bore the trials inflicted by Walter, so all must bear the "sharp scourges of adversity" (IV, E, 1157) by which God tests His creatures.

But as the Canterbury pilgrims have learned from listening to the "Wife of Bath's Prologue and Tale," few wives are as patient as Grisilde nowadays. More up-to-date fourteenth-century women belong to the Wife of Bath's "sect" or counter-religion, which preaches "high mastery" (IV, E, 1171–1172), not Grisilde-like submission. In a passage labeled *Lenvoy de Chaucer* appended to the "Clerk's Tale," the speaker argues that

Grisilde is deed, and eek hire pacience,
And bothe atones buryed in Ytaille;
For which I crie in open audience
No wedded man so hardy be t'assaille
His wyves pacience in trust to fynde
Grisildis, for in certein he shal faille.

Grisilde is dead, as is her patience.
And both together are buried in Italy.
For which I cry in the hearing of all
That no wedded man should be so hardy as to assail
His wife's patience trusting to find
Grisilde, for it's certain he shall fail.

                                                        (IV, E, 1177–1182)

Since the days of patient Grisilde are over, no husband should dare to emulate Walter.

And how should wives treat their husbands? Chaucer knows well that the tale of patient Grisilde was often set forth as a didactic tool meant to shape women's behavior. But he does not agree with its *sentence*, its moral lesson. Instead, he counsels verbal aggression:

O noble wyves, ful of heigh prudence,
Lat noon humylitee youre tonge naille,
Ne lat no clerk have cause or diligence
To write of yow a storie of swich mervaille
As of Grisildis pacient and kynde.

O noble wives, full of high prudence,
Do not let humility nail your tongue,
Nor let any clerk have cause or diligence
To write of you a story of such marvels
As the story of Grisilde, patient and kind.

                                                        (IV, E, 1183–1187)

A smart wife speaks up for herself. The virtue of humility "nails the tongue" of women so that they cannot use their best form of self-defense, their speech. In misogynistic lore of the Middle Ages, women were often criticized for "shrewish" or overly assertive speech. But Chaucer sees this as a proper means of self-defense against the tyrannous behavior of some husbands. By speaking up for themselves, women "take on [themselves] the governance" (IV, E, 1192). "Imprint this lesson in your mind," Chaucer says: become "archwives" (IV, E, 1195). To emulate the Wife of Bath, women must reject Grisilde's speech habits. The cruelty of the image of the nailed tongue shows what Chaucer thinks of men's attempts to control women's speech, their main weapon. Even if the rest of the female body is not suitable for combat, if women "clap like a mill," keep their tongues moving (IV, E, 1200), they will win domestic battles.

The image Chaucer uses is one of penetration:

> *Ne dreed hem nat; doth hem no reverence,*
> *For though thyn housbonde armed be in maille,*
> *The arwes of thy crabbed eloquence*
> *Shal perce his brest and eek his aventaille.*

> Do not dread them; do them no reverence,
> For even if your husband is armed in mail,
> The arrows of your crabbed eloquence
> Shall pierce his breast, and even his neck-guard.

> (IV, E, 1201–1204)

The image of a wife's sharp voice piercing her husband's armor is a psychologically expressive one. The armor Chaucer refers to is chain-link armor, made of small interlocking circles of metal. Such mail covered the chest area, and a separate piece of chain mail formed the neckguard. Armor's true purpose is to defend the knight in battle; but the psychological armor Chaucer describes here is a husband's resistance to his wife's speech. In medieval misogynistic literature, the voices of women, especially when raised in anger, are often described as shrill or sharp. Chaucer imagines a woman's angry words as little arrows. Although a man puts on his emotional "armor" to protect himself from his wife, her sharp shrill voice can breach his defenses, her "arrows" can pierce it. With this weapon, her voice, small but effective, a woman can achieve mastery. A woman who can make her will prevail is, in the Wife of Bath's term, an archwife—a super-wife.

These ideas, still controversial in our own day, were all the more so in Chaucer's. In presenting the Wife of Bath, not Grisilde, as the model of female behavior, Chaucer defies tradition. He sees women as strong-willed, forceful, and authoritative. The reader might wonder if Chaucer's own wife, Philippa, had any part in the development of his proto-feminist theories. While historians provide us with considerable detail about Chaucer's and Philippa's professional lives, personal information is lacking. Barring new discoveries, we will never know if Chaucer's own wife was an archwife like Alisoun, as patient as Grisilde, or somewhere in between.

SUGGESTIONS FOR FURTHER READING

Braswell, Laurel. "Chaucer and the Art of Hagiography." *Chaucer in the Eighties*.
  Eds. Julian N. Wasserman and Robert J. Blanch. Syracuse, N.Y.:
  Syracuse University Press, 1986. 209–221. Braswell sees the "Clerk's
  Tale," the "Second Nun's Tale," the "Man of Law's Tale," and the
  "Prioress's Tale" as operating according to the conventions of the popu-
  lar medieval story type, the *legenda*.

Carruthers, Mary J. "The Lady, the Swineherd, and Chaucer's Clerk." *Chaucer
  Review* 17, no. 3 (1983): 221–234. Carruthers describes how Chaucer
  elects to "tell . . . an unappealing story," and even alters its sources to
  "make it emphatically less attractive than it was to begin with."

Edden, Valerie. "Sacred and Secular in the *Clerk's Tale*." *Chaucer Review* 26, no.
  4 (1992): 369–376. Edden interprets the tale as a "secular story, enriched
  with religious symbolism," not as primarily an allegory of Christian
  patience.

Ellis, Deborah S. "Domestic Treachery in the *Clerk's Tale*." *Ambiguous Realities:
  Women in the Middle Ages and Renaissance*. Eds. Carole Levin and Jeanie
  Watson. Detroit, Mich.: Wayne State University Press, 1987. 99–113.
  Ellis explains how Chaucer "associates domestic insecurity with the
  plight of women."

Gilmartin, Kristine. "Array in the *Clerk's Tale*." *Chaucer Review* 13, no. 3 (1979):
  234–246. Gilmartin explores "the different meanings, political/social or
  spiritual/personal, which Walter and Griselda attach to the clothing."

Hallissy, Margaret. *Clean Maids, True Wives, Steadfast Widows: Chaucer's Women
  and Medieval Codes of Conduct*. Westport, Conn.: Greenwood Press,
  1993. 89–112, 113–134. In Chapter 7, "The Good, the Bad, and the
  Wavering: Women and Architectural Space," Grisilde's movement between father's house and husband's house is analyzed; in Chapter 8,
  " 'Superfluitee of clothynge': Women and Sartorial Excess," her change
  of clothing is examined. Both are seen as metaphors for her helplessness
  and dependency.

Hansen, Elaine Tuttle. *Chaucer and the Fictions of Gender*. Berkeley: University of
  California Press, 1992. 188–207. In Chapter 7, "The Powers of Silence:
  The Case of the Clerk's Griselda," Hansen analyzes the tale as a study of
  the balance of power within the marriage.

Heffernan, Carol Falvo. "Tyranny and Commune Profit in the *Clerk's Tale*."
  Chaucer Review 17, no. 4 (1983): 332–340. Heffernan regards Walter
  and Grisilde as exemplars of two competing "political forces"—Walter as
  "tyranny" and Grisilde as "commune profit."

Kittredge, George Lyman. "Chaucer's Discussion of Marriage." *Chaucer: Modern
  Essays in Criticism*. Ed. Edward Wagenknecht. New York: Oxford University Press, 1959. 188–215. In the classic discussion of the running
  debate on marriage in the "Franklin's Tale," the "Clerk's Tale," the

"Wife of Bath's Tale," and the "Merchant's Tale," Kittredge interprets the tales as dramatic expression of the personal opinions of the tale-tellers.

Levy, Bernard S. "*Gentilesse* in Chaucer's *Clerk's* and *Merchant's Tales.*" *Chaucer Review* 11, no. 4 (1977): 306–318. Levy explains how the various uses of the term *gentilesse* illuminate its significance in the two tales.

Martin, Priscilla. *Chaucer's Women: Nuns, Wives, and Amazons.* Iowa City: University of Iowa Press, 1990. 131–155. In Chapter 8, "The Saints," Martin analyzes the characters of Grisilde, along with that of Custance in the "Man of Law's Tale" and Cecilea in the "Second Nun's Tale," as exemplars of female virtue.

McCall, John P. "The *Clerk's Tale* and the Theme of Obedience." *Modern Language Quarterly* 27 (1966): 260–269. McCall sees Grisilde as the embodiment of the Christian virtues of humility and submissiveness.

Van, Thomas A. "Walter at the Stake: A Reading of Chaucer's *Clerk's Tale.*" *Chaucer Review* 22, no. 3 (1988): 214–224. Van offers a nontraditional reading of the character of Walter as a man "on a quest for growth," seeking, through Grisilde, to "approve of himself."

4. *The wheel of life*. Arundel 83 126v. By permission of the British Library.

The Merchant's Tale

Whan tendre youthe hath wedded stoupyng age,
Ther is swich myrthe that it may nat be writen.

When tender youth has wedded stooping age,
There is such mirth that it may not be written.

(IV, E, 1738–1739)

Medieval people assumed that human life proceeded through orderly, predictable stages: the Ages of Man. One image representing this concept shows men at various stages of life standing on stair steps which proceed upward to a midlife apex, then descend. Or, as in the accompanying photo, the idea of ascent and descent can be combined with the image of the wheel of Fortune. At birth, a man climbs on the wheel of life. Its apex is midlife—full maturity. Thereafter, he declines to old age and death. Both images—stairs and wheel—embody the idea that chronological age is a component of *estat*. Behavior, then, should be appropriate to one's age, as to every other element of *estat*. Each "age of man" had its own characteristics. Impetuosity or lust, though not to be condoned, is to be expected in the young; but an old man with the same character traits would be the more blameworthy in that he should know better.

The lustful old man, the *senex amans* (like John the carpenter in the "Miller's Tale"), was a stock comic character in medieval literature, precisely because his behavior violates norms for his "age of man." A *senex* should be devoting himself to the care of his soul, not indulging the lusts of his body. For "stooping age" to marry at all is foolish; but when he marries "tender youth," a young and lustful girl, "there is such mirth" because medieval people believed that he could not satisfy her sexually and that she would therefore betray him. Age should bring wisdom; when it brought senile lust instead, medieval people saw the resulting events not as pathetic but as comic.

An old knight living in Lombardy in Italy, Januarie had been a "wifeless man" (IV, E, 1248) until the age of sixty. Not that he was a celibate, as was the moral ideal for the unmarried; instead, he satisfied his appetites with various women. Now in his old age he should be repenting of the lusts of his youth. Instead he decides to reform, not by giving up sex but by marrying. This strange notion—whether for "holiness," the desire to lead a sinless life, or "dotage," the senility of old age (IV, E, 1253)—motivates him to seek a wife.

Despite being sixty, Januarie is wildly naive about marriage. He believes that it is "so easy and so pure" that it renders "this world . . . a paradise" (IV, E, 1264–1265). The Merchant-narrator, himself unhappily married (as he reveals in his prologue), cynically describes Januarie as "wise" (IV, E, 1266) for believing this. It would be wonderful if, as the Merchant says, an old man could "take a young wife and a fair, / On which he might engender him an heir" (IV, E, 1271–1272); if marriage always led to "a life blissful and orderly" (IV, E, 1284); if wives were always faithful. "And yet some clerks say it is not so" (IV, E, 1293): antifeminist authors like Theophrastus say that a man would be better off with a good servant than a wife. Worse still, a wife might make her husband into a "cuckold" (IV, E, 1306), a betrayed husband who wears horns on his head visible to everyone but him.

The narrator contrasts Theophrastus' misogynistic viewpoint with an idealistic view of marriage as not only a Christian sacrament but also a state of earthly bliss. In the book of Genesis, God created Eve as a "help" to Adam (IV, E, 1328); so it is with Eve's daughters:

> [A] wyf is mannes helpe and his confort,
> His paradys terrestre, and his disport.

> A wife is man's help and his comfort,
> His earthly paradise, and his sport.
>
> (IV, E, 1331–1332)

The marital relationship is the highest form of earthly joy. Never do a husband and wife disagree, because wives are unfailingly agreeable:

> She seith nat ones "nay," whan he seith "ye."
> "Do this," seith he; "Al redy, sire," seith she.

> Not once does she say "Nay" when he says, "Ye,"
> "Do this," says he; "All ready, sire," says she.
>
> (IV, E, 1345–1346)

Such harmony reigns in this "blissful order of precious wedlock" (IV, E, 1347) that every man should not only have a wife but also take her advice. A long series of biblical and classical examples hymn the praises of devoted wives—while cleverly ignoring the one wife whose advice was fatal: Eve.

Antimarriage propaganda was well known to the medieval audience; so were the high ideals to which married couples committed themselves on their wedding day. But the Merchant's praise of marriage is so extravagant that it undercuts the point he is making. No human relationship can possibly be so perfect as the narrator alleges that marriage is. Everyone in the medieval or modern audience knows this; so the only question is not whether Januarie's proposed marriage will be blissful, but rather what kind of nonbliss will manifest itself.

Januarie announces his intention to marry during a gathering of his friends. He admits that he is "old, / And almost . . . on my grave's brink" (IV, E, 1400–1401). Medieval theologians would agree that it is, as Januarie says, time to think of his soul; none would agree that the remedy for his past lusts should be more lust, this time in marriage. Marriage, though a lesser spiritual *estat* than lifelong chastity, was considered a morally acceptable way of channeling the sexual passions—within strictly defined limits. Januarie, however, does not intend to observe any limitations on sex in marriage. A basic flaw in Januarie's attitude is that he sees marriage only as a way to have excessive sex lawfully, not as a relationship with another human being.

When he announces his intention of getting married, he is not even in love with a specific woman. He has certain qualifications in mind: his wife must be "a maid [virgin] fair and tender of age," no more than twenty years old—surely not thirty, not an "old wife" or an "old widow" (IV, E, 1407, 1416, 1423). Older women are, Januarie thinks, too opinionated, too hard to manage:

> "For sondry scoles maken sotile clerkis;
> Womman of manye scoles half a clerk is.
> But certeynly, a yong thyng may men gye,
> Right as men may warm wex with handes plye."

> "For sundry schools make subtle clerks;
> Women of many schools are half-clerks;

But certainly, men may guide a young thing,
Just as men may ply warm wax with hands."

(IV, E, 1427–1430)

Attending many schools makes a clever student; similarly, experienced women are "half-clerks," almost like learned men. The Wife of Bath has used this same idea of marriage as an education in life. But to Januarie's thinking the Wife of Bath is the least desirable kind of wife. Better to have a "young thing," an inexperienced young girl: guidable, pliable, malleable like "warm wax" (IV, E, 1429–1430), which can be molded into whatever shape suits Januarie. This image of warm wax, here symbolizing the control he hopes to have over his wife, will recur at a crucial point in the narrative—but with a difference.

Another disadvantage that Januarie sees in an old wife sheds light on what medieval people considered immoral motivations for marriage. If his wife were old,

"*I in hire ne koude han no plesaunce,*
Thanne sholde I lede my lyf in avoutrye
And go streight to the devel whan I dye."

"In her I could have no pleasure,
Then I should lead my life in adultery,
And go straight to the devil when I die."

(IV, E, 1434–1436)

Januarie's goal is sexual pleasure only, not as a legitimate part of a loving and committed relationship. As moderns would say, he sees his wife only as a sex object. If she is unattractive (because she is old—like him), he will seek pleasure elsewhere, as has been his pattern of behavior all his life. He has no commitment to his wife as a person; to him, she is a mere instrument of pleasure.

Januarie's only legitimate motivation is his desire to beget an heir. In medieval church law, the desire for procreation was believed to sanction sexual pleasure. In addition, a man in Januarie's position needed an heir, lest his "heritage," his inheritable goods and land, "fall / Into strange hand" (IV, E, 1439–1440). In the "Clerk's Tale," Walter agreed to his liegemen's request that he marry, for this very reason. This, says Januarie, is why he needs a young wife: she would be more likely to have children.

Taming lust and begetting offspring justify marriage theologically. As Januarie knows, to "live in chastity full holily" (IV, E, 1455) would be even better. But Januarie thinks of himself as such a sexy fellow that, even at his advanced age, chastity would be impossible:

> "For—God be thanked!—I dar make avaunt
> I feele my lymes stark and suffisaunt
> To do al that a man bilongeth to."

> "For—God be thanked!—I dare make boast
> I feel my limbs strong and sufficient
> To do all that belongs to a man."

(IV, E, 1457–1459)

For all these reasons, he asks his friends to consent to his marriage.

His counselors disagree: "diverse men diversely told him" stories about marriages, both happy and unhappy, to the point of "altercation" and "disputation" (IV, E, 1469, 1473, 1474) among them. The opposing viewpoints, pro- and antimarriage, are represented by Januarie's two brothers, Placebo and Justinus. Placebo, as would be expected from his name, derived from the Latin verb meaning *to please*, placates Januarie. Justinus, as his name indicates, speaks justly. Before either presents his argument, it is clear that Januarie will only see the viewpoint that supports his own and be blind to the other side.

Placebo's credentials as advisor include being a counselor of lords of "full high *estat*" (IV, E, 1495). It was a commonplace of medieval thought that such lords preferred counselors who served as mirrors reflecting their own images back to them. This is the secret of Placebo's success: he never disagrees with his lord. Obviously, such an advisor offers no advice at all but merely echoes. Accordingly, Placebo pleases Januarie by telling him exactly what he wants to hear:

> "And trewely, it is an heigh corage
> Of any man that stapen is in age
> To take a yong wyf."

> "And truly it takes high spirits
> For any man who is advanced in age
> To take a young wife."

(IV, E, 1513–1515)

Justinus, on the other hand, counsels patience—a character trait thought to be particularly appropriate to an old man:

"I warne yow wel, it is no childes pley
To take a wyf withouten avysement."

"I warn you well, it is no child's play
To take a wife without advice."

(IV, E, 1530–1531)

At his age, Januarie should not be impulsive, should not engage in "child's play" (IV, E, 1530). He should proceed prudently, undertaking a background check to find out if a potential wife has serious flaws: drunkenness, pride, shrewishness, extravagance, lustfulness. Go slowly, Justinus advises: "All this requires leisure," a slow pace, "to enquire" (IV, E, 1544). Justinus knows whereof he speaks; he is unhappily married, despite the fact that his wife is considered the "most steadfast" and the "meekest" in the neighborhood (IV, E, 1551–1552).

But Justinus sees a further problem in Januarie's plan: his intention to marry a young wife. Januarie should know—everyone else does—that male sexual ability inevitably decreases with age. Although Januarie has bragged that he feels "sufficient" (IV, E, 1458) to do all that men do in marriage, he must accept the fact that young women have demanding sexual appetites:

"The yongeste man that is in al this route
Is bisy ynough to bryngen it aboute
To han his wyf allone. Trusteth me,
Ye shul nat plesen hire fully yeres thre—
This is to seyn, to doon hire ful plesaunce."

"The youngest man in all this rout
Is busy enough to bring it about
To have his wife alone. Trust me,
You shall not please her fully for three years—
This is to say, give her full pleasure."

(IV, E, 1559–1563)

This is decidedly not what Januarie wants to hear. Abruptly, Januarie decides he will take Placebo's advice—that is, do what he intended to do all along. Surely this is why the god Cupid is blindfolded, because "love is blind all day, and may not see" (IV, E, 1598), or may choose not to see.

Except for the desire to have a child, Januarie's motivations for marriage are sinful. Thinking about a possible bride, he becomes preoccupied with imagining a physically ideal woman of "fresh beauty and . . . tender age" (IV, E, 1601). By medieval sexual standards, Januarie's thoughts arouse lust and are therefore sinful, without even the partial justification of love for a specific person. Since marriage to him is an earthly paradise of sexual abandon, he worries that he will be so happy that he will not be able to earn heaven:

> *"I have," quod he, "herd seyd, ful yoore ago,*
> *Ther may no man han parfite blisses two—*
> *This is to seye, in erthe and eek in hevene."*

> "I have," said he, "heard it said, very long ago,
> That no man may have two perfect blisses—
> That is to say, on earth and also in heaven."

(IV, E, 1637–1639)

"Perfect bliss" on earth cannot be based on sex because, as Justinus cautions, sex in marriage cannot be excessive. A married man must behave "temperately / . . . not too amorously" (IV, E, 1679–1680), or else he risks his eternal salvation just as much as if he never married at all. So, Justinus assures Januarie, given the well-known imperfections of women and the fact that moderation in marriage limits pleasure, the enthusiastic groom need not worry about being too happy on earth to get to heaven.

But again, despite Justinus' warning, Januarie again accepts the advice of Placebo, who recommends a prospective bride,

> *a mayden in the toun,*
> *Which that of beautee hadde greet renoun,*
> *Al were it so she were of smal degree.*

> a maiden in the town,
> Who had great renown for beauty,
> Although she was of small degree.

(IV, E, 1623–1625)

A beautiful young girl "of small *degree*," or low social class, might well seize the opportunity to marry a wealthy old man like Januarie. For such a woman, this was an easy way to fortune. Even if the marriage was unpleasant, it was unlikely to last long; and widows, especially widows with money, were in a desirable position in the Middle Ages. Freed from the dominance of father and husband, a widow could live independently—or choose a second marriage on her own terms.

The medieval audience would have immediately recognized that this marriage would considerably enhance young May's economic position. Prenuptial financial arrangements, including legal documents, "scrits and bonds," cause May to be "enfeoffed in" (IV, E, 1697–1698) or endowed with

Januarie's land as her marriage portion. In modern times, a bride may have personal possessions or an earning capacity comparable to a groom's; in the Middle Ages, too, many women possessed earned or inherited money or land. But May is young and of low *degree*. She has nothing of her own, and now, not only is she marrying a rich man, but he is an old rich man likely to die soon. Medieval readers would have seen May as an opportunist selling herself in a loveless marriage and counting on an early widowhood.

Januarie and May's wedding day arrives. Wedding guests are expected to feign enthusiasm even for the most outrageous of unions. Here, the effect of the lavish celebration is ludicrous:

> *Whan tendre youthe hath wedded stoupyng age,*
> *Ther is swich myrthe that it may nat be writen.*

> When tender youth has wedded stooping age,
> There is such mirth that it may not be written.
>
> (IV, E, 1738–1739)

Traditional wedding poetry with which the medieval audience would have been familiar stresses the groom's anticipation of the night of love ahead. But when the groom in question has reached "stooping age," his lust is comical. He imagines himself "straining her" in his arms "harder than ever Paris did Helen" (IV, E, 1753–1754). For a *senex* to compare himself to one of history's great lovers would have struck the medieval audience as hilarious; given the diminished potency of old age, Januarie will be lucky if he can consummate the marriage at all, much less exceed the virility of Paris. He thinks of himself as so lusty that he will "offend" his virginal bride; he worries that she will not be able to "endure" his "sharp and keen" lovemaking (IV, E, 1756, 1758–1759). But he will be gentle: "God forbid that I did all my might!" (IV, E, 1761). He can hardly wait to get into bed with his bride. In customary wedding-song fashion, he wishes the day would end:

> "*Now wolde God that it were woxen nyght,*
> *And that the nyght wolde lasten everemo.*
> *I wolde that al this peple were ago.*"

> "Now would God that the night would come,
> And that the night would last forevermore!
> I wish that all these people were gone."
>
> (IV, E, 1762–1764)

At the moment when Januarie thinks he is on the brink of bliss, a threat to that bliss materializes in the form of his squire Damyan. A medieval court typically housed many young men like Damyan, bachelors like the knight in the "Wife of Bath's Tale"; and they are conventionally portrayed in the love poetry of the period as falling in love with the lord's lady. While such a lady is unattainable, the young wife in the contrasting *senex amans* convention is seen as all too attainable. Here, then, are the makings of the *senex–wife–lover* triangle, as in the "Miller's Tale." Januarie, overconfident of his own sexual prowess, cannot see the threat to his marriage, though it is right before his eyes:

> O Januarie, dronken in plesaunce
> In mariage, se how thy Damyan,
> Thyn owene squier and thy borne man,
> Entendeth for to do thee vileynye.
> God graunte thee thyn hoomly fo t'espye!
>
> O Januarie, drunk with pleasure
> In marriage, see how Damyan,
> Thy own squire and thy born man,
> Intends to do thee villainy.
> God grant thee to espy the foe at home!
>
> (IV, E, 1788–1792)

Blind with lust and unwarranted self-esteem, Januarie will not espy the enemy within his house. The rest of the plot will hang on these contrasting images of vision/blindness.

Finally, night falls, and "this hasty Januarie / Would go to bed" (IV, E, 1805–1806). In preparation for the night of love, he takes aphrodisiacs—spiced wines were believed to enhance the sex drive—as recommended in Constantinus Africanus' *De Coitu* (*On Intercourse*), a medieval sex manual. According to medieval custom, members of the wedding party accompany the newlyweds to the bridal chamber, the priest blesses the marital bed, and all discreetly withdraw. What follows is a detailed discussion of Januarie's lovemaking. He takes his "fresh May, his paradise, his mate" into his arms and kisses her, rubbing her with the "thick bristles of his beard unsoft" (IV, E, 1822–1824). He apologizes to her for the "trespass" he is now about to do; he explains that he will take his time, since "there is no workman . . . who may work both well and hastily" (IV, E, 1828–1833); he further assures her that nothing they might do can be sinful, "for we have permission by law to play" (IV, E, 1841).

The grotesqueness of Chaucer's description of his senile antics, the "slack skin shaking about his neck" (IV, E, 1849), is emphasized by the audience's awareness of the youth and beauty of May. This alliance between "youth" and "stooping age" (IV, E, 1738) is inappropriate. Such a relationship can only be comic, not erotic. Januarie's lovemaking cannot please May:

> But God woot what that May thoughte in hir herte,
> Whan she hym saugh up sittynge in his sherte,
> In his nyght-cappe, and with his nekke lene;
> She preyseth nat his pleyyng worth a bene.
>
> God knows what May thought in her heart,
> When she saw him sitting up in his shirt,
> In his night-cap, and with his neck lean;
> She praised not his playing worth a bean.
>
> (IV, E, 1851–1854)

Since May's sexual initiation has not led to her sexual satisfaction, the scene is set for her to become the stock adulterous wife of the *fabliau* tradition.

The plot begins to move quickly toward the inevitable adultery of Damyan and May. But it would not be a good story without complications. Since May and Damyan cannot be alone together, Damyan must find a way to bare his heart to May. Lovesickness weakens him so that he takes to his bed. In her role as lady of the house and therefore in charge of health care for her husband's retainers, May visits Damyan—ironically, with Januarie's encouragement. Since a married woman could not visit a gentleman's bedroom alone, May is accompanied by her women. Nevertheless, Damyan whispers words of love and slips her a purse containing a letter. Privacy was in short supply in the crowded medieval household, so May must pretend a need to visit the only private room—the privy—in order to read Damyan's letter. When she does, she tears it into small pieces "and in the privy softly cast it" (IV, E, 1954). The wordplay on *privee*, which in Middle English means secrecy, the elaborate subterfuge that makes illicit love all the more thrilling, and *pryvee*, the toilet, would have made this scene all the more comic to its original audience.

No unattainable courtly lady, May, like Alisoun in the "Miller's Tale," is a woman of easy virtue. So within a short time,

This gentil May, fulfilled of pitee,
Right of hire hand a lettre made she,
In which she graunteth hym hire verray grace.

This gentle May, filled with pity,
With her own hand she made a letter,
In which she granted him her very grace.

(IV, E, 1995–1997)

"Grace" and "pity," attributes of the courtly lady, meant sympathy for the lover's suffering, nothing more; but May intends to consummate her love for Damyan. As is ever the case with the adulterous *fabliau* liaison, the husband stands in the way.

Januarie had been warned by Justinus that morality required that he "use" the pleasures of marriage "temperately" (IV, E, 1678–1679). Many practices which to moderns provide legitimate variety within a monogamous relationship were, to medieval people, sinful. According to medieval theology, sexual passion was to be controlled, not enhanced. Among the sinful practices were any actions that increased frequency or intensity, such as choosing exciting settings for the marriage act. It is in this context that the medieval audience would see Januarie's garden. The garden metaphor is common in medieval love poetry as a symbol of the delights of love. Januarie's garden is so lovely that it has attracted the attention of the gods: Priapus, the god of masculine potency, and Pluto and Proserpina, famous Olympian lovers. The couple will play an important role in the events taking place in the garden.

In conventional medieval love poetry, the garden is a perfect setting for romantic love. Medieval people particularly found walled gardens attractive, and in the visual arts lovers are often represented therein, attracted by the beauty and privacy of the enclosed space. The privacy of the garden appeals to the lustful Januarie:

he wol no wight suffren bere the keye
Save he hymself; for of the smale wyket
He baar alwey of silver a clyket,
With which, whan that hym leste, he it unshette.

he would allow no one to bear the key
But he himself; for of the small wicket
He always bore a silver clicket,
With which, when he wished, he unshut it.

(IV, E, 2044–2047)

The comical rhyme of "wicket" (gate) and "clicket" (key) calls attention to the sexual nature of the activities in the garden. If a woman's body resembles a gate, Januarie wants to have the only key to it. The key image suggests that Januarie wants exclusive sexual rights to his wife, as is his privilege as her husband; but it also suggests, more vulgarly, that she is a possession, to be unlocked and used whenever he wants.

The issue of sexual excess is crucial in the context of the walled-garden passage. Januarie, ignoring Justinus' advice to the contrary, is overindulging his lust. Medieval moralists would have considered not only the frequency of intercourse but also the inventive use of their surroundings as the deadly sin of lust rather than legitimate expressions of marital love.

> *And thynges whiche that were nat doon abedde,*
> *He in the gardyn parfourned hem.*

> And things which were not done abed,
> He performed them in the garden.

> > > > > > > (IV, E, 2051–2052)

Even apart from strict medieval sexual norms, it is clear that Januarie is exploiting his young wife.

Januarie does not see this, however. He thinks he is a fortunate man, indeed, on top of Fortune's wheel. But the very mention of the word "Fortune" would remind the medieval audience that "worldly joy may not always last / For Januarie, nor for any creature" (IV, E, 2055–2056). "Fortune unstable" (IV, E, 2057) dictates that he who is too high must fall. Januarie's downfall begins with a physical disability: he goes blind. This increases his jealousy, as he worries that he will not be able to supervise his wife carefully enough to keep her from "falling into some folly" (IV, E, 2074). Blindness, a reminder of mortality, leads to anticipatory jealousy of his wife after his death: he wants her to "live ever as a widow in clothes black" (IV, E, 2079). Fearing loss, he redoubles his efforts to keep May near him; "he had his hand on her always" (IV, E, 2091). As the reader can learn from the "Wife of Bath's Prologue" as well as from the "Franklin's Tale" that women hate to be controlled, Januarie's behavior can only have an effect opposite from the one that he desires: May becomes all the more eager for the planned rendezvous.

But Januarie's blindness is more than just another obstacle in the lovers' path. Medieval people believed that physical illness manifested moral iniquity, that in effect the sick got the diseases they deserved. Since in his relationship with May, Januarie has been morally blind, physical blindness is a suitable punishment. As the narrator laments:

> O Januarie, what myghte it thee availle,
> Thogh thou myghtest se as fer as shippes saille?

> O Januarie, what might it avail you,
> Though you might see as far as ships sail?

(IV, E, 2107–2108)

When Januarie saw with his eyes, he was still deceived by the inner "eye" of his incorrect perceptions. Blind to his own moral failings, he has been indulging in sinful behavior. So now the medieval audience would not feel pity for this blind old man, who deserves the fate that now awaits him.

Fortune's wheel turns swiftly as Januarie falls from false bliss. Even in his blindness, Januarie is eager to take his wife to the garden. With "old lewd words" (IV, E, 2149), seductive lyrics imitating the great biblical love lyric, the *Song of Songs*, he attempts to arouse her passions. But meanwhile, May has obtained the "clicket," Januarie's key to the garden gate, "in warm wax has imprinted" it, and given the mold to Damyan, who now has his own "clicket" to the "wicket" (IV, E, 2117–2118). Januarie had believed that young wives were malleable as warm wax. May's use of that very substance proves him wrong: she has a mind of her own and means to use it to get a more suitable lover. Her imprinting of the key to the garden gate shows that being locked away like a possession is not for her.

Thinking that he and May are alone in their garden of love, Januarie reminds May of the importance of keeping her marriage vows. He gives her several reasons, some good, some less so. The audience knows that, whether deliberately or through self-deception, he is misrepresenting his motives for marrying her when he alleges that he did so not for "covetousness" but only for "love" (IV, E, 2166–2167). It is true that May should be faithful for the "love of Christ" and her own "honor" (IV, E, 2171). But given the circumstances of their marriage, Januarie now proceeds to the best reason of all. Fidelity will win her

> "al myn heritage, toun and tour;
> I yeve it yow, maketh chartres as yow leste;
> This shal be doon to-morwe er sonne reste."

"all my heritage, town and tower,
I give it to you; make charters as you will;
This will be done tomorrow before sunset"

(IV, E, 2172–2174)

The term *heritage* in this context can mean one of two things: either
Januarie is making a will to leave her all his worldly possessions on his
death, or he is signing over all his possessions to her right away, "tomorrow
before sunset." Either alternative is an excellent prospect for a girl "of small
degree" (IV, E, 1625) like May. If he is willing her all his estate, that is more
than the usual one-third that widows were entitled to by right under
fourteenth-century British law.

To get this inheritance, she will have to be faithful to him for the rest
of his life—which should not be long, since sexual excess is depleting his
vital spirits. But if his terms *heritage* and *charters* mean that he plans to
execute a legal agreement to turn over his possessions to her tomorrow,
then she has only one more day to be faithful, after which she gets
everything that Januarie owns. In either case, May has only a short time to
wait before her marriage to Januarie pays off in lifelong affluence for her.
The brevity of the time, and the high stakes involved, are played against
May's eagerness to consummate her relationship with Damyan.

In offering May these generous legal arrangements, Januarie has forgotten the reason he advanced for getting married: begetting an heir. At the
beginning of the tale, he professed concern that his "heritage" would fall
into "strange hand" (IV, E, 1439–1440) if he did not marry. So far it is not
clear whether he has succeeded in engendering the desired heir. May hints
that she is pregnant when she asks her husband for a boost into the tree;
but she may be lying to facilitate her adultery.

When Januarie has finished making his financial offer to May, he appeals
for her sympathy:

> "*whan that I considere youre beautee*
> *And therwithal the unlikly elde of me,*
> *I may nat, certes, though I sholde dye,*
> *Forbere to been out of youre compaignye*
> *For verray love.*"

> "when I consider your beauty
> And with it the unlikely age of me,
> I may not, surely, though I should die,

Forbear to be out of your company
For true love."

(IV, E, 2179–2183)

The Middle English term *unlikly* means not only dissimilar but also unnatural. The disproportion between their two ages has obsessed Januarie to the
point that he cannot be out of his wife's company. But the audience knows,
too, that the unnaturalness of the relationship between "tender youth" and
"stooping age" (IV, E, 1738–1739) also means a lack of sexual satisfaction
for the youthful partner, which in turn leads directly to the relationship
with Damyan. Much as he might think he loves her, Januarie has done May
a disservice by placing her in a situation where her infidelity is all but
inevitable. To the medieval audience, his plight does not generate sympathy but "mirth" (IV, E, 1739). Age should confer insight, but Januarie has
been blind all along.

Not that May is a sympathetic character either. A misogynistic commonplace well-known to medieval people was that women are untruthful.
May certainly is, as she professes her intention to remain faithful while she
has already admitted her lover to the garden:

> But first and forward she bigan to wepe.
> "I have," quod she, "a soule for to kepe
> As wel as ye, and also myn honour,
> And of my wyfhod thilke tendre flour."

> But first and foremost she began to weep.
> "I have," said she, "a soul to keep
> As well as you, and also my honor,
> And the tender flower of my wifehood."

(IV, E, 2187–2190)

She assures Januarie further that she would rather be stripped, put in a sack,
and drowned in a river than violate her "honor" and her wifehood: "I am
a gentlewoman and no wench" (IV, E, 2189, 2202). Having thus emphatically declared herself faithful, she proceeds to be unfaithful. Signaling to
Damyan that he should "climb upon a tree / That loaded was with fruit"
(IV, E, 2210–2211), May and Damyan, in the roles of Eve and Satan,
prepare to destroy Januarie's earthly paradise.

Aided by the intervention of divinity, events move rapidly to an exciting
climax. Pluto and Proserpina look down from Mount Olympus at the
activities in the garden. Look, says Pluto to his wife, at "the treasons that

women do to men" (IV, E, 2239). There is May, all ready to deceive her husband. Pluto deplores the situation:

> *"Ne se ye nat this honurable knyght,*
> *By cause, allas, that he is blynd and old,*
> *His owene man shal make hym cokewold.*
> *Lo, where he sit, the lechour, in the tree!"*

> "Don't you see this honorable knight,
> Because, alas, he is blind and old,
> His own man shall make him a cuckold.
> Look, where he sits, the lecher, in the tree!"
>
> (IV, E, 2254–2257)

Not willing to give a deceptive woman such a victory over his fellow male, Pluto resolves to help blind Januarie:

> *"Now wol I graunten, of my magestee,*
> *Unto this olde, blynde, worthy knyght*
> *That he shal have ayen his eyen syght,*
> *Whan that his wyf wold doon hym vileynye."*

> "Now will I grant, of my majesty,
> Unto this old, blind, worthy knight
> That he shall have his eyesight again
> When his wife would do him villainy."
>
> (IV, E, 2258–2261)

But Proserpina, allying herself with her fellow female, is equally determined to help May:

> *"I shal yeven hire suffisant answere,*
> *And alle wommen after, for hir sake,*
> *That, though they be in any gilt ytake,*
> *With face boold they shulle hemself excuse."*

> "I shall give her sufficient answer,
> And all women after, for her sake,
> That, though they be taken in any guilt,
> They will excuse themselves with a bold face."
>
> (IV, E, 2266–2269)

So the bargain between the two deities is this: at the moment of betrayal, Pluto will restore Januarie's sight; but Proserpina will give May (and all women after her) the capacity for such bold-faced lying that she will get away with her "villainy."

Meanwhile, back in the garden, May is still below the tree and Damyan in it. All she needs, for an effective though awkward rendezvous to take place, is a boost into the tree. This she accomplishes by claiming pregnancy cravings:

> "I moste han of the peres that I see,
> Or I moot dye, so soore longeth me
> To eten of the smale peres grene. . . .
> I telle yow wel, a womman in my plit
> May han to fruyt so greet an appetit
> That she may dyen but she of it have."

> "I must have the pears that I see,
> Or I must die, so sorely I long
> To eat the small green pears. . . .
> I tell you well, a woman in my plight
> May have so great an appetite for fruit
> That she may die if she does not have it."
>
> (IV, E, 2331–2333, 2335–2337)

Since May has lied before, we cannot tell whether or not she is really pregnant. But Januarie believes her. Ironically, he wishes he had nearby "a knave / That could climb" (IV, E, 2338–2339); little does he know that he has just that in his squire Damyan. Cruelly but efficiently, May suggests that she step on his back. Into the tree she goes, and the Merchant apologizes for the directness of his description of the consummation of adultery:

> And sodeynly anon this Damyan
> Gan pullen up the smok, and in he throng.

> And suddenly this Damyan
> Pulled up the smock, and in he thrust.
>
> (IV, E, 2352–2353)

Now is the time for both Pluto and Proserpina to make good on their promises. Pluto restores Januarie's sight in time for him to see his wife being *swyved* (IV, E, 2377). Proserpina supplements May's natural gift of feminine speech so that she can excuse herself. She asserts boldly that she had learned that, to cure Januarie's eyesight, she had only to "struggle with a man upon a tree" (IV, E, 2374). If Januarie thought he saw *swyving*, not "struggling," it is only because his eyesight was not completely healed: "You have some glimpsing, and no perfect sight" (IV, E, 2369, 2374, 2382). Januarie's imperfect inner vision leads him to deny the evidence of his newly restored outer vision. What May says is true: "He that misconceives, he misjudges" (IV, E, 2410). And with that pun on misconception, May jumps down from the tree. Convinced by her lie, Januarie is relieved of all suspicion, proving beyond doubt that his blindness is a condition not of his eyes but of his soul.

If May was not pregnant before she climbed into the tree, she well might be now, given the medieval belief in the superior fertility of young men. Doting Januarie looks ludicrous when he "strokes her on the womb very gently" (IV, E, 2414), obviously believing her to be pregnant with his child, not Damyan's. But if May has "misconceived" with Damyan, all Januarie's hopes for an heir of his blood are dashed (although he will, of course, continue to be blind to that fact too). A happy cuckold, he will leave all his "heritage" to the "strange hand" (IV, E, 1439–1440) of Damyan's son—his worst fear realized.

Despite the sorry outcome for Januarie, his story is comic, not tragic, because from the medieval perspective, he has violated several key principles of the moral order. An old man's moral task is to prepare for death. Instead he engages in a degree of sensual behavior that would be inappropriate even in a younger "age of man." The disorder inherent in placing the drives of the body ahead of the needs of the soul is further compounded by a misuse of the pleasures of marriage. Medieval people believed that even legitimate rights must be exercised in *mesure*, or moderation. Since *desmesure*, or immoderation, is a vice, immoderate sex, even within marriage, is an abuse of the marriage partner. Januarie sins in marriage because his feelings for May are based not on love but on lust. In medieval philosophy, true love, or *caritas*, is defined by respect for the other as a person, not merely as a source of sensual gratification. Lust, or *eros*, sees the other person merely as a means to an end.

For all these reasons, Januarie has been more sinning than sinned against; though May is far from admirable, Januarie deserves what he gets. At his age, he should have known better. His behavior is ludicrous, and the audience's laughter recognizes it as such. Thus comedy reasserts a correct moral order that values spirit over body, moderation over excess, love over lust.

SUGGESTIONS FOR FURTHER READING

Benson, Donald R. "The Marriage 'Encomium' in the *Merchant's Tale*: A Chaucerian Crux." *Chaucer Review* 14, no. 1 (1979): 48–60. Benson provides a close analysis of a passage in which meaning depends on an ambiguous point: the identity of the speaker.

Hallissy, Margaret. *Clean Maids, True Wives, Steadfast Widows: Chaucer's Women and Medieval Codes of Conduct*. Westport, Conn.: Greenwood Press, 1993. 135–163. In Chapter 9, " 'Wel at Ese': Widowhood," May's behavior is explained in terms of the social, economic, and legal advantages of the estate of widowhood.

Holman, C. Hugh. "Courtly Love in the Merchant's and Franklin's Tales." *Chaucer: Modern Essays in Criticism*. Ed. Edward Wagenknecht. London: Oxford University Press, 1959. 240–250. Holman examines the two tales "in terms of the medieval concept of courtly love."

Kee, Kenneth. "Two Chaucerian Gardens." *Medieval Studies* 23 (1961): 154–162. Kee examines the "garden tradition in medieval literature" as background to the gardens in the "Merchant's Tale" and the "Franklin's Tale."

Kittredge, George Lyman. "Chaucer's Discussion of Marriage." *Chaucer: Modern Essays in Criticism*. Ed. Edward Wagenknecht. New York: Oxford University Press, 1959. 188–215. In his classic discussion of the running debate on marriage in the "Franklin's Tale," the "Clerk's Tale," the "Wife of Bath's Tale," and the "Merchant's Tale," Kittredge sees the tales as dramatizing the interactions between the tale-tellers.

Levy, Bernard S. "*Gentilesse* in Chaucer's *Clerk's* and *Merchant's Tales*." *Chaucer Review* 11, no. 4 (1977): 306–318. Levy explains how the various uses of the term *gentilesse* illuminate its significance in the two tales.

Martin, Priscilla. *Chaucer's Women: Nuns, Wives, and Amazons*. Iowa City: University of Iowa Press, 1990. 84–105. In Chapter 6, "The Merchandise of Love: Wives and Merchants," Martin examines the correlation between sex and money in the "Wife of Bath's Tale," the "Merchant's Tale," and the "Shipman's Tale."

The Franklin's Tale

"Trouthe is the hyeste thyng that man may kepe."
"Troth is the highest thing that man may keep."

(V, F, 1479)

Both the "Franklin's Tale" and the "Physician's Tale" center on a major cultural preoccupation: women's chastity. Throughout all the stages of her life, a woman's sexual purity was believed to be not only her greatest virtue, but also the only virtue she needed. According to Chaucer's formula in *The Legend of Good Women* (G Prol., 282–283), as a daughter in her father's house a woman should be a "clean maid," a virgin until marriage. During her marriage, she should be a "true wife," faithful to her husband. At her husband's death, she should be a "steadfast widow," not remarrying, but loyal to her husband's memory. In the lives of saintly women, the heroines were depicted as enduring unbelievable suffering to preserve their chastity. In fact, suffering was seen as enabling such women to reach heights of virtue otherwise unattainable. In the "Franklin's Tale," Chaucer explores what to his culture was a self-evident principle: that chastity is a woman's only important virtue, and that suffering for chastity is both necessary and good.

The relationship of Dorigen and Arveragus begins conventionally. Arveragus is the stock courtly lover,

> *a knyght that loved and dide his payne*
> *To serve a lady in his beste wise.*

> a knight who loved and suffered pain
> To serve his lady in his best manner.

(V, F, 730–731)

Even their courtship is conventional. Arveragus does great deeds to win his lady's love, suffering "woe," "pain," and "distress" (V, F, 737). Dorigen too is the typical romance heroine, "the fairest under the sun" and of "high kindred" (V, F, 734–735) as well—stock attributes of the character type. In courtship, the lady must neither yield too readily nor be too unyielding. So eventually, recognizing Arveragus' "worthiness" and "meek obedience," Dorigen responds with the reciprocal feminine virtue, "pity," and agrees to "take him for her husband and her lord" (V, F, 738–742). So far, the relationship is utterly typical, proceeding as it does through predictable stages from courtship to marriage.

As the term *lord* indicates, marriage reverses the courtly love relationship. In courtship, the man must "serve" and "obey" the lady; but in marriage, men have "lordship . . . over their wives" (V, F, 731, 739, 743). But Arveragus loves Dorigen so dearly that he attempts a new kind of marriage—unknown in Chaucer's day and rare in ours:

> *Of his free wyl he swoor hire as a knyght*
> *That nevere in al his lyf he, day ne nyght,*
> *Ne sholde upon hym take no maistrie*
> *Agayn hir wyl, ne kithe hire jalousie,*
> *But hire obeye, and folwe hir wyl in al,*
> *As any lovere to his lady shal.*

> Of his free will he swore to her as a knight
> That never in all his life, not day or night,
> Would he take upon himself mastery
> Against her will, nor show her jealousy,
> But obey her, and follow her will in all,
> Like any lover to his lady.

(V, F, 745–750)

Arveragus swears to reject the power that men in his culture traditionally assume in marriage. Unlike Walter in the "Clerk's Tale," he recognizes that his wife has her own will, as he does, and vows never to ask her to act against it. Moreover, he agrees to continue to "follow her will" as he did in courtship. Arveragus promises this "as a knight," on the honor of his knighthood; thus this commitment is backed by all the weight of his high *estat.*

Arveragus' promise constitutes a major modification of the rigid rules governing an ancient institution. In modern times, men and women still struggle to adapt the traditional expectations of marriage to their own needs. Thus it is not surprising that, since Arveragus' promise is a radical act for his time, he does not want to publicize it. He wants the "name of sovereignty," the appearance of husbandly dominance, "for shame of his *degree*" (V, F, 751–752) because it would embarrass him for others to know that a man of his *estat* had overturned what medieval people thought was a divinely ordered hierarchy: husbands in authority. Male dominance was assumed in medieval marriage, as the language of Dorigen's acceptance shows. She thanks him, humbly, for offering her a greater scope of freedom, "so long a rein" (V, F, 755). Dorigen's image of a rein, a leash for an animal, embodies the ideas of the superiority of the holder of the leash, the inferiority of the leashed animal, and the control of the latter by the former. A long rein is a rein still, and a husband could, in that culture, still put his wife on a short rein if he wished. By using this image, Dorigen shows her awareness that she only has as much freedom as her husband chooses to give her. No matter what he says about giving up "mastery," he is still her "lord" in the eyes of society (V, F, 747, 742).

Despite this inherent contradiction, the marriage begins on the highest possible plane of idealism. The couple believes that their marriage will be different. They will be "friends," equals; instead of the wife obeying her husband (as Grisilde does Walter), they will "obey each other" reciprocally (V, F, 762). Unilateral vows of wifely obedience destroy true love:

> *Love wol nat been constreyned by maistrye.*
> *Whan maistrie comth, the God of Love anon*
> *Beteth his wynges, and farewel, he is gon!*
> *Love is a thyng as any spirit free.*
> *Wommen, of kynde, desiren libertee,*
> *And nat to been constreyned as a thral.*

> Love will not be constrained by mastery.
> When mastery comes, right away the God of Love
> Beats his wings, and farewell, he is gone!
> Love is a thing like any spirit—free.
> Women, by nature, desire liberty
> And not to be constrained like a slave.

(V, F, 764–769)

Dominance kills love because women like to be free, "and so do men" (V, F, 770). By force of repetition, this concept of women's love for freedom becomes a major theme in *The Canterbury Tales*. In this, women and men are very much like each other. So Arveragus and Dorigen begin their marriage with a sense of similarity and mutuality, as friends.

The plot revolves around a test of the couple's commitment to this new kind of marriage vow. A separation triggers the plot events. Her husband away, Dorigen behaves as a good wife is expected to do: "She mourns, lies awake, wails, fasts, laments" (V, F, 819). Because she is suffering from "heavy thought" (V, F, 822), what moderns would call depression, her friends encourage her to console herself. But by the conventional norms for wifely behavior, she is supposed to be exactly as she is: inconsolable. When her friends urge her to walk on the seashore, she becomes even more sorrowful, lamenting at the sight of every passing ship. Dorigen focuses her fears for her husband's safety on the "grisly fiendly black rocks" (V, F, 868) that line the seashore. She comes to see them as a symbol of evil in the universe:

> "*grisly feendly rokkes blake,*
> *That semen rather a foul confusion*
> *Of werk than any fair creacion*
> *Of swich a parfit wys God and a stable.*"

> "grisly fiendish black rocks
> That seem rather a foul confusion
> Of work than any fair creation
> Of such a perfect, wise, and stable God."

(V, F, 868–871)

The rocks seem more an ugly destroyer of the good than a good in themselves. How could a good and loving God create something that could destroy His own fair creation, her husband Arveragus? Solving the age-old philosophical problem of the existence of evil is beyond Dorigen who, like most medieval women, has not been educated in philosophy or logic. She must "leave disputation" on this complex subject to learned "clerks," educated men (V, F, 890). All she can do is wish "that all these black rocks / Were sunk into hell for his sake!" (V, F, 891–892). So anxious is Dorigen that she would do anything to get rid of those rocks.

Her friends see that it is doing her no good to walk by the sea, where she can see the rocks. They offer a new suggestion: to attend a cheerful social event, involving typical medieval pastimes, dancing and playing chess and backgammon, all in a lovely garden, a "very paradise" (V, F, 912). Like English people today, medieval English people loved their gardens. The garden was envisioned as a place where human skills, the "craft of man's hand," embellished or "arrayed" the natural world (V, F, 909–910). As in the "Merchant's Tale" and the "Knight's Tale," the garden setting, especially in the spring, is associated with love. So, when Dorigen attends the garden party on a May morning, she is placing herself in a setting conducive to love.

This is a mistake. Violating the seclusion appropriate to a woman whose husband is away, she is seen at the party by Aurelius, a "lusty squire" who had "loved her best of any creature / Two years and more" (V, F, 937–939). Unlike Damyan in the "Merchant's Tale," Aurelius has behaved as the conventional young bachelor, hopelessly in love with his lord's lady:

> *He was despeyred; no thyng dorste he seye,*
> *Save in his songes somwhat wolde he wreye*
> *His wo, as in a general compleynyng;*
> *He seyde he lovede and was biloved no thyng.*

> He was in despair; he dared to say nothing,
> Except in his songs he would somewhat reveal
> His woe, as in a general complaining;
> He said he loved and was not beloved at all.

(V, F, 943–946)

After these years of musical, but fruitless, lamentations, the garden party gives him a chance to offer his "service" to Dorigen and ask for "mercy," lest he die for her love (V, F, 972, 978). Perhaps influenced by the romantic setting, Dorigen responds to his appeal. Despite an initial protestation of utter fidelity—"I shall never be an untrue wife," she says (V, F, 984)—she suggests jokingly, "in play," that if Aurelius "removes all the rocks," she will "love [him] best of any man" (V, F, 988, 993, 997). To this she pledges her *trouthe* (V, F, 998).

To pledge one's troth, as when Arveragus makes his unusual nuptial promise, is to bind oneself according to the highest standard of medieval codes of honor. But Dorigen's troth-plight hinges on her conditional promise to break her troth to her husband. To Dorigen, however, the possibility of the condition being met seems nonexistent. How could Aurelius remove those "grisly fiendly black rocks" (V, F, 868)?

Aurelius tries all sorts of prayers and supplication to various gods to remove the rocks, or at least send a flood sufficient to cover them. Finally, Aurelius' despair is such that he becomes physically ill, suffering for "two years and more" (V, F, 1102). Fearing for Aurelius' life, his brother conveniently remembers a clerk he knows, a student of "natural magic," a "science / By which men make diverse appearances," visual illusions (V, F, 1125, 1139–1140). Perhaps such a clerk might cause the rocks to seem to disappear. The brother tells Aurelius, who "up starts" (V, F, 1168) from his sickbed immediately to see if this magical illusion can be arranged.

Like some modern people, many medieval people believed in magic, astrology, and the occult. Magicians such as the one Aurelius consults could use "white" or "natural" magic (V, F, 1125) to help others; more sinister "black" magic called upon the power of demons to do evil. Aurelius' magician is an astrologer, a student of the effect of planetary influences on human life. Through "calculating" the position of the planets, the magician is able to "make illusions" (V, F, 1284, 1264). Aurelius agrees to pay this master of magic for creating an illusion that the rocks are gone. When he does so, Aurelius promptly goes to Dorigen with the news—and to remind her that it is now time to make good on her pledge.

Dorigen is shocked:

> "Allas," quod she, "that evere this sholde happe!
> For wende I nevere by possibilitee
> That swich a monstre or merveille myghte be!
> It is agayns the proces of nature."

> "Alas," quoth she, "that this should ever happen!
> I never thought it a possibility
> That such a monster or a marvel might be!
> It is against the process of nature!"

(V, F, 1342–1345)

Although magical practices and beliefs flourished in the Middle Ages, Dorigen never anticipated, when she made her pact "in play" (V, F, 988), that Aurelius would employ sorcery to achieve his goals.

Dorigen sees only two alternatives to resolving her dilemma: "death or else dishonor" (V, F, 1358). In her long "complaint" (V, F, 1354) or speech of lamentation, she shows her inability to conceive of any third alternative. Over and over she repeats the formula, varying the words but not the thought: death or dishonor. Even the alliteration of the terms of the dilemma contributes to her sense of inevitability, since neatly phrased ideas somehow seem truer. Like most medieval people, Dorigen is the more persuaded by the many examples she can cite of women who killed themselves "rather than do trespass with their body" (V, F, 1366). The great number of these old tales shows the force of the cultural mandate: women must suffer to defend their chastity. After considering these many examples of suffering women, she comes to a decision:

"I wol conclude that it is bet for me
To sleen myself than been defouled thus."

"I will conclude that it is better for me
To slay myself than be defiled thus."

(V, F, 1422–1423)

Having come to this conclusion, however, Dorigen does not kill herself but waits for Arveragus to come home, and she tells him "all" (V, F, 1465).

What happens is a complicated shift in the relationship of the marriage partners. Under the terms of their agreement, Dorigen and Arveragus are friends, and friends share problems. But Dorigen also seeks Arveragus' help in solving a problem she cannot solve alone. She is in effect handing over a difficult decision to Arveragus. In doing so, she risks that, at worst, he will reject her, acting like a stereotypical betrayed husband. But at best, he may act like the friend he promised to be when they married.

Arveragus behaves beautifully. First, he hears her out, listening carefully and calmly, "with glad cheer, in friendly wise" (V, F, 1467). When Dorigen finishes her tale, Arveragus responds in a way that shocks even his wife: "Is there anything else, Dorigen, but this?" (V, F, 1469). Is that all? The understatement here is all the more pronounced when set against the background of the horror with which moralists of Chaucer's day responded to the merest hint of wifely unchastity. Dorigen knows this, which is why she says that what she has already told her husband is "too much" (V, F, 1471). Then, against all prevailing medieval belief, Arveragus maintains that not chastity but *trouthe* is "the highest thing that man may keep" (V, F, 1479), the highest virtue of humanity, male and female. Moreover, he applies this principle even to his own wife, asserting that she must hold her *trouthe* as of higher value than her chastity—and act upon that belief by keeping her pledge to Aurelius. Again, all he asks is that no one be told of this second radical deviation from prevailing social mores.

Regretful but ready to keep her promise, Dorigen delivers herself to the romantic setting where her problem began: the garden. When the squire Aurelius hears about Arveragus' noble behavior, Aurelius "had great compassion" for both husband and wife (V, F, 1515). Such exemplary behavior on their part demands a comparably noble response from him. "Considering the best on every side," he decides that he would rather deny his "lust" for Dorigen than engage in "churlish wretchedness," low, animal-like behavior, in response to the "great *gentilesse*" of the married couple (V, F, 1521–1527). So he pledges his troth to release Dorigen from hers, thereby proving that a "squire can do a gentle deed / As well as can a knight" (V,

F, 1543–1544). Dorigen, relieved and thankful, returns home to Arveragus, and they live happily ever after.

But Aurelius, for all his own *gentilesse*, is left with a financial problem. He had agreed to pay the magician "a thousand pounds of pure gold" for his services, a sum so great as to bankrupt him: "My heritage I must sell, / And be a beggar" (V, F, 1560, 1563–1564). True to his own *trouthe*, he does not intend to shirk payment, but hopes to work out terms of payment (a downpayment of 500 pounds, with the balance paid on "certain days, year by year" [V, F, 1568]). When he makes this offer, the magician asks if indeed he "had [his] lady" (V, F, 1589) as he wished. When Aurelius answers that he did not, the magician asks why. Upon hearing the story, the magician is so impressed with the *gentilesse* of all three that he thinks similar behavior is now required of him:

> This philosophre answerde, "Leeve brother,
> Everich of yow dide gentilly til oother.
> Thou art a squier, and he is a knyght;
> But God forbede, for his blisful myght,
> But if a clerk koude doon a gentil dede
> As wel as any of yow."

> The philosopher answered, "Dear brother,
> Each of you did nobly to the other.
> You are a squire, and he is a knight;
> But God forbid, for his blissful might,
> If a clerk cannot do a gentle deed
> As well as any of you."

> (V, F, 1607–1612)

The clerk's "gentle deed" is to release Aurelius from his debt.

The tale concludes with the Franklin's rhetorical question to the Canterbury pilgrims: of these four characters, Dorigen, Arveragus, Aurelius, and the magician, who was "the most free" or generous (V, F, 1622)? The moral atmosphere of the tale is positive. Despite lapses, the characters finally embrace the highest standards of ethical behavior. They evaluate the competing claims of various virtues; they make tough moral choices; they accept responsibility for the consequences; they forgive trespasses; they respond to good behavior with even better behavior. The Franklin invites the reader to consider which character surpasses all the rest.

Chaucer intended each member of his audience to decide which of the four was most "free." From the perspective of Chaucer's ongoing examination of marriage in his so-called "marriage group," Arveragus is clearly the most unusual. He has rejected the dominance in marriage that his culture told him was his right. He has made a difficult moral decision according to the highest moral principles. Although his wife had placed herself in a situation that was painful and potentially embarrassing for him, he forgives her wholeheartedly thereafter and "cherishes her as though she were a queen" (V, F, 1554). Chaucer's advancement, through the character of Arveragus, of the idea that chastity is only one of the virtues appropriate to a woman is a sharp divergence from the norms of his time. The tale develops a theory that perceives men and women as equally capable of all virtues, with no virtue seen as gender-specific. Arveragus, in generous love for his wife, does not allow her to suffer for a mistake that threatens her chastity. Given medieval preoccupations with women's sexual purity, this is certainly as "free" an act as any other depicted by Chaucer. But Chaucer's open-ended question invites other interpretations too.

SUGGESTIONS FOR FURTHER READING

Carruthers, Mary J. "The Gentilesse of Chaucer's Franklin." *Criticism* 23, no. 4 (1981): 283–300. Carruthers shows the relationship between the tale-teller's *degree* and the tale's theme of *gentilesse*.

Fyler, John M. "Love and Degree in the *Franklin's Tale*." *Chaucer Review* 21, no. 3 (1987): 321–337. Fyler explains the significance of the concept of *degree*.

Hallissy, Margaret. *Clean Maids, True Wives, Steadfast Widows: Chaucer's Women and Medieval Codes of Conduct*. Westport, Conn.: Greenwood Press, 1993. 25–42. In Chapter 3, "Suffering Women and the Chaste Ideal," Hallissy examines Dorigen's "death-or-dishonor" choice in the context of the medieval belief in the value of women's suffering.

Holman, C. Hugh. "Courtly Love in the Merchant's and Franklin's Tales." *Chaucer: Modern Essays in Criticism*. Ed. Edward Wagenknecht. London: Oxford University Press, 1959. 240–250. Holman examines the two tales "in terms of the medieval concept of courtly love."

Kee, Kenneth. "Two Chaucerian Gardens." *Medieval Studies* 23 (1961): 154–162. Kee examines the "garden tradition in medieval literature" as background to the gardens in the "Merchant's Tale" and the "Franklin's Tale."

Kittredge, George Lyman. "Chaucer's Discussion of Marriage." *Chaucer: Modern Essays in Criticism*. Ed. Edward Wagenknecht. New York: Oxford University Press, 1959. 188–215. In his classic discussion of the running debate on marriage in the "Franklin's Tale," the "Clerk's Tale," the "Wife of Bath's Tale," and the "Merchant's Tale," Kittredge sees the tales as dramatizing interactions between the tale-tellers.

Lee, Anne Thompson. " 'A Woman True and Fair': Chaucer's Portrayal of Dorigen in the *Franklin's Tale*." *Chaucer Review* 19, no. 2 (1984): 169–178. Lee sees the tale as a "study [of] one marriage relationship . . . from a woman's perspective."

Luecke, Janemarie. "Dorigen: Marriage Model or Male Fantasy." *Journal of Women's Studies in Literature* 1 (1979): 107–112. Luecke contends that, compared to two historical medieval women, Christine de Pisan and Margaret Paston, as well as to her own fictional husband Arveragus, Dorigen is "neither an adult person nor one capable of any willed action."

Raybin, David. " 'Wommen, of Kynde, Desiren Libertee': Rereading Dorigen, Rereading Marriage." *Chaucer Review* 27, no. 1 (1992): 65–86. Raybin interprets Dorigen's behavior as independent, active, decisive; her characterization stresses "primacy of free choice in the fashioning of a successful marriage."

Rudat, Wolfgang E. H. "Aurelius' Quest for Grace: Sexuality and the Marriage Debate in the *Franklin's Tale*." *CEA Critic* 45, no. 1 (1982): 16–21. Rudat speculates on Dorigen's motivation in making the rash promise, and examines the effect of the episode on both of the marriage partners and on Aurelius.

The Physician's Tale

For in hir lyvyng maydens myghten rede,
As in a book, every good word or dede
That longeth to a mayden vertuous.

For in her living maidens might read,
As in a book, every good word or deed
That belongs to a virtuous maiden.

(VI, C, 107–109)

A popular form of didactic literature in the Middle Ages was the *legenda*. When the saint was female, the plot usually revolved around a threat to chastity. In the typical *legenda*, a virgin refuses either marriage or an illicit sexual relationship. As a result, she enrages male authority figures, often including her own father. Pitted against the strength of powerful men, figures representing intractable authority, the saint paradoxically triumphs in her weakness through humbly submitting to her fate. The martyrdom of St. Catherine of Alexandria, depicted in photo 5, is a visual representation of a typical virgin martyr *legenda*. Her humility, visible in the curved line of her bent back, contrasts with the arrogance of the erect male figures. The sexual nature of the situation is stressed by the exaggerated gender-specific details of the painting: male aggression is signified by the unusually long sword, female attractiveness by the saint's unnaturally long hair. Stories of martyrs like Catherine were well known to the medieval audience and would have shaped their responses to Virginia in the "Physician's Tale." Two significant differences, however, between the typical *legenda* and the tale of Virginia is that it is not the sexual predator but her own father who martyrs her; and the religious element is minimized. The variation in

5. *The martyrdom of a virgin*. "St. Catherine of Alexandria is Beheaded." From *The Belles Heures of Jean, Duke of Berry* (ca. 1410–1413), 54,1,1, fol. 19v. By permission of the Metropolitan Museum of Art, the Cloisters Collection (1954).

the common plot throws attention on the special relationship between the virgin daughter and her father.

In medieval literature, the marriageable young virgin belongs to her father until he "gives" her in marriage. When a woman is "given" and "taken" in marriage, the father transmits his authority over her and his responsibility for her to her husband. Just as modern parents often fear for the safety of their daughters, so the medieval father would want to protect his daughter in a world unsafe for women. While *authority over* is a concept repugnant to many moderns, it was a universal principle of order to medieval people. To understand *responsibility for* as they did, we must remember that age's longing to be part of a group united under a strong protector, a father-figure. The right and duty of protecting women must be seen against the background of a society in which the stronger were expected to protect the weaker, in return for which the weaker owed loyalty and service. Women, perceived as weaker, had the duty to obey, as well as the right to be protected by, strong men: fathers, then husbands.

A major component of the father/daughter relationship was the father's duty to protect his daughter's virginity until such time as he gave her in marriage to a man of his choosing. Of crucial importance is the smooth transition of a virgin from father-protector to husband-protector. The young girl in transition is in a borderline state. Until her only journey is safely completed, she is in danger. The successful "virgin's story" ends in marriage to a man chosen by her father. But any disruption of the transition can lead to dreadful alternatives: death or dishonor. The plot of the "Physician's Tale" revolves around the father's response to the threat to his daughter's chastity posed by the evil judge Appius. Virginius, the father, operating on the cultural assumption that chastity is women's highest virtue, believes he must choose death or dishonor for his daughter Virginia. To preserve his daughter's virginity, he kills her.

The tale begins with the introduction of the two key characters. Virginius is a man of high social position, a knight

Fulfild of honour and of worthynesse,
And strong of freendes, and of greet richesse.

Full of honor and of worthiness
And strong of friends, and of great wealth.

(VI, C, 2–4)

Virginia is his only child. The "onliness" of a child in medieval tales marks such a child off as special. Since he has no other child, it is psychologically believable that Virginius' identity would be wrapped up in Virginia, and Chaucer underlines this bond by giving them male and female variants of the same name. Since the two are as one, whatever happens to her is tremendously threatening to him. And as her name also signifies, her virginity is essential to her identity. Without it, she cannot be Virginia; virginity is her very self.

In terms of the standards of appearance and behavior expected of the medieval virgin, Virginia is perfect. Nature's child, she is without artifice. Cosmetics were seen as a falsification of nature's handiwork, a form of deception; so it is a high compliment to Virginia that no artist could "paint" or "counterfeit" such a creation as she (VI, C, 12–13). She is perfectly beautiful and very young; her skin is white, her cheeks are red, her hair is golden, her limbs are graceful. She possesses the ideal feminine virtues according to the standards of the time: humility, abstinence, temperance, patience, moderation, discretion in speech, modesty, constancy, "busyness" (to keep her out of trouble [VI, C, 56]). But above all, as her name indicates, she is the epitome of chastity.

The Physician digresses here to advise those in charge of protecting the chastity of young women: their mothers, fathers, and governesses. The virtue of the young, the Physician thinks, can be protected either by those who are perfectly pure themselves, have "kept [their] honesty," or, paradoxically, by those who "have fallen in frailty" (VI, C, 77–78). The fallen who repent can teach others to avoid the same mistakes, just as a reformed poacher can make a good game warden. Parents must be careful to give good example to their children; but no matter how carefully a girl is supervised, she is never safe from threats to her chastity.

Virginia's story is an example of the vulnerability of even the well-protected virgin girl. To trigger the plot events, Chaucer must account for Virginia's being seen at all by the lecherous judge:

> *This mayde upon a day wente in the toun*
> *Toward a temple, with hire mooder deere,*
> *As is of yonge maydens the manere.*

> One day this maid went into town
> Toward a temple, with her mother dear,
> As is the custom of young maidens.

> (VI, C, 118–120)

In the Middle Ages, some advisors to young girls forbade even churchgoing because of the risk of being seen by a lecher, who might, as Appius does,

"cast his eyes / Upon this maid" (VI, C, 123–124). More common, however, was the idea that churchgoing was permissible as long as it was "the
manner," local custom; and as long as the "maid" was properly chaperoned,
as Virginia is, by "her mother dear" (VI, C, 119). Virginia's mother, having
played her brief but crucial role, vanishes from the action. Henceforth
Virginia's chastity is a matter between her father and her would-be seducer.

Appius' lust threatens both Virginius' sense of morality and his position
in the community. Appius has not asked Virginius for Virginia's hand in
marriage. What he intends is concubinage. The devil prompts him to
attempt to "win" the "mayden to his purpose" by deception (VI, C, 132).
Neither force nor bribery would work because of her well-known virtue and
the fact that she is "strong of friends," socially well-connected (VI, C, 135).
So Appius plans a "conspiracy" (VI, C, 149) to seduce Virginia. He hires
a "false churl" (VI, C, 164) to perjure himself before Appius' court by
claiming that Virginia was not Virginius' daughter at all but rather a slave
stolen from the churl's house. Appius abuses his official position as judge
to rule in the churl's favor, whereupon

> *this worthy knyght Virginius*
> *Thurgh sentence of this justice Apius*
> *Moste by force his deere doghter yiven*
> *Unto the juge, in lecherie to lyven.*
>
> this worthy knight Virginius
> Through sentence of this justice Appius
> Was made by force to give his daughter
> To the judge, to live in lechery.
>
> (VI, C, 203–206)

This transaction is a grotesque parody not only of the justice that Appius
is supposed to represent, but also of the proper giving and taking of a
daughter in marriage. A knight who was honored, worthy, and "strong of
friends" (VI, C, 4) would be disgraced by his daughter's becoming a
concubine, "living in lechery" rather than in matrimony.

Instead of considering how he might muster his and Virginia's strong
friends to save her from this shame, Virginius turns his attention toward
his daughter and away from her would-be seducer. Like Dorigen in the
"Franklin's Tale," Virginius assumes that in a situation where female
chastity is threatened, "there are two choices, either death or shame" (VI,
C, 214). He also assumes that it is his daughter, not the unjust judge, who
must die or be shamed. Caught in this conventional response, Virginius

(unlike Arveragus in the "Franklin's Tale") sees no third alternative to the two dreadful choices.

Virginius suffers greatly himself. Athough he believes that she must die, he loves his daughter:

> *"O gemme of chastitee, in pacience*
> *Take thou thy deeth, for this is my sentence.*
> *For love, and nat for hate, thou most be deed;*
> *My pitous hand moot smyten of thyn heed."*

> "O gem of chastity, in patience
> Take your death, for this is my sentence.
> For love, and not for hate, you must be dead;
> My pitying hand must smite off your head."

(VI, C, 223–226)

The Latin root of the word "patience" is a verb meaning "to suffer." In the saints' lives, virtuous women suffer for their chastity. Virginius makes himself the judge of his daughter's fate as he hands down a "sentence" of death. He kills her out of love and pity, believing in all sincerity that she is better off dead than alive as Appius' concubine. Many medieval theologians would have seen Virginius as morally justified in taking upon himself the responsibility for his daughter's eternal salvation—in effect, making her a martyr.

Even Virginia agrees. Perfect, as usual, she acknowledges the supreme value of chastity and the absoluteness of her father's authority over her:

> *"Blissed be God that I shal dye a mayde!*
> *Yif me my deeth, er that I have a shame;*
> *Dooth with youre child youre wyl, a Goddes name!"*

> "Blessed be God that I shall die a virgin!
> Give me my death, before I am shamed;
> Do with your child as you will, in God's name!"

(VI, C, 248–250)

Then Virginius takes his sword and beheads his fourteen-year-old daughter.

Reasoning on the basis of the death-or-dishonor principle leads both father and daughter to conclude that Virginius' paternal duty requires him to kill his beloved only child, a girl "fostered up with such pleasure" (VI, C, 219). But matters have come to this because of the twin cultural assumptions that a dead woman is preferable to a dishonored woman, and that if anyone suffers, it must be Virginia. Why is it that Virginius never considers smiting off Appius' head? Virginius is no peasant like Janicula in the "Clerk's Tale," helpless to defend his daughter; he is a powerful knight with many friends. Such a man should be able to preserve his daughter's honor—or die himself in the attempt. A further piece of evidence that an aggressive response directed against Appius might have been successful is that, when Appius' role in Virginia's death is discovered, he is not strong enough to get away with his crime. The people promptly cast him into prison, whereupon he slays himself; his henchman the churl, originally condemned to death, is exiled. These details show that there is no drastic imbalance of power between the father and his daughter's would-be seducer. Why then must Virginia die, and not Appius?

As is typical of the ending of a medieval tale, the Physician draws a moral: "Here may men see how sin has its reward" (VI, C, 277). But Appius has sinned, not Virginia. In an imperfect world, virtue is punished right along with vice. The injustice of this surely must have been apparent, if not to Chaucer's Physician, then to Chaucer. From a modern perspective, the tale can be seen as yet another example of the "blaming the victim" syndrome. Virginia, a virgin, is nevertheless attractive enough to arouse lust; and both she and her father behave as though it is self-evident that she is the one who must suffer for this. The illogic of Virginius' reaction— indeed, the moral confusion of the entire tale—is a consequence of the overwhelming importance attached to women's purity in medieval culture. That Chaucer saw another possible response to the death-or-dishonor situation is evidenced by the "Franklin's Tale."

SUGGESTIONS FOR FURTHER READING

Crowther, J.D.W. "Chaucer's *Physician's Tale* and Its 'Saint.' " *English Studies in Canada* 8, no. 2 (1982): 125–137. Crowther argues that Virginia is depicted in terms of typical characteristics of medieval women saints; but that her father, by his precipitous action, fails to allow her to demonstrate the full extent of her virtue by resisting Appius herself.

Hallissy, Margaret. *Clean Maids, True Wives, Steadfast Widows: Chaucer's Women and Medieval Codes of Conduct.* Westport, Conn.: Greenwood Press, 1993. 43–58. In Chapter 4, "Perfect Virgin, Perfect Wife," Virginia is seen as an example of the danger involved in the transition from daughter to wife.

Lumiansky, R. M. *Of Sondry Folk: The Dramatic Principle in the Canterbury Tales.* Austin: University of Texas Press, 1955. 195–200. In support of his famous thesis, that the tales are developments of the character of the tellers, Lumiansky explores this relatively weak connection between teller and tale.

Mathewson, Jeanne T. "For Love and Not for Hate: The Value of Virginity in Chaucer's *Physician's Tale*." *Annuale Medievale* 14 (1973): 35–42. Mathewson explains that Virginia is valued not for herself but as an embodiment of the "transient conditions of beauty, youth, and virginity."

The Pardoner's Prologue and Tale

"Thus spitte I out my venym under hewe
Of hoolynesse, to semen hooly and trewe."

"Thus I spit out my venom under hue
Of holiness, to seem holy and true."

(VI, C, 421–422)

Religion, whether in the Middle Ages or today, is a broad term encompassing a variety of beliefs and practices. The medieval Christian, like his
modern counterpart, might be an internationally renowned scholar, an
uneducated peasant, or somewhere in between. Religious practices that
make theological sense to the well-informed seem like magical thinking
when employed by the uncomprehending—or exploited by the unscrupu-
lous. The key religious elements in the "Pardoner's Prologue and Tale"—
the sermon itself, the belief in the power of relics, and the traffic in
"pardons" or indulgences—were, ideally, intended to bring the Christian
soul closer to God. But the Pardoner misuses these instruments of God's
forgiveness for his own gain. Because he abuses the faith of simple believers,
he who should be an agent of God's pardon is himself unpardoned.

By trade the Pardoner is a preacher. His task is to use his rhetorical gifts
to persuade his hearers to repent and be saved. The sermon, then and now,
is a major part of the Christian liturgy. The homilist selects a scriptural
passage on which to expound, typically one selected from that day's liturgy.
Since the Pardoner is an itinerant preacher and not a parish cleric, his
audience changes. So he uses not only the same text but also the same
sermon over and over. His scriptural passage is always the same: *"Radix
malorum est Cupiditas"* (VI, C, 334); cupidity, the inordinate desire for or
excessive love of money, is the root of all evil. Nothing is wrong with this

text, or even with the Pardoner's sermon on it. Something is very wrong with the Pardoner's intention, however. He deliberately uses his considerable homiletic skills to persuade his audience to demonstrate their ability to overcome *cupiditas* by generously giving their money away—to him.

Churchmen whose job it was to wander from place to place soliciting contributions abounded in the Middle Ages. At their best, such medieval churchmen collected money for worthwhile projects such as the support of religious orders or the building of great cathedrals like the one at Canterbury to which the pilgrims journey (see photo 1). As identification, solicitors for funds would carry, as the Pardoner does, "bulls" and "patents" (VI, C, 336–337). Then they would preach, exhorting believers to generosity in support of the organization—in the Pardoner's case, a hospital, St. Mary's of Roncevalles. An honest pardoner would be much like a fundraiser for any religious or charitable organization today. But a dishonest pardoner like this one had many opportunities to profit at the expense of the naive. Once he was able to "stir them to devotion" (VI, C, 346), he could pull out his "relics," odds and ends, bits of stones and bones and cloth, and offer them for sale.

Relics—objects or fragments of objects associated with a saint, or even parts of the body of a saint—are still available today. Medieval people would go to great lengths (even digging up long-buried corpses) to get a piece of a saint's body. Even an object touched by a saint was prized. A church would often contain a relic of the saint to which it was dedicated. Craftsmen built elaborate jeweled reliquaries, containers for relics, medieval examples of which can still be seen in museums such as New York's Metropolitan Museum of Art. A theologian would not believe a relic to have any magical power in and of itself. Its purpose was, rather, to encourage the believer to pray to the saint, who would in turn intercede with God. But this degree of theological sophistication was often beyond simple believers, who were all too likely to believe such far-fetched stories as the Pardoner tells of one relic, an alleged "shoulder bone" from the sheep of a "holy Jew" or Old Testament character (VI, C, 350–351). This object, according to the Pardoner, was effective against the diseases of animals; merely washing the bones in a well would give the well waters curative powers. Moreover, if the owner of the animals drank that same water on an empty stomach, his animals would reproduce faster. And besides, this same water would heal jealousy in husbands with adulterous wives. Surely, suggests the Pardoner, this cure-all was well worth the price.

Anyone simple enough to believe this sales pitch might very likely also believe the Pardoner's further allegation that

" 'If any wight be in this chirche now
That hath doon synne horrible, that he
Dar nat, for shame, of it yshriven be,
Or any womman, be she yong or old,
That hath ymaked hir housbonde cokewold,
Swich folk shal have no power ne no grace
To offren to my relikes in this place.' "

" 'If any person now in this church
Has done a sin so horrible that he
Dare not to be forgiven of it, for shame,
Or any woman, whether she is young or old,
Has made her husband a cuckold,
Such folk shall have no power nor no grace
To offer to my relics in this place.' "

(VI, C, 378–384)

Unforgivable sinners and adulterous wives would be unable, says the
Pardoner, to buy his relics. Presumably, a desire to prove themselves neither
unforgivably sinful nor adulterous would lead to a great rush of customers.

The Pardoner's behavior would not be as evil if he believed, however
misguidedly, in the power of the relics he was hawking. But he does not:

"Of avarice and of swich cursednesse
Is al my prechyng, for to make hem free
To yeven hir pens, and namely unto me."

"Of avarice and of such cursedness
Is all my preaching, in order to make them generous
To give their pennies, and namely unto me."

(VI, C, 400–402)

Sin lies in the Pardoner's intention. He uses his ecclesiastical authority for
his own purposes, not for the spiritual good of his audience:

"For myn entente is nat but for to wynne,
And nothyng for correccioun of synne."

"For my intention is only to win,
And not for correction of sin."

(VI, C, 403–404)

The Pardoner consciously identifies himself with the devil, the serpent of Eden, whose "venom" of sin brought suffering and death to the whole human race:

> *"Thus spitte I out my venym under hewe*
> *Of hoolynesse, to semen hooly and trewe."*

> "Thus I spit out my venom under hue
> Of holiness, to seem holy and true."
>
> (VI, C, 421–422)

The Pardoner described his own words as poisonous. As a churchman, he should employ his considerable speech skills in the service of God. Instead he sees himself as Satan's agent, a serpent "stinging" his audience with his "sharp tongue / In preaching" (VI, C, 413–414). He misuses his God-given talent to nurture the very *Cupiditas* against which he preaches:

> *"What, trowe ye, that whiles I may preche,*
> *And wynne gold and silver for I teche,*
> *That I wol lyve in poverte wilfully?*
> *Nay, nay, I thoghte it nevere, trewely!. . .*
> *I wol noon of the apostles countrefete;*
> *I wol have moneie, wolle, chese, and whete,*
> *Al were it yeven of the povereste page,*
> *Or of the povereste wydwe in a village,*
> *Al sholde hir children sterve for famyne."*

> "What, do you think that while I may preach,
> And win gold and silver for what I teach,
> That I will live in poverty willfully?
> No, no, I never thought it, truly! . . .
> I will imitate none of the apostles,
> I will have money, cheese, and wheat,
> Even if it were given by the poorest page,
> Or by the poorest widow in a village,
> Even if her children should starve for famine."
>
> (VI, C, 439–442, 447–451)

The Pardoner's hypocritical behavior is comparable to that of a corrupt evangelist today who, not even believing what he preaches, takes money from the poor to live in wealth.

But the Pardoner would not be as successful a sinner if he were not a talented preacher. Though a "vicious man," he can tell a "moral tale," full of the "examples" that "lewd" or common people love (VI, C, 435–437, 459–460). The "Pardoner's Tale" is a typical medieval sermon. Such a sermon often begins with a story or illustrative anecdote. The Pardoner's opens with a tale set in Flanders of "a company / Of young folk" (VI, C, 463–464) who commit the typical "tavern sins": drunkenness, gluttony, gambling, lechery, and swearing. Instead of going to church, they dwell in the "devil's temple," the inn; instead of practicing *mesure*, or moderation, they are guilty of "abominable superfluity" (VI, C, 470–471). This theme of the "tavern sins" leads the Pardoner away from his anecdote and into a long digression on drunkenness, gambling, and swearing. Given that his sermon is on cupidity, Chaucer may well be satirizing the tendency of preachers to wander from their main theme.

The Pardoner develops his digression on the tavern sins by example. This popular medieval method of argumentation involves piling up a series of cases. The assumption seems to have been that multiplying examples proves the point, and the more examples cited, the more forcefully the point is proven. Examples are typically chosen from such authoritative sources as the Bible, history, mythology, and literature, as well as from personal experience.

A typical use of the example method is seen in the Pardoner's connection of gluttony with drunkenness and lechery. The biblical story of Lot, who, "so drunk" that he "did not know what he was doing," had sex with his own two daughters (VI, C, 484–485), illustrates the point. So does that of Herod, who, "replete with wine at his feast," ordered the death of John the Baptist (VI, C, 489). Conversely, all the "sovereign acts . . . / Of victories in the Old Testament" were done in sobriety, "in abstinence and in prayer" (VI, C, 574–577). History proves, too, that drunkenness is evil:

> Looke, Attilla, the grete conquerour,
> Deyde in his sleep, with shame and dishonour,
> Bledynge ay at his nose in dronkenesse.

> Look, Attila, the great conqueror,
> Died in his sleep, with shame and dishonor,
> Bleeding at his nose in drunkenness.

(VI, C, 579–581)

Personal experience also confirms the disgusting nature of this behavior:

> O dronke man, disfigured is thy face,
> Sour is thy breeth, foul artow to embrace.

O drunk man, your face is disfigured,
Your breath is sour, you are foul to embrace.

(VI, C, 551–552)

This is how the example method works: the more instances that can be cited to support the proposition "Drunkenness is evil," the truer it must be. The other tavern sins related to drunkenness are developed similarly. While drunk, men swear and gamble, and examples are cited proving the evil of these practices too.

Finally, the Pardoner returns to his tale of the company of young revelers, sinning enthusiastically in their tavern in Flanders. He focuses on three of them, who, while drinking, "heard a bell clink / Before a corpse being carried to his grave" (VI, C, 664–665). Only those under the influence of alcohol could make so irrational a plan as theirs: to pursue and kill "a secret thief called Death" who has "slain a thousand this pestilence" (VI, C, 675–676, 679). When Chaucer uses the charged term *pestilence*, he sets the action against one of the major demographic disasters of medieval history, the recurrent outbreaks of plague in the fourteenth century known collectively as the Black Death.

Modern historians of medicine estimate that during Chaucer's century the pestilence reduced the population of Europe at least by half. Given the abysmal state of medical care in the Middle Ages, there was very little chance that a victim, once infected, would survive. The concept of infection or contagion itself was only understood in a rudimentary fashion. Plague victims were quarantined, suggesting that communicability was feared. But before the invention of the microscope around 1600, no one could have known that disease was communicated by tiny organisms too small to be seen by the unaided eye. So pestilence was a mystery; unpredictable, unavoidable, unmanageable, it was surely a formidable "adversary" (VI, C, 682),

"for he hath slayn this yeer,
Henne over a mile, withinne a greet village,
Bothe man and womman, child, and hyne, and page;
I trowe his habitacioun be there."

"for he has slain this year,
Over a mile from here, within a great village,
Both man and woman, child, peasant and page;
I think his place of residence is there."

(VI, C, 686–689)

In the face of this threat, people could take one of two approaches. They could maintain themselves in a state of spiritual readiness for death and thank God if they survived (possibly by doing what the Canterbury pilgrims were doing, traveling to the shrine of the saint "who helped them when they were sick" [I, A, 18]). Or they could do as the three revelers do: eat, drink, and be merry.

Thinking in their drunkenness that they can slay Death, they set out on their journey. Soon they meet an old, poor man, an image of Age itself. The revelers, contemptuous of the old as are so many of the young, mock him: "Why do you live so long in such great age?" (VI, C, 719). The old man sees Death differently than do the three young men. While the three rioters see Death as the enemy, a "false traitor" (VI, C, 699) to be slain if possible, the old man sees Death as a blessed relief from suffering. So he wanders the world in search of Death, which is, ironically, avoiding him:

> "Thus walke I, lyk a restelees kaityf,
> And on the ground, which is my moodres gate,
> I knokke with my staf, bothe erly and late,
> And seye 'Leeve mooder, leet me in!' "

> "Thus I walk like a restless captive,
> And on the ground, which is my mother's gate,
> I knock with my staff, both early and late,
> And say 'Dear mother, let me in!' "

(VI, C, 728–731)

The young cannot believe that they will ever feel trapped in an aging body, hoping for a return to their "dear mother," the earth, in a reversal of the birth process. The old man reminds the revelers that, if only because they too might one day be old, they should respect the aged,

> "Ne dooth unto an oold man noon harm now,
> Namoore than that ye wolde men did to yow
> In age, if that ye so longe abyde."

> "Nor do an old man any harm now,
> No more than you wish men did to you
> In age, if you live so long."

(VI, C, 745–747)

The irony in the revelers' continued contemptuous behavior lies in the fact that, despite their youth, they have less time left to live than the old man does.

The old man directs the revelers to a place where they can find Death as they requested: a tree, under which is a treasure trove of gold coins. As in folklore, their discovery of hidden treasure is a mixed blessing. Lest someone think they stole it, it cannot be carried home openly, in daylight, to be enjoyed "in high felicity" (VI, C, 787); instead, it must be transported in darkness, "slyly" (VI, C, 792). They do not ask how a thing that must be concealed could be good. To them, it is self-evident that the gold is a "treasure" that "Fortune [has] given unto us" (VI, C, 779). They have already forgotten that they were directed to the fortune while seeking Death.

Because they have to wait until nightfall to return home with the treasure, they devise a plan to draw lots for which of them will go back to town to "bring us bread and wine full secretly" (VI, C, 797) while the other two guard the treasure. The youngest draws the lot and goes off to town. No sooner is he gone than the other two, remembering that they are "sworn brothers" to each other (VI, C, 808) but forgetting that the absent one shares in this brotherhood also, conspire to kill him upon his return so that they might divide the gold by two instead of three. Their greed in murdering to reap even more reward from what was a windfall in the first place is despicable; but so is the behavior of the third reveler, younger but no more innocent.

His plot begins with his wishful thought that he might not have to share the treasure. "The fiend, our enemy," the devil, seeing in him a vulnerability to temptation, "put in his thought that he should buy poison" and with it, kill his two companions (VI, C, 844). Temptation proceeds to decision, as the young reveler resolves "to slay them both and never to repent" (VI, C, 850)—in theological terms, to commit a sin so serious as to merit eternal damnation. To carry out his plan, the young reveler goes to the medieval version of the neighborhood pharmacist—an apothecary. Claiming to have problems with rats, a polecat, and vermin, he seeks a strong poison. The apothecary sells him one that is "so strong and violent" (VI, C, 867) that no one can survive ingesting even a fragment the size of a kernel of wheat. Taking this poison, the young reveler puts it in the two bottles of wine he intends for his "sworn brothers," while keeping the third "clean for his [own] drink" (VI, C, 873).

The inevitable happens. Upon the third reveler's return, his two companions kill him, then cheerfully sit down beside the corpse to eat and drink their victim's bread and wine, in a grotesque parody of the Eucharistic meal of fellowship. Poetic justice requires that they be punished:

> *But certes, I suppose that Avycen*
> *Wroot nevere in no canon, ne in no fen,*
> *Mo wonder signes of empoisonyng*
> *Than hadde thise wrecches two, er hir endyng.*

> But surely, I suppose that Avicenna
> Never wrote in any canon, nor in any fen,
> More wondrous signs of poisoning
> Than these two wretches had before their ending.
>
> (VI, C, 889–892)

Avicenna (980–1037) was a highly respected medical authority in the Middle Ages, and one of his works was a long and detailed treatise on poisoning with which Chaucer seems to have been familiar. Divided into "canons" and "fens," divisions and subdivisions, Avicenna's treatise summarizes hundreds of "signs of poisoning." So what Chaucer is saying, in an understated fashion, is that the two suffered greatly "before their ending." Not that the audience should feel sorry for them: all three evildoers deliberately sought Death for the sake of the gold. The Pardoner's text is surely true: *Radix malorum est Cupiditas*—the love of money is the root of all evil.

The sermon's rousing conclusion culminates in a sales pitch:

> *Now, goode men, God foryeve yow youre trespas,*
> *And ware yow fro the synne of avarice!*
> *Myn hooly pardoun may yow alle warice,*
> *So that ye offre nobles or sterlynges,*
> *Or elles silver broches, spoones, rynges.*

> Now, good men, forgive you your trespass,
> And guard you from the sin of avarice!
> My holy pardon may preserve you all,
> As long as you offer nobles or sterlings [coins],
> Or else silver brooches, spoons, rings.
>
> (VI, C, 904–908)

This, according to the Pardoner, is how he preaches. He appears to be ready to end his sermon to the Canterbury pilgrims when he assures them that he knows that Jesus Christ is the "soul's leech" (VI, C, 916), the only true Physician of the spirit, the only real Pardoner. This Pardoner is a sinner, but he is not an unbeliever: he believes in the power of Christ to do in fact what he himself only pretends to do.

Having assured the Canterbury pilgrims that he "will not deceive" them
(VI, C, 918), he immediately attempts to do just that, by offering his
traveling companions an opportunity to buy the same spurious "relics and
pardons" (VI, C, 920) that he hawks to others. He reminds them that
traveling is dangerous, and it might come in handy to have someone around
who can forgive their sins:

> *Paraventure ther may fallen oon or two*
> *Doun of his hors and breke his nekke atwo.*
> *Looke which a seuretee is it to yow alle*
> *That I am in youre felaweshipe yfalle.*
>
> Perhaps one or two may fall
> Down from his horse and break his neck in two.
> Look what security it is to you all
> That I have fallen into your fellowship.

(VI, C, 935–938)

Has the Pardoner forgotten that only Christ can pardon, as he just said?
Perhaps he thinks that his sermon has been so effective that he can gull
even the well-informed pilgrims into "unbuckling [their] purse" (VI, C,
945).

This is too much for the ordinarily genial Host, Harry Bailly. Harry
attacks the Pardoner in the most vulgar terms. You would "make me kiss
your old britches / And swear it was the relic of a saint," even if it were
"painted" with the evidence of improper toileting habits (VI, C, 949–950).
Harry wishes he could detach private parts of the Pardoner's anatomy
"instead of relics" and enshrine them in an unusual reliquary, a "hog's turd"
(VI, C, 948–956). Crude though they are, Harry Bailly's words are closer
to the truth than are those of the smooth-talking but deceptive Pardoner.
For once, the Pardoner is speechless.

Chaucer does not mean for his audience to sympathize with the embarrassed Pardoner. Like his three drunken and greedy revelers, the Pardoner
deserves what he gets. Harry Bailly's insults are merely a foretaste of the
eternal punishment merited by such sins as the Pardoner commits. The
religious practices the Pardoner exploits represent high spiritual ideals. A
relic should serve as a reminder of a saint, leading the believer to imitation
of the saint's virtues. Indulgences were imagined as a share in the spiritual
benefit of the good deeds of all Christians. When these practices became
associated with financial contributions, abuses may have been inevitable.

But the abuser is still guilty. Fully aware of sin, the Pardoner freely chooses it, and chooses also, like his youngest reveler, "never to repent" (VI, C, 850). Paradoxically, however, the Pardoner, though corrupt himself, may be an agent of pardon to another through Christ, the soul's Physician, whose power transcends the defects of the ministers of His church. But the Physician of the soul can only heal one who presents himself for cure. Pardon only comes to one who repents; and this the Pardoner will never do. Unrepentant, the Pardoner is unpardonable. To the medieval Christian, he is a damned soul—perhaps Chaucer's only one.

SUGGESTIONS FOR FURTHER READING

Beidler, Peter G. "The Plague and Chaucer's Pardoner." *Chaucer Review* 16, no. 3 (1982): 257–269. Beidler sees the plague setting as crucial not only to the tale but also to the Pardoner's "motivation in telling it," and to "Harry Bailly's violent reaction to the Pardoner's request for money."

Bloom, Harold, ed. and intro. *Geoffrey Chaucer's "The Pardoner's Tale."* New York: Chelsea House, 1988. This collection of essays illustrates a variety of critical viewpoints.

Faulkner, Dewey R., ed. and intro. *"The Pardoner's Tale": A Collection of Critical Essays.* Englewood Cliffs, N.J.: Prentice-Hall, 1973. This collection of essays illustrates a variety of critical viewpoints.

Hallissy, Margaret. "Poison Lore and Chaucer's Pardoner." *Massachusetts Studies in English* 9, no. 1 (1983): 54–63. Hallissy sees the poison image as embodying beliefs in medicine, biblical interpretation, sermon literature, and animal lore.

Howard, Donald R. *The Idea of the Canterbury Tales.* Berkeley: University of California Press, 1976. 333–387. Howard regards the Parson and the Pardoner, and their respective tales, as representing the polar opposites: good and evil.

Kittredge, George Lyman. "Chaucer's Pardoner." *Chaucer: Modern Essays in Criticism.* Ed. Edward Wagenknecht. New York: Oxford University Press, 1959. 117–125. Kittredge explains why Chaucer gave his most despicable villain such an eloquent tale.

Noll, Dolores L. "The Serpent and the Sting in the *Pardoner's Prologue and Tale.*" *Chaucer Review* 17, no. 2 (1982): 159–162. Noll demonstrates the importance of the serpent image.

Rowland, Beryl. "Chaucer's Idea of the Pardoner." *Chaucer Review* 14, no. 2 (1979): 140–154. Rowland presents medieval scientific interpretations of the Pardoner's sexual abnormality.

The Shipman's Tale

"How longe tyme wol ye rekene and caste
Youre sommes, and youre bookes, and youre thynges?
The devel have part on alle swiche rekenynges!"

"How long will you reckon and cast
Your sums, and your books, and your things?
The devil have part in all such reckonings!"

(VII, 216–218)

Economics has been termed the "dismal science"—but money was not a dull topic to Chaucer. In his career, he was a salaried employee of the crown and had responsibility for overseeing financial transactions. Possibly as a result of his practical experience in the world of getting and spending, he refers to money in his poetry more often than is typical of the medieval writer. Chaucer was always careful to situate his characters in terms of their economic as well as social *estat*. In the "General Prologue," for example, he makes the reader aware of proper and improper sources of his characters' income as well as their appropriate and inappropriate expenditures. In doing so, he situates his characters firmly in an economic and social milieu very much like our own.

During the fourteenth century, a drastic economic change was taking place all over Europe. In its simplest terms, it can be described as a change from a land-based to a money-based economy. Power was shifting from a landed and hereditary nobility to a monied and upwardly mobile bourgeoisie. Self-made men, like the Shipman, his character the merchant, indeed like Chaucer himself, were increasing both in number and in importance. Such men saw their world in economic terms. Thus the "Shipman's Tale" is permeated with the language of money and the rapidly developing science of accounting. Unfortunately, however, some saw their world only in terms of money. The root of the comedy in this tale is that all relationships—friendship, marriage, even adultery—depend on what moderns call cash flow, the movement of money from one person to another.

Chaucer sets his scene in France, not in England, as if to distance his countrymen from the venery and venality of the action. The central character, the merchant, is rich, "for which men held him wise" (VII, 2)—a misapprehension that the tale will correct. The merchant has "a wife . . . of excellent beauty"; to the Shipman, such a woman is merely a "thing that causes . . . expense" (VII, 3, 5). To the mercantile mind, women are expensive "things," possessions. They do not make money but only spend it. Expenditures made by and for one's wife must therefore be firmly regulated. This is particularly important in the matter of *array*. On the one hand, a wife's *array* must suitably reflect the social position and purchasing power of her husband; his "worship" (VII, 13), or reputation, in the community depends on it. On the other hand, husbands tend to regard money spent on clothing as "wasted and lost" (VII, 17). If women overspend, then—the narrator momentarily shifting into the point of view of the wife of a tightwad—"another must pay for our cost, / Or lend us gold, and that is perilous" (VII, 18–19). The husband of a spendthrift wife has two unpleasant choices: pay up, or risk that a lover will. The language of finance—cost, expense, payment, loss, cash, credit—defines the relationship between husband and wife, and between wife and lover.

It is a commonplace of medieval misogynistic lore that wives will spend their husbands into bankruptcy. It is also a commonplace that women like generous, free-spending men. (The Wife of Bath prays that all the women in her audience will be spared the pain of stingy husbands.) A common assumption in the misogynistic lore is that women have no means of acquiring money except from men, and therefore have no means of repayment but sex. On this complex of beliefs hangs the comedy of this commercial *fabliau*.

Despite his frugality with his wife, the merchant is a man of *largesse* with others (VII, 22). His public display of wealth takes the form of generous entertaining. Among his habitual guests is a young monk, Daun John. With this character is introduced a language contrasting with the jargon of finance: the language of interpersonal relationships. Only Daun John has a name; the other characters are known by trade titles (merchant) or family relationships (wife). Daun John is "familiar," like a family member; he "claims" the merchant "for cousinage," as a kinsman, and "thus they are knit with eternal alliance" and a pledge of "brotherhood" (VII, 31, 36,

40–42). Despite the friendlier tone of the terminology describing it, this relationship, like the marriage of the merchant and his wife, is affected by money. Daun John is himself "free" with money and "manly of dispense" (VII, 43); when he comes to the merchant's house, he is no freeloader, but spends freely on tips for the help and gifts for the host.

The complication in this comfortable arrangement occurs when the merchant needs to make a business trip to Bruges. It was a *fabliau* commonplace that the absence of a husband gave his wife and her would-be lover opportunity for sexual misbehavior. Foolishly, given this well-known situation, the merchant invites Daun John to visit him and his wife "a day or two / Before he went to Bruges" (VII, 60–61), thus calling the young monk's attention to the merchant's planned absence. Like several of Chaucer's other roaming ecclesiastics, Daun John has an exemption from the monastic rule of enclosure. But since a monk who wanders in one way might do so in another, it seems inevitable that the monk will make use of his freedom to seize his opportunity with the wife of the absent merchant.

Before the merchant's departure, Daun John lays the groundwork for a closer relationship with the wife than his familiar status has thus far allowed him. He pays a visit, bringing hospitality gifts as a good guest should: two kinds of wine and a fowl for roasting. During the monk's visit, the merchant is a poor host, more interested in his finances than in his guest—or his wife. In his description of the merchant's activities, Chaucer uses accounting terminology to reinforce the idea of the merchant's preoccupation with money:

> up into his countour-hous gooth he
> To rekene with hymself, wel may be,
> Of thilke yeer how that it with hym stood,
> And how that he despended hadde his good,
> And if that he encressed were or noon.

> up to his counting-house goes he
> To reckon with himself, it well may be,
> How it stood with him this year,
> And how he has expended his good,
> And if he were increased or not.

(VII, 77–81)

In his counting-house, the merchant is preparing annual financial records to evaluate his financial position, weighing his "spending" against his "increase." This activity, while surely necessary for a business owner, is not immediately urgent and could be deferred in order that he might pay more attention to the people around him.

But by the props surrounding the merchant, as if he were an image in a painting, his values are known:

> His bookes and his bagges many oon
> He leith biforn hym on his countyng-bord.
> Ful riche was his tresor and his hord,
> For which ful faste his countour-dore he shette.

> His books and his bags, many of them,
> He lay before him on his counting-board.
> So rich was his treasure and his hoard,
> That he shut his accounting-room door quite tightly.

(VII, 82–85)

Shut away in his accounting-room, surrounded by record books and bags of money, he is the very image of greed.

Then too, the timing of the merchant's financial activities is important. He gets up early and does his bookkeeping "till it was past prime," nine in the morning (VII, 86–88). During that time, the monk (having, with the odd but typically medieval combination of religious piety and moral flexibility, said his morning prayers) meets the merchant's wife in the garden, that seductive locale. After some chitchat about their respective sleeping habits, the monk teases the wife for her "pale" visage (VII, 106), suggesting that she is exhausted after a night of love. Quite the contrary, says she: she has no "lust for that sorry play" (VII, 117). The monk, swearing secrecy upon his prayerbook, urges the wife to confide in him. The medieval audience would have enjoyed the parallel to the relationship between confessor and sinner in the sacrament of penance. When the monk "swear[s] . . . on his profession" (VII, 155), his religious vows, he is abusing those vows to seduce his friend's wife; priests were often suspected of doing such things in the intimacy of the confessional. The wife, for her part, is also violating a strong medieval tradition against violating the *privetee* (VII, 164) of the marital relationship. The one exception to this prohibition against confiding marital secrets was, in fact, in confession. But the confessional relationship established here is a burlesque of the sacrament: Daun John intends not to forgive sin but to encourage it.

The wife confesses that she is unhappily married. Ironically, given the merchant's great concern with money, his wife's despair—she says she is considering either running away or killing herself—is due, she says, to both

sexual and economic deprivation. She agrees with the Wife of Bath's
definition of a good husband:

> *"And wel ye woot that wommen naturelly*
> *Desiren thynges sixe as wel as I:*
> *They wolde that hir housbondes sholde be*
> *Hardy and wise, and riche, and therto free,*
> *And buxom unto his wyf and fressh abedde."*

> "And well you know that women naturally
> Desire six things as much as I do;
> They wish that their husbands should be
> Hardy and wise, and rich, and generous with it,
> And obedient to their wives, and fresh in bed."

(VII, 173–177)

From a wife's viewpoint, a husband's wealth is of little use if he is not "free"
with it. One of the main purposes for which women spend money is,
according to misogynistic lore, on *array*. The merchant's wife says she has
a debt for her *array*, purchased "for his honor" (VII, 179), to reflect his
earning capacity and *estat*. The bill amounts to one hundred francs, and
the due date is the following Sunday.

The assumptions on which the tale is based are that a spendthrift wife
must get money either from her husband or from another man, and that
she has no means of repaying it other than sexual. The merchant's wife asks
the monk for a hundred francs, promising to repay him with sexual favors
even if she repays the money too; so, from the monk's point of view, the
sex becomes comparable to interest on a loan:

> *"Pardee, I wol nat faille yow my thankes,*
> *If that yow list to doon that I yow praye.*
> *For at a certeyn day I wol yow paye,*
> *And doon to yow what pleasance and service*
> *That I may doon."*

> "By God, I will not fail to thank you,
> If you agree to do what I ask;
> On a certain day, I will pay you,
> And do for you whatever pleasure and service
> That I may do."

(VII, 188–192)

Notice that she will pay him *and*, not *or*, have sex with him. This seems to be a no-lose proposition for the monk, who seals the bargain with a downpayment on the interest due to him:

> And with that word he caughte hire by the flankes,
> And hire embraceth harde, and kiste hire ofte.

> And with that word he caught her by the flanks,
> And embraced her hard, and kissed her often.

(VII, 202–203)

The only problem for the monk at this point is that technically, because he is under a vow of poverty, he is not supposed to have any money. But, clever as he is, he will soon remedy that.

Meanwhile, the wife seeks out her miserly husband. It is breakfast time, and he is still in his accounting-room—oblivious to the fact that his friend and his wife have made both a business deal and a sexual assignation. His wife's nagging points to a serious flaw in the merchant's character. He has spent too much time "reckoning" and "casting sums," tending to his account-book when he should be tending to his marriage (VII, 216–217). He demonstrates stinginess in both the financial and the sexual senses instead of the generosity that medieval people admired. In medieval canon law, one of the (few) legitimate justifications for having sex in marriage (paying the marital debt, as was the curiously monetary phrase in canon law) was to prevent the partner from committing adultery. By allowing himself to become overly preoccupied with his accounts, the husband is simultaneously allowing his wife to become sexually frustrated, thus exposing her to temptation. As the wife claims in exasperation, "the devil [has] part in all such reckonings" (VII, 218) in that the husband's greed places the wife's soul in jeopardy.

Nevertheless, Chaucer, himself a man of business, does not oversimplify this stingy and money-obsessed husband. On the husband's side of the matter, it is clear that he is pompous about his manly responsibility: "Little can you understand," he patronizes his wife, "the curious business that we have" (VII, 224–225). While the merchant's attitude is condescending, it is also true that business deals are risky. He who takes the risk gets the reward, but also conversely: "hap and fortune" (VII, 238) can lead to business failure as well as success. The merchant is telling the truth about the difficulties of playing the financial-provider role. In addition, the merchant assigns only such tasks to his wife as were routinely expected of the competent medieval housewife whose husband was away on business:

to be careful of their possessions, their "good"; to "honestly govern well [their] house" (VII, 243–244). He has, he says, provided her with the wherewithal to do both:

> *"Thou hast ynough, in every maner wise,*
> *That to a thrifty houshold may suffise.*
> *Thee lakketh noon array ne no vitaille;*
> *Of silver in thy purs shaltow nat faille."*

> "You have enough, in every way,
> That may suffice for a thrifty household.
> You lack neither clothing nor food;
> You shall not fail to have silver in your purse."

> (VII, 245–248)

Chaucer leaves unresolved whether what the merchant considers "enough" is really enough to run a "thrifty household." In the misogynistic lore satirizing wifely extravagance, no amount of money is enough to provide for a wife who is the medieval equivalent of a "shopaholic." It is clear that the merchant's wife must have exceeded her household allowance because she needs an extra hundred francs. But whether her extravagance or her husband's stinginess is the cause of the problem is never specified. In any case, despite what her husband feels is his adequate provision, she feels she does not have enough, and must turn to another man for money.

Daun John, being a monk, has no money; so he must borrow it from one who has: the intended cuckold, his friend the merchant. The monk's excuse to the merchant is that he needs the money to buy "certain beasts" (VII, 272)—an unflattering allusion to the essentially subhuman nature of the relationship financed with it. Ignorant of the money's true purpose, the merchant nevertheless cautions Daun John about the importance of money to a businessman:

> *"But o thyng is, ye knowe it wel ynogh*
> *Of chapmen, that hir moneie is hir plogh.*
> *We may creaunce whil we have a name,*
> *But goldlees for to be, it is no game."*

> "But one thing is—you know it well enough—
> For businessmen, their money is their plough.
> We may get credit while we have a reputation,
> But to be goldless is no joke."

> (VII, 287–290)

The merchant is conscious of the risk he is taking in lending money to a poor monk. As in the case of modern credit-granting practices, the more money a person has in the bank, the higher his or her salary, the more credit is available. Without what moderns call a positive cash flow, the sources of credit will dry up. Businessmen use money to make money; money is to them as a plow is to a farmer, the tool of their trade. Since without money they can make no more, it behooves them to make cautious and objective business deals. Out of friendship, the merchant lends money to a poor credit risk. Because the usual financial transaction between a businessman and a monk is a donation, not a loan, the merchant reminds the monk that this is a loan. "Pay it again when it lies in your ease" (VII, 291), says the merchant; pay when you are comfortable in doing so—but pay.

Having made this unsecured loan, the merchant goes off on his business to Bruges. While there, as if to restate Chaucer's habitual concern with "hap and fortune" (VII, 238), the merchant gets involved in a particularly risky and complicated business deal. The merchandise he wants to buy is so expensive that he needs a *chevyssaunce*, a loan to cover a cash shortfall, confirmed by a *reconyssaunce*, or repayment pledge (VII, 329). To repay the loan, he needs to return to Paris to borrow enough francs to pay off the debt. The business deal is made more complex by the different values of the two currencies, the Flemish shield and the French franc, and the use of Lombard bankers as intermediaries. Chaucer must have been familiar with such transactions in his own international travels. The merchant, upon his return to Saint-Denis, goes to see his friend Daun John,

> Nat for to axe or borwe of hym moneye,
> But for to wite and seen of his welfare.

> Not for to ask or borrow of him money,
> But to know and see about his welfare.

> (VII, 338–339)

In the course of the conversation the merchant tells his old friend the monk about his business loan.

During the merchant's absence, the monk has used his own loan from the merchant. He gave it to the wife and, in return, got his night of love, his "interest"; but the wife did not repay the principal. Now the monk is poor again. He assures the merchant that, to help him pay off the business loan, he would give him 20,000 Flemish shields—if he had them. Since he has no money of his own, he can repay only the hundred francs that he has borrowed (without interest). Since the wife has not repaid the monk, the monk has no cash to give her husband. So he tells the merchant what is technically the truth: that he already gave the hundred francs to the merchant's wife. The monk knows that, given the sexual terms of the financial transaction, his secret is safe.

Some risks lead to rewards. The merchant pulls off a good deal by renegotiating his loan with Lombard bankers in Paris, the complex transaction calling attention to the increasing sophistication of international trade in the Middle Ages. He expects now to make "a thousand francs above his cost" (VII, 372). Flushed by success, the merchant is welcomed home by his wife, and the two, mutually inspired by a positive cash flow, enjoy a night of love:

> *His wyf ful redy mette hym atte gate,*
> *As she was wont of oold usage algate,*
> *And al that nyght in myrthe they bisette;*
> *For he was riche and cleerly out of dette.*

> His wife, all ready, met him at the gate,
> As she was used to do according to old custom;
> And all that night they set themselves to mirth,
> For he was rich, and clearly out of debt.

(VII, 373–376)

Earlier, worried about money, the merchant spent a morning counting in his counting-room. Now, confident and affluent, he is attracted away from his money bags and toward his wife—and she toward him. The sexual enthusiasm of both fluctuates with the merchant's income.

Their night of love over, they, like many another married couple, revert to everyday business. The merchant tells his wife that he is "a little wroth," a bit angry, at her for not telling him that Daun John had paid her "by ready token," in cash, the hundred francs (VII, 383, 390). The merchant says he was embarrassed at discussing a loan with a man who had already repaid it, and he urges his wife to keep him better informed in the future. The wife seems to be in a tight spot; but she, "not fearful nor afraid," answers "boldly" (VII, 400–401). She cannot return the money to her husband, because she has used it to pay her *array* bill. So she claims to have understood the money to be a personal gift, "for cousinage" (VII, 409) or kinship (similar to those gifts that Daun John habitually brought to the household), not as a repayment for a loan. But in this mercantile milieu human relationships have no value other than the monetary. The wife now knows that Daun

John bought her sexual favors with her own husband's money. The merchant, however, does not.

The complexities of this transaction rival those of the merchant's international loan. According to the marital debt concept in medieval canon law, a husband and wife owe each other sexual payment. The wife has erred in paying that debt to another in the form of interest on money borrowed from her own husband. She cannot repay her husband in cash, because she has no cash. All she has is the same currency that she used to pay the monk: her own body. The medieval audience would have found it highly comical that the term for a line of credit was a "tail" (VII, 416)—the same term also used as a vulgarism for the female genitalia. So the wife offers to pay her debt to her husband in the same coin she used to pay the monk: "I am your wife; score it upon my tail" (VII, 416). In this coin she professes herself a better credit risk than other "slacker debtors" (VII, 413) to whom her husband has lent money in the past. And besides, says she, using a typical excuse of wives with large clothing bills,

> *"For by my trouthe, I have on myn array,*
> *And nat on wast, bistowed every deel;*
> *And for I have bistowed it so weel*
> *For youre honour, for Goddes sake, I seye,*
> *As be nat wrooth, but lat us laughe and pleye."*

> "For by my troth, I have on my array,
> And not on waste, spent every bit;
> And because I have spent it so well
> For your honor, for God's sake, I say
> Don't be angry, but let us laugh and play."

> (VII, 418–422)

This is an ambiguous reconciliation. On the one hand, the husband's preoccupation with money might now get him into bed with his wife more often, that he might get his hundred francs' worth. It is the only way, after all, that he can get value for his money, according to his wife:

> *"Ye shal my joly body have to wedde;*
> *By God, I wol nat paye yow but abedde!"*

> "You shall my jolly body have to wed;
> By God, I will not pay you except in bed!"

> (VII, 423–424)

Further humor is derived from the fact that, even without the hundred francs "scored" upon her "tail," the husband has a right to the payment of the marital debt simply by virtue of being married. Conversely, although the wife has a right to the use of her husband's money, the idea that sex is a wife's *quid pro quo* is a vulgarization of the marriage relationship. Moreover, the wife's use of her "jolly body" as a mode of paying off her husband does not obliterate her adultery with the monk. When the merchant chides his wife for her too-generous ways, his cautionary words contain a double meaning of which he is himself unaware:

> *"Now wyf," he seyde, "and I foryeve it thee;*
> *But, by thy lyf, ne be namoore so large.*
> *Keep bet thy good."*

> "Now wife," he said, "I forgive you it,
> But by your life, don't be so generous any more.
> Keep your good better."

(VII, 430–432)

He is unwittingly forgiving adultery as well as forgiving a debt. The wife's generosity with her only "good," her sexual favors, is a direct result of the fact that it is the only currency on which she can trade in a world in which money belongs to men.

Another comic irony lies in the fact that in all this ebb and flow of cash, only the man of business has been bested. He has paid good money for something he already owns. The monk, in contrast, has received interest without investing his own principal. The wife has gotten her bills paid, plus more of what she wants: sex. But in the whole commercial transaction, real value, real "good" has been lost. Friendship between men, love between husband and wife, even adulterous passion, have been exchanged for cash.

SUGGESTIONS FOR FURTHER READING

Adams, Robert. "The Concept of Debt in *The Shipman's Tale*." *Studies in the Age of Chaucer* 6 (1984): 85–102. Adams argues that the term *debt* has a theological as well as an economic meaning in the tale as an indicator of the need for repentance, defined as paying a debt to God.

Coletti, Theresa. "The *Mulier Fortis* and Chaucer's *Shipman's Tale*." *Chaucer Review* 15, no. 3 (1981): 236–249. Coletti interprets the merchant's wife as comic analogue of the biblical "valiant woman" (Prov. 30:10–31).

Hahn, Thomas. "Money, Sexuality, Wordplay, and Context in the *Shipman's Tale*." *Chaucer in the Eighties*. Eds. Julian N. Wasserman and Robert J.

Blanch. Syracuse, N.Y.: Syracuse University Press, 1986. 235–249. Hahn's close analysis of the language of the tale reinforces the "linkage of sex and money."

Martin, Priscilla. *Chaucer's Women: Nuns, Wives, and Amazons.* Iowa City: University of Iowa Press, 1990. 84–105. In Chapter 6, "The Merchandise of Love: Wives and Merchants," Martin examines the correlation between sex and money in the "Wife of Bath's Tale," the "Merchant's Tale," and the "Shipman's Tale."

Whittock, Trevor. *A Reading of the Canterbury Tales.* Cambridge: Cambridge University Press, 1968. 195–201. Whittock contends that the tale was "not originally intended for the Shipman but was to be told by a woman."

The Prioress's Prologue and Tale

But as a child of twelf month oold, or lesse,
That kan unnethes any word expresse,
Right so fare I.

But like a child of twelve months old, or less,
Who can hardly say a word,
Just so am I.

(VII, 484–486)

Like the "Man of Law's Tale" and the "Second Nun's Tale," the "Prioress's Tale" belongs to that popular medieval story type, the *legenda*, or saint's life. Simple believers loved these tales of heroic virtue, and the "Prioress's Tale," focusing on the martyrdom of a holy child, is one of these. It also belongs to another subspecies of pious medieval tale, the "miracle of the Virgin" story, in which Christ's mother Mary intercedes in human events at moments of crisis. Mary's central role in the tale is prefigured by the Prioress's prologue, which is just such a prayer as might win Mary's intercession on behalf of her earthly children. In it, the Prioress begs for the aid of Jesus and his mother, "the white lily flower / Who bore thee, and is a maid always" (VII, 461–462), to help her tell her story. Imagining herself as "a child of twelve months old," "weak" of "cunning" (VII, 484, 481), she sees herself not as a mature tale-teller like the other pilgrims, but rather as a childlike instrument of praise for Jesus and his mother. Her tale exalts the holiness of the child-saint and the motherly love and concern of the Virgin Mary.

The image of the child in both prologue and tale suggests the high value attached to virginity in the Middle Ages. The child's purity is associated with that of Mary, the "white lily flower" who, medieval Christians believed, retained her virginity despite being Jesus' mother. To the modern reader, however, the childlike purity of both teller and tale is sullied by the portrayal of Jews as enemies of Christians and killers not only of this innocent child-martyr but of Mary's son too. Modern readers often wonder how the vicious anti-Semitism of the tale can be reconciled with the character of the Prioress or, for that matter, with that of genial Chaucer himself.

According to the conventions of the medieval *legenda*, the saint, principle of virtue, is pitted against a principle of evil. Evil is depicted as much more powerful than the saint, so that, paradoxically, weakness can triumph, with God's help. In the stories of saints martyred during the persecutions of the early Christian centuries, the villains were Roman governors, generals, or consuls. Since the *legenda* is a didactic tool, the villain is always depicted as totally evil, with no redeeming virtues whatsoever; the audience is not encouraged to grow in understanding of, for example, the Roman governor, but rather to see him in simple, stark, black-and-white terms. There are no moral nuances in the saint's life: the saint is Virtue Personified; the saint's persecutor is Evil Personified.

In the "Prioress's Tale," the role of the saint's opponent is played by the inhabitants of an urban "Jewry," or ghetto (VII, 489). As happened in various European countries during the Middle Ages, these Jews, dwelling in a city somewhere in Asia, were "sustained by a lord of that country" (VII, 490), maintained under his protection, because they provided a needed service: lending money at interest. This practice, regarded as a simple matter of business in modern times, was termed "foul usury" (VII, 491) and forbidden to Christians under medieval church law. Christians could not lend money but often needed to borrow money. Jews were not bound by Christian canon law and could lend money. But moneylenders did not inspire love. It was all too easy to impute evil motives to people who appeared to be profiting by one's own loss—and who, in addition, practiced a different religion.

Religious toleration was not a value to medieval people. The idea that people of different backgrounds and beliefs should learn to understand each other and enrich their own lives by doing so would have seemed utterly incomprehensible to medieval people. Indeed, it is not even universally accepted today. A simple believer like the semi-educated Prioress would have been taught in school and in church that Christianity was the one true faith, that only Christians could go to heaven, that non-Christians were obliged to convert to Christianity, and that if they did not do so, if they persisted in what was seen as their unbelief, they were simply "hateful

to Christ and to his company" (VII, 492) of Christians, as the Prioress
describes the Jews. This set of beliefs led to dreadful persecutions, not only
inflicted on Jewish communities by Christians, but also by Christians on
other Christians of unorthodox belief. It was a cruel age in which nonconformity was often eliminated by killing the nonconformist.

Did Chaucer believe, as the Prioress does, that Jews were "hateful to
Christ and to his company" (VII, 492)? From the evidence within the
"Prioress's Tale" it is hard to say. It cannot be assumed that a person who is
innovative as a literary artist will be advanced in his thinking on religious
and social issues as well. Chaucer does not, as Shakespeare would two
centuries later in *The Merchant of Venice*, create a Shylock, a complex
character who expands the audience's range of empathy toward an individual Jewish moneylender. The Prioress regards Jews in general as villains;
without further evidence regarding Chaucer's private beliefs, we cannot say
whether Chaucer would have done the same. All we can note is that
Chaucer is speaking through a character in the "Prioress's Tale," not in his
own voice, and that he is working in a genre that requires an easily
recognizable villain. Would Chaucer have noted the irony that modern
readers perceive in the prologue, that the Prioress prays to Jesus, born a Jew,
and to Mary, a Jewish mother?

In the Asian city where the action of the tale occurs, Christians and
Jews live in close proximity without growing closer in understanding or
affection. The Jewry is on the same street as a "little school of Christian
folk" (VII, 495), an elementary school or song-school. The curriculum is
simple:

> Swich manere doctrine as men used there,
> This is to seyn, to syngen and to rede,
> As smale children doon in hire childhede.

> Such kind of teaching as people learned there,
> This is to say, to sing and to read,
> As small children do in their childhood.
>
> (VII, 499–501)

Among these children was "a little *clergeoun*," a clerk-let or tiny scholar,
"seven years of age" (VII, 503). Seven was considered an age of transition
in medieval theology: at seven, a child was considered capable of achieving theological understanding and accepting moral responsibility. In a
vestige of this medieval belief, children today usually make their first
Communion in Roman Catholic parishes at the age of seven. Thus a seven

year old is capable of both sin and virtue. But such a child, as yet sexually unawakened, was still pure, like the "white lily flower" (VII, 461), the Virgin Mary.

In the saints' lives, saints who lived to adulthood were usually depicted as having been remarkably pious children. The "little *clergeoun*," like little St. Nicholas, shows a preternatural capacity for devotion. All he wanted to learn in school was the *Alma Redemptoris*, a hymn in praise of Mary. So "young and tender . . . of age" (VII, 524) is he that he does not understand the Latin words of the hymn. An older fellow student explains that the song is a prayer to Mary "to be our help and succour when we die" (VII, 534). The "little *clergeoun*" vows to learn the song even if in doing so he is "beaten thrice in an hour" for neglecting his "primer," his other lessons (VII, 541–542)—an insight into medieval educational methods. But the apprentice martyr must be prepared to suffer for his faith.

The "little *clergeoun*" learns his hymn and practices it as he walks "to schoolward and homeward" (VII, 549) twice a day—that is, as he walks through the Jewry which is between his home and the school. To intone a Christian hymn under such circumstances might be seen today as insensitive, but to the medieval audience, the "little *clergeoun*" is offering the Jews an opportunity to be edified by Christian doctrine. In keeping with the role of villain to which the conventions of the *legenda* consign them, "the Jews have conspired / To chase this innocent out of the world" (VII, 565–566). They seize him, "and cut his throat, and in a pit him caste" (VII, 571). To add insult to injury, the pit is a privy, a cesspool. The Prioress expostulates against these "cursed folk" and their "evil intent" (VII, 574–575). They will not get away with this infamous deed; "murder will out" (VII, 576).

As mentioned earlier, the "little *clergeoun*" lives with his mother and comes home from school every day. Although the audience knows that martyrdom unites the child in his innocence with the Lamb of God, on earth the anxious mother seeks her lost boy. She, a widow (a detail adding more pathos), searches for her "little child, but he came not" (VII, 587). She calls on Jesus' mother Mary, also the widowed mother of an only son, and takes practical measures as well, questioning the inhabitants of the Jewry, her son's habitual route to and from school. Although they falsely deny seeing him, she finds him anyway, in the pit. Miraculously, although his throat is cut, he begins to sing his favorite hymn, the *Alma Redemptoris*.

To medieval people, the age of miracles did not lie in the past. For the inspiration of his people, God interceded in daily life. So here a child "with throat carved" (VII, 611) sings a hymn in praise of the Virgin. This supernatural event has the desired effect: the increased devotion of "Christian folk," who "come to wonder at this thing" and "with honor of a great procession / . . . carry him unto the next abbey" (VII, 614–615, 623–624). Processions in honor of a saint are still popular religious practices in Catholic communities today. This one features the grieving mother, "swooning by his bier" (VII, 625).

This pious scene has a darker side, however. The provost or civil officer has been called to witness the miracle, and he in his role as representative of secular government takes swift and violent retaliation against not only those Jews who did the deed but even those who only knew about it. The civil law apparently did not admit of distinguishing degrees of guilt—or distinguishing one Jew from another, for that matter. All are deemed guilty for the crime of some, and all are swiftly and cruelly punished. Such mass retribution would come to be called a pogrom.

Meanwhile, the child continues his hymn-singing. Then as now, a representative of the church hierarchy must be called upon to judge the authenticity of an alleged miracle; hence the transportation of the singing martyr to the abbey. The abbot begins to "conjure" (VII, 644) or question the child. Preternaturally wise as well as holy, he explains how this miracle confirms the faith of Christian people in Christ and his mother Mary,

> "My *throte is kut unto my nekke boon*,"
> *Seyde this child, "and as by wey of kynde*
> *I sholde have dyed, ye, longe tyme agon.*
> *But Jesu Crist, as ye in bookes fynde,*
> *Wil that his glorie laste and be in mynde,*
> *And for the worship of his Mooder deere*
> *Yet may I synge* O Alma *loude and cleere."*

> "My throat is cut unto the neck bone,"
> Said this child, "and by way of nature
> I should have died, yes, a long time ago,
> But Jesus Christ, as you find in books,
> Wills that his glory last and be kept in mind,
> And for the worship of his Mother dear
> I may yet sing O *Alma* loud and clear."

>   (VII, 649–655)

Jesus allows this miraculous suspension of nature's laws to encourage devotion to his Mother.

The idealization of the Virgin Mary was a dominant theme in medieval religion. The "little *clergeoun*," despite his tender years and minimal edu-

cation, is on theologically sound ground when he explains that it is Christ's
power operating through Mary that has caused the miracle. Mary's role is
as intermediary between man and God. But she is also an embodiment of
the nurturing, caring, mothering side of God, helping her children in
moments of crisis. The "little *clergeoun*" had learned the hymn because he
had been assured that the musical prayer would bring Mary's "help and
succour when we die" (VII, 534). At the moment of his death—and the
"Hail Mary," a prayer still recited by Catholics today, beseeches Mary's help
"at the hour of our death"—Mary comes to him in the squalid pit:

> "*And whan that I my lyf sholde forlete,*
> *To me she cam, and bad me for to synge*
> *This anthem verraily in my deyynge,*
> *As ye han herd, and whan that I hadde songe,*
> *Me thoughte she leyde a greyn upon my tonge.*"

> "And when I should lose my life
> She came to me and bade me for to sing
> This anthem verily in my dying
> As you have heard; and when that I had sung,
> I thought she laid a grain upon my tongue."

> (VII, 658–662)

This miraculous grain preserves his ability to sing until it is removed. Now
he need not fear death, for Mary is with him.

The miracle accomplished, the abbot removes the grain, and the holy
child dies. A modern miracle story would end with the child being saved
in the sense of earthly survival. But to the medieval believer salvation
meant going to heaven. In that context, the child martyr should not be
restored to a life in which he might grow up to lose his childhood
innocence. Better to die now, as a "gem of chastity" (VII, 609). So although
the abbot is overcome with emotion to the point of tears and swooning, he
does the right thing by allowing this little boy to leave his earthly mother
and join his heavenly Mother.

The postmortem function of the saint is to provide continuing inspiration for the faithful. To this end, shrines to saints were built and still are,
in honor of holy martyrs like this "little *clergeoun*":

> *And in a tombe of marbul stones cleere*
> *Enclosen they his litel body sweete.*
> *Ther he is now, God leve us for to meete!*

> And in a tomb of marble stones clear
> Enclosed they his little body sweet.
> There he is now, God grant us for to meet!

(VII, 681–683)

The theological principle involved here and in the Prioress's concluding prayer is that, if Christian believers are inspired by the life and death of the saint, they will meet the saint in heaven.

So, if the Canterbury pilgrims are inspired by the tale, they too might, through Jesus and Mary, be saved. That is the goal of the pilgrimage of the Christian life. Many modern readers are offended by the Prioress's typically medieval idea that the path to God can only be walked by Christians. Read in the context of the prevailing beliefs of its age, however, the tale is a moving expression of childlike faith in Mary's motherly concern for her "little *clergeoun*."

SUGGESTIONS FOR FURTHER READING

Braswell, Laurel. "Chaucer and the Art of Hagiography." *Chaucer in the Eighties*. Eds. Julian N. Wasserman and Robert J. Blanch. Syracuse, N.Y.: Syracuse University Press, 1986. 209–221. Braswell sees the "Clerk's Tale," the "Second Nun's Tale," the "Man of Law's Tale," and the "Prioress's Tale" as operating according to the conventions of the popular medieval story type, the *legenda*.

Daichman, Graciela S. *Wayward Nuns in Medieval Literature*. Syracuse, N.Y.: Syracuse University Press, 1986. Given the dissolute state of convent life in the Middle Ages, Daichman argues that the reader cannot assume a nun's innocence or purity.

Friedman, Albert B. "The *Prioress' Tale* and Chaucer's Anti-Semitism." *Chaucer Review* 9, no. 2 (1974): 118–129. Friedman explores the issue of whether the tale is in fact anti-Semitic, and if so, whether it reflects its author's own views.

Hanning, Robert W. "From *Eva* and *Ave* to Eglentyne and Alisoun: Chaucer's Insight into the Roles Women Play." *Signs* 2 (1977): 580–599. Hanning sees the Wife of Bath and the Prioress as representing "two apparently irreconcilable contraries" in medieval men's view of women: the "emblem of all man's striving" as represented by the Prioress, and the "cause of his loss of self-control, freedom, and happiness" as represented by the Wife of Bath.

Rex, Richard. "Chaucer and the Jews." *Modern Language Quarterly* 45, no. 2 (1984): 107–122. Rex argues that, compared to his contemporaries, Chaucer was a "master manipulator of stereotypes" and recognized the evil of anti-Semitism.

The Nun's Priest's Prologue and Tale

For Seint Paul seith that al that writen is,
To oure doctrine it is ywrite.

For Saint Paul says that all that is written
Is written for our doctrine.

(VII, 3441–3442)

The "Nun's Priest's Prologue" begins with an interruption. The Knight cannot bear to hear any more of the "Monk's Tale," a deliberately tedious series of examples of the rise and fall of great men (see Appendix V). The Monk, who appeared jolly, told a dull tale. "No more of this!" says the Knight; "a little heaviness" or seriousness is "right enough for many people" (VII, 2767–2770). Now it is time for a "lighter" tale. Playing the role of literary critic, the Knight explains the distinction between "heavy" tragedy and "light" comedy. Not surprisingly, he uses his own tale's central metaphor: Fortune's wheel. Tragedy is the tale of downward turning of the wheel; it tells of the "sudden fall" of "men [who] had been in great wealth and ease"; its audience feels "great disease," dis-ease or discomfort (VII, 2771–2773). Comedy, its "contrary," tells of the opposite spin of Fortune's wheel,

As whan a man hath been in povre estaat,
And clymbeth up and wexeth fortunat,
And there abideth in prosperitee.

When a man had been in poor estate,
And climbs up and becomes fortunate,
And abides there in prosperity.

(VII, 2775–2777)

Such a "gladsome tale" gives its audience "joy and great solace" (VII, 2778, 2774). This is the kind of tale the pilgrim audience needs now, as an antidote to the "Monk's Tale."

Harry Bailly, Host and moderator, agrees with the Knight and offers the Monk another chance. Less polite than the Knight, the Host tells the Monk that his tale was so dull that, were it not for the clinking of the bells on the Monk's horse's bridle, he would have fallen asleep. The Monk, discouraged, refuses to tell a new tale, so the Host selects another pilgrim, the Nun's Priest. Not characterized in the Prologue, the Priest, Sir John, is only briefly described here as a "sweet priest" and a "goodly man" (VII, 2820). Responding to the Knight's definitions of the two contrasting dramatic types, he proposes to give the audience a comedy. Further developing the idea of contrariety, the Nun's Priest links his comedy to the Monk's tragedy by merging the structure of the fall-from-fortune story with the content of another popular medieval genre, the beast fable. So Sir John tells what the title describes as the "Tale of the Cock and Hen, Chaunticleer and Pertelote," with the rooster Chaunticleer cast as hero.

The tale begins with a description of the owner of the cock and hen, then the fowls themselves. The "poor widow" (VII, 2821) is an ideal exemplar of her *estat*. The description of her habits contrasts the human character's simplicity with her barnyard animals' pretentiousness. Her "simple life" includes humble activities (tending her animals) and plain food ("slender meals" unembellished by "poignant" sauces [VII, 2826, 2833–2834]). Her avoidance of excess in food and drink contrasts with the dietary excess of which Pertelote will accuse Chaunticleer later. Similarly, the widow's humility contrasts with Chaunticleer's pridefulness. As everyone knows, roosters announce the arrival of morning. Chaucer inflates his rooster—pushing him ever higher on Fortune's unstable wheel—by attributing to him specific knowledge of the astrological forces governing the rotation of the planets. After considering these scientific factors, he crows.

Chaunticleer is superior in other ways to his unassuming owner. Not only is he a well-informed rooster, but he is a handsome one. His appearance is described in terms of the bright colors medieval people associated with royalty: red, black, blue, white, gold. Besides being intelligent and handsome, he is successful in love, leading a comfortable life with a harem of seven hens, his chief consort being the most colorful among them, the "fair damsel Pertelote" (VII, 2870). In medieval romance, the best knight gets the most beautiful woman. So when Chaucer employs the romance term "damsel" to describe Pertelote, he enhances Chaunticleer's status too. If Pertelote is a courtly lady, "courteous . . . discreet, and debonair" (VII,

2871), Chaunticleer is a courtly lover, serenading her in courtly fashion with a popular love song.

Grand though they are, Chaunticleer and Pertelote interact like a typical long-married couple. One morning, Chaunticleer, lordly "among his wives . . . in the hall," nonetheless is in a bad mood, "groaning in his throat" (VII, 2883–2884, 2886). His wife, hearing him, responds in good-wife fashion: "Dear heart, / What ails you, to groan in this manner?" (VII, 2889–2890). I've had a bad dream, says he, and I'll tell it to you, that you may "interpret aright" (VII, 2896) what it means:

> "Me mette how that I romed up and doun
> Withinne our yeerd, wheer as I saugh a beest
> Was lyk an hound, and wolde han maad areest
> Upon my body, and wolde han had me deed.
> His colour was bitwixe yelow and reed,
> And tipped was his tayl and bothe his eeris
> With blak, unlyk the remenant of his heeris;
> His snowte smal, with glowynge eyen tweye.
> Yet of his look for feere almoost I deye;
> This caused me my gronyng, doutelees."

> "I dreamed that I roamed up and down
> Within our yard, where I saw a beast
> Like a hound, who would have captured
> My body, and would have me dead.
> His color was between yellow and red,
> And his tail and both his ears were tipped
> With black, unlike the rest of his hair;
> His snout was small, with two glowing eyes.
> I almost die still for fear of his look;
> This caused my groaning, doubtless."

(VII, 2898–2907)

Medieval people believed that dreams were possible messages from the other world. Biblical dreamers were warned of danger: Joseph, the Virgin Mary's husband, was warned of King Herod's threat to Jesus by an angel appearing in his dream. Being on the receiving end of a communication from God, even if the message itself is threatening, is flattering. Because of the dreams, Chaunticleer sees himself as a potential tragic hero, threatened by a fall from fortune.

His wife deflates him, as wives will. Fearing a dream is unmanly, mocks Pertelote. Women want brave men, not cowards:

"How dorste ye seyn, for shame, unto youre love
That any thyng myghte make yow aferd?
Have ye no mannes herte, and han a berd?
Allas! And konne ye been agast of swevenys?"

"How dare you say, for shame, unto your love
That anything might make you afraid?
Have you no man's heart, despite your beard?
Alas! And can you be afraid of dreams?"

                                                    (VII, 2918–2921)

Pertelote disagrees with Chaunticleer's opinion that dreams have super-natural significance. She sees a dream as a purely physiological phenome-non caused by an imbalance of the bodily fluids, the "humours" (VII, 2925), correct proportions of which were believed to ensure health. The humours could become imbalanced owing to excess of food and drink, and this is what Pertelote believes to be Chaunticleer's problem. Since Chaunticleer has had dreams featuring the colors red and black, he must be suffering from a superfluity of red ("choleric" [VII, 2928]) and black ("melancholic" [VII, 2933]) humours. In addition to her common-sense diagnosis, Pertelote, learned as is Chaunticleer, has read an authority on dreams, Cato, who said to ignore them. To her, her husband's dreams are merely a sign of physical illness, to be corrected by medicines.

Traditionally, medieval women were responsible for their families' health care. They would know the herbs and potions that would solve common health problems. Since Pertelote's diagnosis is that Chaunticleer suffers from an excess of both choleric and melancholic humors, treatment involves purging his body of those superfluous and noxious fluids. "For God's love, take some laxative," she exclaims (VII, 2943). There is no pharmacist in the town, but she will make an herbal potion. What Pertelote is saying is that Chaunticleer needn't fear that his dreams constitute a prophecy; he merely needs a "purge . . . beneath and also above" (VII, 2953), that is, a laxative/emetic combination, to straighten out his diges-tive system. Although Chaunticleer has asked for his wife's interpretation of his dream, he doesn't like what he hears. How undignified for a tragic hero to be told he merely needs the medieval equivalent of Ex-Lax!

Fortunately, he too is learned, well-read like his wife in the work of authorities on dreams. Chaunticleer, forming his opinions in the best tradition of the medieval educational system on the basis of what "men may read in old books" (VII, 2974), disagrees with Pertelote. He thinks that

> *"dremes been significaciouns*
> *As wel of joye as of tribulaciouns*
> *That folk enduren in this lif present."*

> "dreams are significations
> As well of joy as of tribulations
> That folk endure in this present life."

(VII, 2979–2981)

To prove this, Chaunticleer launches into a long and involved argument involving anecdotal evidence combined with citations of learned authorities. Argumentation as practiced by medieval rhetoricians relied heavily on these two modes of "true proof" (VII, 2983). A good tale proved a point as well as any logic; citations from learned men of the past—the farther in the past, the better—substituted for scientific evidence. Pertelote herself has cited Cato on dreams, and since he lived from 234 to 149 B.C., Cato surely qualifies as an *auctoritee* by virtue of antiquity alone. Chaunticleer's two stories, taken from his own ancient authority, constitute tales within the tale on the same theme: the importance of dreams as prophecies of the future.

In the first tale, two pilgrims arrive at a town so crowded that they must lodge separately, one in an ox's stall and one in comfortable accommodations. The comfortable pilgrim has a dream in which his companion appears to him, warning of the companion's murder later that night in the ox's stall. The dreamer pays no attention to this first dream and goes back to sleep; he treats a second dream the same way. But the third dream is different: the companion announces that he has indeed been slain and that his body will be found in a dung-cart. Sure enough, when the sluggish dreamer finally pays attention, it is too late: the companion's body is indeed found in a dung-cart. The moral of the story is clear: "dreams are to dread" (VII, 3063).

Chaunticleer continues with a second illustrative tale. Two men await favorable winds for their departure on a sea voyage. But before they sail, one of the two has an ominous dream warning them not to go; if they do, they will be drowned. The dreamer awakens his companion, reports the dream, and begs him to abandon the journey. The companion is scornful:

> *"I sette nat a straw by thy dremynges,*
> *For swevenes been but vanytees and japes."*

> "I set not a straw by your dreamings,
> For dreams are but vanities and japes."

(VII, 3090–3091)

The skeptic boards ship, the believer does not; as might be expected, the ship sinks and the skeptic drowns.

Chaunticleer's conclusion follows inexorably from the two anecdotes:

> *"And therfore, faire Pertelote so deere,*
> *By swiche ensamples olde maistow leere*
> *That no man sholde been to recchelees*
> *Of dremes."*

> "And therefore, fair Pertelote so dear,
> By such old examples you may learn
> That no man should be too reckless
> Of dreams."

(VII, 3105–3108)

In each anecdote, Pertelote is comparable to the skeptic. In the anecdote of the two pilgrims, if the dreamer had believed his first dream, he could have saved his companion. In the second anecdote, the voyager could have saved himself if he had not scorned the dream of his companion. Both anecdotes demonstrate that being "reckless of dreams" leads to destruction.

So important is it to Chaunticleer that Pertelote be converted from this attitude that he piles up still more examples, references, and citations. Dreams figure importantly in the life of St. Kenelm; in an authoritative ancient work, Macrobius' *Dream of Scipio*; in the biblical books of Daniel and Joseph; in the myth of Croesus; in the story of Hector and Andromache from *The Iliad*. So do not, says Chaunticleer to his wife, talk to me of laxatives; dreaming is serious business. By the conventions of medieval rhetoric, Chaunticleer has thoroughly proved his point. At this juncture in the story, so impressive is the marshalling of arguments on both sides that it is hard to remember that the intellectual adversaries are a cock and a hen.

Chaunticleer shows that he has acquired a thorough medieval education by citing sources that would only have been known to clerks, those literate in the classical languages, Latin and Greek. Human females (much less hens) were excluded from the system of formal education in the Middle Ages. So when Chaunticleer turns from argument to lovemaking, he indulges himself in a little joke at Pertelote's expense. After praising her beauty, he treats her to what he apparently hopes will be an impressive Latin quote: "*In principio, / Mulier est hominis confusio*" (VII, 3163–3164). The correct translation is: "From the beginning [of time], woman is the confusion of man." But Chaunticleer deliberately mistranslates this bit of clerkly misogyny in a way that will flatter Pertelote and thus forward his seduction attempts: "Woman is man's joy and all his bliss" (VII, 3166). Pertelote has shown herself to be an intelligent hen, knowledgeable in practical matters like health care. This is the sort of training a medieval woman might have had: informal, home-based, and requiring either no literacy or literacy in the vernacular, not the scholarly, languages. But Chaunticleer, a medieval male, has an advantage over her in his knowledge of Latin. Although Pertelote had cited Cato, she apparently knows his work only second-hand and not in the original Latin; this is obvious from the fact that she cannot spot Chaunticleer's mistranslation of the Latin phrase. Whether Pertelote's awe at her husband's erudition is the reason we are not told; but Chaunticleer's advances toward his wife are successful.

The satisfied rooster is now at his best, "royal, as a prince is in his hall" (VII, 3184), that is, at the top of Fortune's wheel. His rooster's paradise persists until one sunny morning in early May. The birds are singing, the flowers are growing, and Chaunticleer is walking in the yard "in all his pride" (VII, 3191). Realizing how happy he is, Chaunticleer simultaneously perceives himself as being at that most perilous perch, atop Fortune's wheel:

> *For evere the latter ende of joye is wo.*
> *God woot that worldly joye is soone ago.*
>
> For ever the latter end of joy is woe.
> God knows that worldly joy is soon gone.
>
> (VII, 3205–3206)

As if in response to these feelings, a being appears who seems the embodiment of Chaunticleer's threatening dream: "a colfox, full of sly iniquity" (VII, 3215). The narrator waxes effusive, comparing the fox to famous traitors of literature and history, helplessly apostrophizing the unhearing Chaunticleer, warning him to be mindful of the prophetic dream.

At the same time, the Nun's Priest, a clerk well-educated in philosophy and theology, reflects on the problem of predestination. If an event was prophesied in a dream, then both the dream and the event must have been foreknown by an omniscient God. Since "what God foreknows must necessarily be" (VII, 3234), anything prophesied must necessarily happen. But then "necessity" can be interpreted in two ways, as simple or conditional. Simple necessity can be defined as a situation that is always true: for example, humans die. Conditional necessity is more complex, involved with the freedom of man's will:

> *if free choys be graunted me*
> *To do that same thyng, or do it noght,*
> *Though God forwoot it er that I was wroght.*

> if free choice be granted me
> To do something, or do it not,
> Even though God foreknew it before I was made.
>
> (VII, 3246–3248)

But does God's foreknowing cause an individual's free-will choice? This conundrum puzzles the Nun's Priest as it did his authorities, Augustine, Boethius, and Bradwardyn. So the narrator drops his philosophical digression and returns to his main plot, his "tale . . . of a cock" who "took counsel of his wife, with sorrow" (VII, 3252–3253).

Heeding the advice of women was roundly condemned by misogynistic writers of Chaucer's day. The precedent for such a situation was Adam, who, because he listened to Eve, lost Paradise:

> *Wommennes conseils been ful ofte colde;*
> *Wommannes conseil broghte us first to wo*
> *And made Adam fro Paradys to go,*
> *Ther as he was ful myrie and wel at ese.*

> Women's counsels are very often cold;
> Women's counsel brought us first to woe
> And made Adam go from Paradise,
> Where he had been quite merry and well at ease.
>
> (VII, 3256–3259)

The Nun's Priest, a man who works for a female boss, must take care to assure an audience which includes her that Chaunticleer's opinions on women may not coincide with the priest's own.

But Pertelote's skepticism plays a role in the tale's climax. Her contempt might, despite his elaborate arguments to the contrary, have influenced Chaunticleer to take his dream less seriously and consequently to let down his guard. Furthermore, Chaunticleer is loath to show fear before his wife—all the more because she feels that there is nothing to fear. Manly bravado supplements wifely influence to motivate Chaunticleer's rash deed. Yet the relationship between Pertelote's opinion and Chaunticleer's misfortune cannot be reduced to simple causality. Human marriage partners often find it convenient to blame each other for personal faults. Chaucer, a married man himself, might have noted such behavior and transplanted it into his "tale of a cock."

Pertelote's responsibility must also be seen against the conventional definition of tragedy and of the tragic hero. The *Poetics* of Aristotle (384–322 B.C.), an authoritative work on tragedy to this day, was widely accepted as definitive in the Middle Ages. Aristotle defines tragedy as a fall from high position and the tragic hero as a man whose fall is precipitated by a personal failing or error in judgment. It is obvious that Chaunticleer's character flaw is what moderns would term overconfidence, what medievals would call the deadly sin of pride. So far Chaunticleer has been presented as a creature puffed up with pride, full of himself, self-congratulatory: all faults that beg for correction. Chaunticleer actually *is* the way a rooster *looks* when crowing; indeed, even today the term "to crow" is used to describe self-praise. Like a hero in ancient Greek tragedy, Chaunticleer, overconfident, overreaches by attempting to outwit rather than flee from the agent of his fall, the fox.

In keeping with the motif of the fall from atop Fortune's wheel, the action speeds up as Chaunticleer confronts his prophesied nemesis, the colfox. Observing the rooster's pompous crowing pose, the fox senses that an appeal to pride will work on Chaunticleer. So the fox claims that his only purpose in approaching Chaunticleer is to listen to him sing. Learned like the cock and the hen, the fox compares Chaunticleer's feeling for music to that of the Roman philosopher Boethius (c. 480–524). The fox sentimentally reminisces about Chaunticleer's late father and mother. Both have been in the fox's house "to his great ease" (VII, 3297)—apparently the fox has eaten them. Chaunticleer's father, observes the fox, was a master crower. Is it possible that Chaunticleer could give an exhibition of his own crowing, "counterfeit" his father (VII, 3321)? The fox's purpose in getting Chaunticleer to perform is to get him to expose his throat and close his eyes, as Chaunticleer's father had done. When Chaunticleer assumes this same vulnerable position, the fox seizes him by the throat and carries him away.

Since this is not only a beast fable but also a mock tragedy, the climactic action—the fall from fortune—must be accompanied by emotional outpourings and grandiose moralizations. The tragic flaw, pride, threatens lords and roosters. The narrator's apostrophes, exclamations addressed to abstract qualities ("O destiny! . . . O Venus!" [VII, 3338, 3342]), set the barnyard action in the context of great historical tragedies: the death of King Richard I, the fall of Troy. The latter disaster, recounted in *The Iliad*, was accompanied by the cries of "lamentation" of wailing women. Now, Chaunticleer's "woful hens" (VII, 3369) shriek like the bereaved women of classical tragedy. This jarring sound deflates the action, bringing it down abruptly from classical tragedy to barnyard mishap.

The hens' cries alert the human characters, the poor widow and her two daughters. All three come running, and with them an undignified rabble consisting of the dog, the cow, the calf, pigs, ducks, geese, even bees. The bedlam is such that the narrator compares it to the Peasant's Revolt of 1381—a revolt of the lesser against the greater which, to medieval people, represented the epitome of cosmic disorder. All rush, with the noise of trumpets amplifying their own shrieking, to the rescue of poor Chaunticleer.

Much medieval humor turned on the idea of retaliation in kind—the guiler beguiled, the jealous husband cuckolded, the miser cheated. If this tragic tale of Chaunticleer's fall from fortune is to end as a comedy, somehow the enemy must be beaten at his own game, the fox outfoxed. The rooster, in the fox's clutches, is an example of "how fortune turns suddenly" (VII, 3403). Chaunticleer's only hope is to cause Fortune to spin her wheel once more, raising him from his current wretched state.

Chaunticleer's downfall was caused by his pride and his consequent susceptibility to flattery. Since this is a common character flaw of those atop Fortune's wheel, it could in turn work on the fox in his current state of superiority. So Chaunticleer urges his captor to boast of his success to the ineffectual humans running about the barnyard:

> "*Sire, if that I were as ye,*
> *Yet sholde I seyn, as wys God helpe me,*
> *'Turneth agayn, ye proude cherles alle!*
> *A verray pestilence upon yow falle!*
> *Now I am come unto the wodes syde;*
> *Maugree youre heed, the cok shal heere abyde.*
> *I wol hym ete, in feith, and that anon!' "*

> "Sire, if I were like you,
> I would say, as God help me,
> 'Turn away, all you proud churls!
> A very pestilence fall upon you!
> Now I am come to the edge of the woods,
> In spite of you, the cock shall abide here.
> I will eat him, in faith, and right away!' "

(VII, 3407–3413)

The fox is as easily persuaded to open his mouth and boast as was Chaunticleer to throw back his head and crow:

The fox answerede, "In feith, it shal be don."
And as he spak that word, al sodeynly
This cok brak from his mouth delyverly.

The fox answered, "In faith, it shall be done."
And as he spoke that work, all suddenly
This cock broke from his mouth quite agilely.

(VII, 3414–3416)

Escaping to a high perch, Chaunticleer is safe again. The fox, wanting to recoup his loss, apologizes for capturing Chaunticleer; just come down once more, he pleads. Wiser now, Chaunticleer refuses, and the disappointed fox draws the expected moral:

"God yeve hym meschaunce,
That is so undiscreet of governaunce
That jangleth whan he sholde holde his pees."

"God give him mischance
Who is so indiscreet of governance
That he chatters when he should hold his peace."

(VII, 3433–3435)

The narrator chimes in with a moral of his own:

Lo, swich it is for to be recchelees
And necligent, and truste on flaterye.

Lo, such it is to be reckless
And negligent, and trust in flattery.

(VII, 3436–3437)

All good stories, to the medieval way of thinking, pointed to a realm of truth beyond literature. Both of these snippets of proverbial wisdom fulfill the purpose of literature: to teach a lesson applicable to life. Just as the examples in the "Monk's Tale" of the fall of great men stress the precariousness of all earthly fortune, so does the "Nun's Priest's Tale." The narrator, a priest, reminds the audience that his tale is not a "folly," a bit of foolishness of a "fox, or of a cock and hen"; rather, it is useful and important in having a "morality" of its own (VII, 3438–3439, 3440).

For Seint Paul seith that al that writen is,
To oure doctrine it is ywrite.

For Saint Paul said that all that is written
Is written for our doctrine.

(VII, 3441–3442)

As St. Paul said, everything written has a deeper theological or "doc-trinal" meaning, contained within but extending beyond it. The hearer is drawn to a tale by its pleasing or entertaining quality. But this surface narrative (what moderns would call the plot or story line) is not all there is. Just as the visible, tangible body contains a soul; just as, in the Nun's Priest's image, the external husk contains the more important grain of wheat, so the story contains "morality" and "doctrine" (VII, 3440, 3442). The "chaff" or covering of the wheat is thrown away, but the "fruit," the important part, must be retained (VII, 3443). Chaucer has stressed this point before by contrasting *ernest* and *game*.

Thus the Nun's Priest further articulates the theory of the purpose of literature that was introduced earlier in *The Canterbury Tales*. Even a light comedy, intended as a relief from the heaviness of the "Monk's Tale" preceding it, has in reality a high and noble purpose, nothing less than the eternal salvation of its audience. Even a tale of a fox, a rooster, and a hen can, in God's eternal plan, "make us all good men, / And bring us to his high bliss! Amen" (VII, 3445–3446).

SUGGESTIONS FOR FURTHER READING

Brown, Peter. *Chaucer at Work: The Making of the Canterbury Tales*. London: Longman, 1994. 164–175. Taking a self-study approach, Brown explores the built-in ambiguities in the text.

Hotson, J. Leslie. "Colfox vs. Chaunticleer." *Chaucer: Modern Essays in Criticism*. Ed. Edward Wagenknecht. New York: Oxford University Press, 1959. 98–116. Hotson finds a historical analogue to the events of the tale in the 1397 murder of the duke of Gloucester, in which a Richard Colfox was involved.

Howard, Donald R. *The Idea of the Canterbury Tales*. Berkeley: University of California Press, 1976. 282–288. Howard sees the tale as a parody of medieval intellectual pretensions, especially concerning the study of rhetoric.

Huppé, Bernard F. *A Reading of the Canterbury Tales*. Albany: State University of New York Press, 1964. 174–184. Huppé explores the relationship of the tale to the ongoing "marriage debate."

Lumiansky, R. M. *Of Sondry Folk: The Dramatic Principle in the Canterbury Tales*. Austin: University of Texas Press, 1955. 105–117. In support of his famous thesis, that the tales are developments of the characters of the tellers, Lumiansky argues that this tale is a "suitable one for a cleric," especially one "under the petticoat rule" of the Prioress.

Mann, Jill. *Geoffrey Chaucer*. Atlantic Highlands, N.J.: Humanities Press, 1991. 186–194. Mann sees the tale as an illustration of "Chaucer's originality in creating models of both female and male behavior that erase traditional gender boundaries."

Whittock, Trevor. *A Reading of the Canterbury Tales*. Cambridge: Cambridge University Press, 1968. 228–250. Whittock argues that the tale "echoes, renews, and raises themes dealt with in other stories."

The Second Nun's Prologue and Tale

"But ther is bettre lif in oother place,
That nevere shal be lost, ne drede thee noght."

"But there is a better life in another place
That never shall be lost, fear not."

(VIII, G, 323–324)

At certain points the reader is reminded that *The Canterbury Tales* is an incomplete work, and the "Second Nun's Prologue" is one of these points. Since the Second Nun is not described in the "General Prologue," it is unclear how the prologue serves as other prologues do, to develop the character of the tale-teller. As for its relationship to the tale, the prologue's three parts—a sermonette on idleness; a prayer to the Virgin; and an interpretation of the heroine's name—are like three separate threads lightly joined to each other and to the main body of the tapestry.

The saying, "An idle mind is the devil's workshop," is current even today; idleness has long been viewed as a moral vacuum into which evil penetrates. Idleness is the porter at the gate of pleasure; it gives the devil a chance to catch a man by the hem of his garment. Physical idleness is a manifestation of a sinful spiritual state "of which there never comes good or increase" (VIII, G, 18). One of the Seven Deadly Sins, sloth is "rotten sluggardry" (VIII, G, 17), spiritual complacency. The slothful person is too contented with himself; lacking the desire for spiritual improvement, he lives only on a physical plane, "only to sleep, and to eat and drink" (VIII, G, 20). Such self-satisfaction was condemned in medieval Christianity because it ended the quest for perfection. The slothful do not increase; the spiritually ambitious do. Since St. Cecile's story stresses the growth of Christianity through her influence, the theme of idleness in the prologue contrasts with the main theme of the tale: increase. The Second Nun herself is part of the same process of increase. To carry on Cecile's work, the Second Nun has taken on her own work, translating the saint's life for the edification of the faithful. Thus, through her own "faithful" or faith-filled "busy-ness" (VIII, G, 24), she too hopes to contribute to the spiritual increase of her audience.

The second element of the prologue is a prayer to the Virgin, which is especially appropriate to begin the story of a virgin as told by another virgin. The Second Nun's prayer is reminiscent of the similar invocation at the beginning of the "Prioress's Tale," underlining the similarities between the two saints' lives. The prayer cites Mary's standard virtues: her mercy toward sinners, her unparalleled purity, her role as intercessor with her divine son. Mary's virginity allies her not only to the Second Nun but also to St. Cecile. Mary, the Nun, and Cecile are linked to each other, and this community of holy women, extended further back in time by including Mary's mother St. Anne, inspires the nun to tell her tale. But even if her own limited writing ability leads to an imperfect result, the Nun begs the reader to "forgive" her failings and "amend" or supplement her work (VIII, G, 79, 84) with their own knowledge of the well-known story.

The third part of the prologue, the etymological analysis of the saint's name, points to a popular medieval habit of mind. Based on the assumption that the names of people or objects somehow contain their esssence, medieval name-analysis stressed phonetic similarity, not what moderns would consider demonstrable linguistic affinities. The Second Nun attributes her etymology to a Brother Jacob of Genoa, in yet another example of the medieval preference for citing a source book rather than speaking on personal authority. The explication of Cecile's name is based on a combination of free association of sounds and creative logic. "Cecilia" means "heaven's lily" (VIII, G, 87); the combination of the place and the white flower connotes virginity. The lily's green foliage signifies "conscience" and "good fame" (VIII, G, 90). But this one interpretation, however elaborate, is insufficient. The Nun gives two more possible etymologies, each slightly different in emphasis, but also stressing her "wise works," "excellence," and "whole[ness] in good persevering" (VIII, G, 105, 112, 117). Increase, virginity, and wholeness, themes sounded in the prologue, are picked up and developed in the tale. Perhaps they should be thought of as musical themes, since Cecile's traditional role is as patron saint of music.

Since, like the "Prioress's Tale," the "Second Nun's Tale" is a *legenda*, its purpose is didactic: to teach the faithful proper values and behavior by presenting a strong—often even exaggerated—example. Like the Physi-

cian's story of Virginia, the Second Nun's story of Cecile stresses the high
value placed on female virginity and the lengths to which women were
expected to go to defend it. The traditional life of the virgin martyr follows
a predictable pattern, beginning with a preternaturally holy childhood.
The crisis arises in adolescence, when a marriage is planned and the saint
refuses it, declaring her commitment to lifelong virginity. Often the father,
whose authority is challenged by his daughter's rebelliousness, becomes her
persecutor. If not he, then other male authority figures (her betrothed, her
husband if she has already been married, or a political superior) strive to
force the virgin to abandon her holy calling. No compromise is possible
between the two absolutes: virginity and nonvirginity. The drama lies in
the disparity of the opponents: the weak woman versus the strong man. As
is visualized in the photo of St. Catherine (see photo 5), the virgin's death
seems to constitute the victory of the forces of evil, embodied in the male
authority figure. But strengthened by her faith in God, the heroine triumphs in apparent defeat by winning a martyr's crown.

Cecile's story is a typical example of this form. Cecile is born to a noble
Roman family. Raised a Christian, "up fostered from her cradle in the
faith / Of Christ" (VIII, G, 122–123) in a Roman community, she is a
member of a persecuted religious minority group. These two facts prepare
for her inevitable conflict with Almache, the representative of secular
authority. As a noblewoman, she is eminently marriageable; in fact, it is
her duty as the daughter of a noble family to forge an alliance with another
noble family through her marriage. Often in the legenda, the father of the
saint becomes chief persecutor when she rejects the marriage he has
arranged, even inflicting sadistic tortures on his hitherto beloved daughter
in an attempt to change her mind. Here, however, the conventional father
character is suppressed, and the focus shifts to other male authority figures.
In the stock legenda plot, the villain would be her betrothed, the pagan
Valerian.

Cecile does not outwardly rebel against the arranged marriage. When
her wedding day arrives, she is appropriately dressed for it "in a robe of gold"
(VIII, G, 132). But under the gold dress she wears a hair shirt, an uncomfortable, itchy garment worn to inflict concealed suffering—a common
discipline of the flesh practiced by medieval saints. While the wedding
music plays, Cecile prays that, though married, she may yet preserve her
virginity. How is this to be?

"The night came, and to bed must she go / With her husband" (VIII, G,
141–142). Now Cecile must save her virginity or lose it. In the legendae,
the marriage of a Christian woman to a pagan man has two possible

outcomes: persecution by the husband, or his conversion. Here, however, Cecile's goal is not only to convert Valerian to Christianity but also to cause him to accept a higher, more demanding spiritual *estat*, celibacy. Cecile will need all the supernatural help she can get. Cecile begins the conversion process by telling Valerian that she has a secret:

> "I have an aungel which that loveth me,
> That with greet love, wher so I wake or sleepe,
> Is redy ay my body for to kepe.
>
> "And if that he may feelen, out of drede,
> That ye me touche, or love in vileynye,
> He right anon wol sle yow with the dede,
> And in youre yowthe thus ye shullen dye."

> "I have an angel, who loves me
> With such great love that, whether I wake or sleep,
> He is always ready to keep my body safe.
>
> "And if he feels, out of dread,
> That you touch me, or love unworthily,
> He will kill you as soon as you do the deed,
> And in your youth thus you shall die."

(VIII, G, 152–158)

Valerian, not raised a Christian as was Cecile, is understandably skeptical about this angel who will kill him in his youth for exercising his legitimate marital rights. So he asks to see the angel. Cecile explains that if Valerian goes to Pope St. Urban on the Appian Way, proclaims belief in Christ, and accepts baptism, he will see the angel.

Valerian does as instructed and searches out St. Urban in the catacombs, the burial places of the saints. The saint is moved to tears by Valerian's having sought him out, this being evidence of how the "seed of chastity" planted in Cecile is bearing "fruit" in Valerian (VIII, G, 193). This inversion of the imagery of human fertilization emphasizes a key concept: that, since the spirit's products are better than those of the flesh, chastity is more truly generative than is sexuality. Valerian, who could have been "like a fierce lion" in marriage, comes to Urban "as meek as ever was any lamb" (VIII, G, 198–199) and embraces celibacy. This radical transformation is a tribute to Cecile's positive influence on her husband.

Miracles, medieval Christians believed, were suspensions of the natural order permitted by God for His own purposes. Here, the conversion of Valerian is assisted by the miraculous appearance of an "old man, clad in white clothes" and carrying a book proclaiming in gold letters that Christianity is "above all and over all everywhere" (VIII, G, 201, 209). The vision converts Valerian, and Pope St. Urbain "christened him right there" (VIII, G, 217), on the very spot of his conversion. Valerian, who left home a pagan husband, returns a Christian celibate. True to her promise, Cecile awaits him in their marital bedroom, with the angel. The angel in the bedroom is a clear signifier of marital chastity. The angel reinforces his own meaning by giving Valerian and Cecile two invisible crowns, one of roses and one of lilies, along with a lecture on the value of the virtue which the crowns represent.

So cooperative has Valerian been that the angel offers him a special request. The sincerity of Valerian's conversion is indicated by his asking for a favor for another: the conversion of his beloved brother Tiburce. The angel grants him this, as well as an additional reward for both brothers: "the palm of martyrdom" (VIII, G, 240), guaranteeing both eternal happiness in heaven (VIII, G, 239–240). With that, Tiburce, arriving opportunely at his brother's house, miraculously smells the roses and lilies of his brother's and sister-in-law's invisible crowns of chastity. Like the miraculous appearance of the old man to Valerian, the miracle inspires "wonder" (VIII, G, 245), an openness to spiritual experience. With his whole being, Tiburce responds:

> "The savour myghte in me no depper go.
> The sweete smel that in myn herte I fynde
> Hath chaunged me al in another kynde."

> "The savor might penetrate me no deeper;
> The sweet smell that I find in my heart
> Has changed me completely into another kind."
>
>   (VIII, G, 250–252)

The word *conversion* is derived from the Latin verb *convertere*, meaning to turn about. Conversion is a total reversal of mind and spirit, in Tiburce's words, transforming the convert into "another kind" of being (VIII, G, 252). His spirit opened to conversion by the miracle, Tiburce questions his brother, who explains his own conversion experience, retelling the whole story again in brief—an effective didactic technique. Tiburce is somewhat harder to convince than was his brother, however. When Valerian suggests that Tiburce go to Pope St. Urbain as he had, Tiburce demurs:

> "Ne menestow nat Urban," quod he tho,
> "That is so ofte dampned to be deed,
> And woneth in halkes alwey to and fro,

And dar nat ones putte forth his heed?
Men sholde hym brennen in a fyr so reed
If he were founde, or that men myghte hym spye,
And we also, to bere hym compaignye."

"Do you not mean Urban," he said then,
"That is so often condemned to death,
And runs to hiding places to and fro,
And dare not once put forth his head?
Men would burn him in a fire so red
If he were found, or if men might spy him,
And we also, to bear him company."

(VIII, G, 309–315)

Tiburce's hesitation differentiates him from his brother and reiterates the idea that Christianity is a persecuted sect operating underground—literally, as Urbain, though pope, has earlier been described as hiding in catacombs. The opportunity to win the crown of martyrdom does not initially appeal to Tiburce as much as it did to his brother. He needs some indoctrination, some further instruction in Christian doctrine, which Cecile "boldly" teaches (VIII, G, 319). It might be reasonable to dread death, she says, if this were our only life. But "there is better life in other place" (VIII, G, 323), in heaven, with the Trinity, Father, Son, and Holy Ghost. Tiburce requires further explication of the theology of the Trinity, which Cecile gladly provides. Tiburce's reluctance enables Cecile to demonstrate theological expertise, and her teaching educates the audience in turn. Tiburce is converted, baptized by Urbain, and even exceeds his brother in learning and in holiness, so much so that he sees the angel every day (not just once), and receives promptly "every manner of boon" (VIII, G, 356) that he requests.

Conventions of the *legenda* obviously do not include realism and probability. Miraculous events trigger prompt conversions; visions appear; young girls teach theology (a phenomenon only slightly less remarkable to medieval people than visions of angels with golden books). The conversion of Valerian and his brother shows the beneficent influence of the saint: "The maid hath brought these men to bliss above" (VIII, G, 281) through the shining example of her chastity. But the three cannot, in the nature of the genre, live happily and chastely ever after. Since all have been promised the "palm of martyrdom" (VIII, G, 240), persecution and death are not only inevitable but also desirable.

Insofar as the three represent the forces of good, a force of evil must emerge. The three saints' reputation for miracles brings them to the attention of the secular authorities. The trio has violated the laws of the Roman state in refusing to worship Roman gods. Almache, the prefect, demands that they sacrifice to Jupiter or else lose their heads. No compromise is possible. But further spiritual successes are: Maximus, ordered to enforce the law on the three saints, instead takes them to his own house, listens to their "preaching," and is converted, along with "his folk," the members of his household (VIII, G, 375, 377). Their ranks swelled by further converts, their resolve increased by Cecile's motivational speech, the martyrs are led forth to martyrdom.

Martyrdom scenes in the *legenda* are typically gory affairs in which violence, especially against women, is depicted with sadistic relish. Ingenious tortures are followed by miraculous recoveries, to be followed in turn by escalating violence. The foregone conclusion is the death of the martyr, but in the process, in awe at the martyr's endurance of suffering, bystanders, even torturers, are converted *en masse*. The martyrdom scene in the "Second Nun's Tale" is a tame affair compared to typical representatives of its genre. The two brothers' deaths, followed by that of the recent convert Maximus, are described only briefly. With her husband and brother-in-law dead, and she the more vulnerable because of their deaths, all attention now focuses on Cecile.

In a pair of contrasting images characteristic of the medieval tendency to think in terms of polar opposites, Cecile has described conversion as "casting completely away the works of darkness" and "arming" oneself in the "armor of brightness" (VIII, G, 384–385). The forces of darkness are embodied in the Roman prefect Almache and the force of brightness in Cecile (she who, in the prologue, was described as "white," "light," and "bright" [VIII, G, 89, 100, 118]). The dramatic encounter between these two forces is a required element in the martyr story. A further element of the drama is the gender of the opponents. Spiritual strength in the person of a physically weak and unprotected woman is pitted against political power. Because she represents Christ himself and his church, Cecile must be assertive; she cannot play a deferential female role here. Almache accuses her of "answering so rudely" (VIII, G, 432), by which he means as compared to the standard of deferential, placating speech encouraged in medieval women. In this context, Cecile's defiant speech is, paradoxically, both unladylike and saintly:

> "Youre myght," quod she, "ful litel is to dreede,
> For every mortal mannes power nys
> But lyk a bladdre ful of wynd, ywys.

> *For with a nedles poynt, whan it is blowe,*
> *May al the boost of it be leyd ful lowe."*

> "Your might," said she, "is very little to dread,
> For every mortal man's power is
> But like a bladder full of wind, I know.
> For with a needle's point, when it is blown,
> May all the boast of it be laid quite low."

(VIII, G, 437–441)

Human authority, when compared to the higher authority of God, is like a "bladder full of wind," which can easily be popped, laying low the "boast" or pretentiousness of power. The trivializing image—a popped balloon—enrages Almache all the more. The saint does not fear the death he can inflict, but actively seeks it. When Almache issues an ultimatum—"Do sacrifice, or renounce Christianity"—Cecile "began to laugh," not only rejecting but mocking the power of institutionalized evil (VIII, G, 459, 462). Cecile's unladylike rebelliousness is stressed by the terms Almache uses to criticize her: "rude," "proud," and "bold" (VIII, G, 432, 472, 487). She will not obey; she does not agree; she disputes his every point, corrects his erroneous assumptions, presumes to educate him. Because Cecile speaks here not in her own person but as Defender of the Faith, she is a saint, not a shrew. The weak woman is right, the strong man wrong.

Cecile's example does not, however, convert Almache as it did her husband and brother-in-law; he represents those who reject the word of God. Almache condemns Cecile to be placed in a cauldron and "burned in a bath of red flames" (VIII, G, 515). Unusual modes of execution are common in the saints' lives, as is the saint's miraculous imperviousness to torture. A day and a night later,

> *For al the fyr and eek the bathes heete*
> *She sat al coold and feelede no wo.*
> *It made hire nat a drope for to sweete.*

> For all the fire and also the bath's heat
> She sat all cold and felt no pain.
> It made her not a drop for to sweat.

(VIII, G, 520–522)

Not only does the bath's fiery heat not kill her, but, miraculously, it does not even make her sweat. So Almache sends an executioner to smite off her head. After three strokes, he has not killed her; and since the law forbids a fourth stroke, he leaves her there, "half dead, with her neck carved" (VIII,

G, 532). By a further miracle, she lives in this condition for three days, "and never ceases to teach them the faith / That she had fostered" (VII, G, 538–539). In a third miracle, Cecile is allowed three more days "to preach" and "to teach" (VIII, G, 538–539) on this spot of her martyrdom, in order that her house may become a shrine. The growth of a saint's cult depended on such marvels, as it did on the belief in the power of the saint's relic. That is why "Christian folk" try to capture the martyr's blood in their "sheets," or cloths (VIII, G, 535–536).

As in the miraculous postmortem singing of the "little *clergeoun*" in the "Prioress's Tale," the prolongation of the saint's earthly life by supernatural means must end, that the martyr's crown be attained. So Cecile dies, and indeed her house becomes a shrine; St. Urban "hallowed" or blessed it, and, says the Second Nun, "men do service to Christ and to his saint" therein to this day (VIII, G, 551, 553).

In modern times, the feast of St. Cecile is still observed on November 22. She and her legend are still part of Christian lore. Her tale teaches the value not only of chastity, but also of the ramifying influence of strong faith. The increase in the ranks of the faithful through her influence reminds the medieval Christian of the power of his own faith to influence others. But it is inevitable that some, like Almache, will be blind despite the brightness of Cecile's example. Not all can emulate Valerian and Tiburce, Maximus, and all the other converts: men brought out of the darkness by a woman's "great light" (VIII, G, 100).

SUGGESTIONS FOR FURTHER READING

Beichner, Paul E. "Confrontation, Contempt of Court, and Chaucer's Cecilia." *Chaucer Review* 8, no. 3 (1974): 198–204. Beichner sees Cecile as a rebel against the "Roman establishment," with speech as her weapon.

Braswell, Laurel. "Chaucer and the Art of Hagiography." *Chaucer in the Eighties.* Eds. Julian N. Wasserman and Robert J. Blanch. Syracuse, N.Y.: Syracuse University Press, 1986. 209–221. Braswell sees the "Clerk's Tale," the "Second Nun's Tale," the "Man of Law's Tale," and the "Prioress's Tale" as operating according to the conventions of the popular medieval story type, the *legenda*.

Collette, Carolyn P. "A Closer Look at Seinte Cecile's Special Vision." *Chaucer Review* 10, no. 4 (1976): 337–349. Colette fills in the theological background to the imagery of sight in the tale.

Longsworth, Robert M. "Privileged Knowledge: St. Cecilia and the Alchemist in the *Canterbury Tales*." *Chaucer Review* 27, no. 1 (1992): 87–96.

Longsworth's thesis is that the relationship between the two tales is based on the common theme of transformation.

Martin, Priscilla. *Chaucer's Women: Nuns, Wives, and Amazons.* Iowa City: University of Iowa Press, 1990. 131–155. In Chapter 8, "The Saints," Martin analyzes the character of Cecile along with that of Custance in the "Man of Law's Tale" and Grisilde in the "Clerk's Tale" as examples of perfect womanly virtue.

The Canon's Yeoman's Prologue and Tale

We faille of that which that we wolden have,
And in oure madnesse everemoore we rave.
And whan we been togidres everichoon,
Every man semeth a Salomon.
But al thyng which that shineth as the gold
Nis nat gold.

We fail to get what we would have,
And in our madness evermore we rave.
And when we are together, every one,
Every man seems like a Solomon.
But all things which shine like the gold
Are not gold.

(VIII, G, 958–963)

"All that glitters is not gold": the proverb is still current today as a warning against the deceptiveness of appearances. Wealth is the object of many a quest. When all engaged in that quest remain within their own self-contained world, the journey seems sensible and the pilgrims wise. But in contrast to the search for salvation for which the Canterbury pilgrimage is metaphor, the search for mere material gold is madness, and the searchers lunatic. The central image of the "Canon's Yeoman's Prologue and Tale" is gold: shining, beautiful, as valuable as any earthly possession can be. The glitter of gold is so alluring that it distracts those who seek it from the higher goals of human life. This, to the medieval mind, would be tragic even if the seeker obtains the gold he seeks; it is the very image of futility when even on the lower material level, the questors "fail of that which [they] would have" (VIII, G, 958). The Canon and his Yeoman have made gold their god. This is bad enough; but in their failed quest the Canon, and possibly the Yeoman, have lost both gold and God.

An ill-chosen goal, a misdirected journey: the arc of motion in the "Canon's Yeoman's Prologue and Tale" reverses that of the Canterbury pilgrimage itself. The prologue begins with Canon and Yeoman joining the Canterbury pilgrimage, probably for the wrong reasons. It would be nice to think that these two malefactors had seen the error of their ways and were now redirecting their lives, not only to the beautiful cathedral at Canterbury (see photo 1), but also to the heavenly city of which the cathedral is a foretaste. But the main point of the basic contrast in both prologue and tale between true and false gold is that visible appearances may or may not reflect reality. Not everything that shines like gold is gold; on the other hand, some things that glitter are gold. Appearances sometimes reflect reality, but not always. The moral complexity of the tale involves the reader's sorting out which appearances accurately reflect reality and which do not; which goals are worth the questing, which not. This is a difficult process, and the "Canon's Yeoman's Prologue and Tale" is a difficult work. With its sophisticated combining and recombining of elements from the whole body of the tales, it resembles the complex alchemical processes it describes.

The Middle Ages was not a time of rapid progress in the sciences, and for several reasons. Given the hierarchical values of the time, the best minds were encouraged to pursue what were regarded as "higher" studies, those concerned with the spirit: first theology, then philosophy. These were considered the apex of education in the burgeoning medieval university system. The physical sciences, in contrast, were held in contempt precisely because they were physical. They sought knowledge (Latin, *scientia*) of the material world, which was regarded as inherently inferior to the spiritual world studied by the theologians and philosophers. Because science was not considered worthy of the best efforts of the best minds, what moderns would regard as progress was discouraged. But progress is itself a modern concept. As has been noted in regard to the "Wife of Bath's Prologue," medieval people saw truth in the old books of the ancient authorities, not in observations of the physical world. To them, "scientific" knowledge meant restating authoritative opinions, not discovering something new. In fact, novelty rendered an idea suspect.

Paradoxically, only the alchemists were looking for something new, and that for the wrong reason. What the alchemists sought was termed the "philosopher's stone"—a wondrous substance that transmuted base metals into gold. Their motive was not the advancement of learning but rather their own profit. By medieval moral standards, this made them impure on two counts. Even if they had intended only to advance scientific knowledge, they would have been misguided in directing their efforts toward the material world, rather than the spiritual world. But the alchemists did not intend even this lesser good. Like Chaucer's evil Pardoner, all they wanted was to make money. The profit motive was not considered a legitimate engine of human activity, but rather sin. As the Pardoner's text warns, "*Radix malorum est Cupiditas*" (VI, C, 334)—the love of money is the root of all evil.

Since the quest for money costs money, the alchemist seeks investors willing to finance his experiments in hopes of achieving a substantial reward. Modern guides to investment stress the relationship between high rewards and high risk. Any reward at all depends on the success of the venture: an investor in an oil well loses money if there is no oil at the drilling site. Similarly, investors in the alchemist's venture lose their investment if the philosopher's stone is not found. If such a substance were found, however, the investors would be wealthy beyond imagining. The lure of great wealth draws gamblers to Las Vegas today; the lure of the philosopher's stone misdirected the efforts of the scientific minds of the Middle Ages. The quest proved futile. But even if it had succeeded, the pursuit of the philosopher's stone was a less worthy goal than that on which the Canterbury pilgrims are embarked when the Canon and his Yeoman join them.

Chaucer breaks the established pattern of *The Canterbury Tales* by adding these two characters to the original pilgrim group and then subtracting one of them again. Thus he modifies what might have become a monotonously rigid structure by accommodating a principle of disorder: unexpected intrusion from without. Combined with the different strategies employed in the links between the tales, this technique makes the overall structure seem to develop organically and naturally, not mechanically and artificially. Life does not proceed according to orderly plan, and neither does this pilgrimage.

After hearing the tale of St. Cecile (the "Second Nun's Tale"), the pilgrims reach Boughton under Blee, a town about five miles from Canterbury. Cecile's story must be fresh in the mind of both pilgrim and reader, as two key images from the saint's life are important also in the lives of these two sinners: fire and sweat. In the story of St. Cecile, the evil Roman prefect Almache condemns her to death for her refusal to renounce Christianity. When Cecile is placed in a cauldron of water over a "great fire" (VIII, G, 518), however, a miracle occurs: not only is she not burned to death, but she doesn't even perspire. Her virginal body, self-contained and cool, does not respond to heat.

In contrast to this miraculous suspension of the natural order, the Canon, and even his horse, are unusually responsive to the natural processes of heat. Alchemy, the ancestor of modern chemistry, depended on fire to facilitate the hoped-for chemical reactions between the combined elements. Hunched daily over his still or distillation vessel, the alchemist would naturally perspire from the heat of the fire. Even though the Canon is not in his laboratory now, he is sweating: "His forehead dripped like a still" (VIII, G, 580). It is as if the Canon has been transformed into the tool of his trade—and his horse with him. Unlike the heavenly Cecile, the Canon emanates the fires of hell.

Aside from this symbolic association with fire, there is a realistic reason why the Canon is sweating: he is a man in a hurry. The pilgrimage has been proceeding at a sedate pace: the Wife of Bath rides an ambler, a comfortable walking horse, and the Cook has fallen asleep on his horse, suggesting slow, rhythmic rocking motion. Were it true, as the Yeoman asserts, that the Canon was hurrying to catch up with the pilgrims because he wanted to ride with them for "disport" and "daliance," companionable entertainment (VIII, G, 592), why did he have to ride so fast to catch up with them? The Yeoman's story—that he had seen the pilgrims leave that morning and urged his Canon to catch up with them—has the air of concoction.

As the Yeoman reveals later, alchemists require equally greedy investors to fund their experiments, and enticing such investors often involves chicanery. So the Canon's haste seems more likely to be motivated by a desire to escape a disgruntled investor than to catch up with ambling pilgrims. Covered in a black cape, he might hope to blend in with this diverse group, thus escaping detection. Geffrey also notices that the Canon is traveling light, dressed "in light array / As if for summer" (VIII, G, 567–568). As the first line of *The Canterbury Tales* announces that the pilgrims set forth in April, not a warm month in England then or now, the Canon's light summer array is unusual. His clothing suggests that he is fleeing in haste and that the effort involved in the flight adds to the fiery heat of his own corrupt moral nature.

Once the two join the pilgrimage, it can be surmised by the tone of the Yeoman's conversation with the other pilgrims that the Canon is not within hearing distance of the Yeoman. Harry Bailly incorporates the Yeoman into the group by encouraging him to describe his boss. The Canon, says the Yeoman, is a man who works "craftily" (VIII, G, 603). The term *craft*, which the Yeoman uses several times more in his description of the Canon, has a double meaning in Chaucer. A craft is a trade skill; in the "Knight's Tale," Chaucer uses the term "crafty man" to describe a builder

(I, A, 1897). This meaning of the term also suggests another meaning, as in the modern "crafty": deceptive, sneaky, cunning, tricky. Unlike the craftsmen in the "Knight's Tale" who, however craftily, build real buildings, the crafty alchemist uses his cunning and guile to chase fool's gold, accomplishing nothing.

At first, it seems that the Canon's Yeoman is prepared to be as tricky as his master, for he claims that the Canon could turn the roads leading to Canterbury into silver and gold. But Harry Bailly, whose trade as an innkeeper makes him a shrewd observer, is quick to point out the discrepancy between the Canon's alleged ability to generate precious metals and his current disheveled appearance:

> *"Why is thy lord so sluttissh, I the preye,*
> *And is of power bettre clooth to beye,*
> *If that his dede accorde with thy speche?"*

> "Why is your lord so sloppy, I pray you,
> If he has power to buy better cloth,
> If his deeds accord with your speech?"

> (VIII, G, 636–638)

Evading the question, the Yeoman cites the need for secrecy and the great wisdom of the Canon. Picking up on the negative meaning of the Yeoman's term "crafty," the Host probes him further for a description of how the Canon employs his "cunning . . . / Since he is so crafty and so sly" (VIII, G, 653–655). The location of the Canon's trade bodes ill: What legitimate craft could require a location outside of town (the "suburbs"), in a concealed location ("lurking in hiding places and blind alleys"), in short, a "private fearful residence" (VIII, G, 657–660)? No legitimate tradesman would thus avoid the public areas in the medieval town where business was customarily done.

In addition to the discrepancy between his poor array and his alleged talent at paving roads with gold and silver, the sharp-eyed Host also notices another suspicious piece of evidence about these two late arrivals. "Why," says Host to Yeoman, "are you so discolored in your face?" (VIII, G, 664). For no apparent reason, the Yeoman drops his pose of complicity with the Canon and adopts the confessional mode:

> *"I am so used in the fyr to blowe*
> *That it hath chaunged my colour."*

"I am so used to blowing in the fire
That it has changed my color."

(VIII, G, 666–667)

Unlike the saintly Cecile, the Canon and his Yeoman have absorbed the fire's heat. Morally, too, they have been infected by their hellish enterprise:

"We blondren evere and pouren in the fir,
And for al that we faille of oure desir,
For evere we lakken oure conclusioun.
To muchel folk we doon illusioun,
And borwe gold, be it a pound or two,
Or ten, or twelve, or manye sommes mo,
And make hem wenen, at the leeste weye,
That of a pound we koude make tweye."

"We blunder ever and stare into the fire
And for all that we fail of our desire,
For we always lack our conclusion.
We do illusion to many folk,
And borrow gold, maybe a pound or two,
Or ten, or twelve, or many sums more,
And make them think, at the very least,
That of a pound we could make two."

(VIII, G, 670–677)

Despite a track record of failure, the Canon and Yeoman cannot stop. Like compulsive gamblers, in ever seeking to recoup their losses, they lose more. Worse still, they craftily persuade others to do the same by promising them unrealistic rewards: double their money. A 200 percent return on investment requires a high degree of risk indeed.

Like the Pardoner and the Summoner, the Canon and the Yeoman are involved in a financial scam; unlike the former pair, the latter have been deceiving themselves as well. It seems as if, at the point of joining the pilgrimage, the Canon and his Yeoman are ready to take separate paths. The Yeoman seems disillusioned and ready to end his apprenticeship. Even if he is not exactly repenting, he is at least abandoning his past sins. But the Canon indicates by his behavior that he does not really intend to join the pilgrimage, symbolically changing his life. Rather, he intends to use the pilgrimage as a method of concealment, and he is irate at his apprentice for revealing as much as he has. Drawing near and overhearing part of the conversation, he berates his Yeoman for "uncovering" what should be "hidden" (VIII, G, 696). While training in all crafts involves the passing along of specialized knowledge from master to apprentice (one Middle English term for a trade was *mistere*, mystery), this degree of secrecy marks the Canon off as no legitimate craftsman. Guilt, not craft solidarity, makes him "suspicious / Of men's speech" (VII, G, 686–687) and fearful of having his "private business" revealed (VIII, G, 701). When Harry Bailly urges the Yeoman to tell them even more, the Canon can take it no longer and "fled away for very sorrow and shame" (VIII, G, 702). Like one of his own alchemical elements, the Canon in effect evaporates, leaving his Yeoman free to divulge all the secrets of their *mistere*.

Structurally, the "Canon's Yeoman's Prologue" is like one of the links between tales (see Appendix I). Part I of the tale serves the same function as the prologue in some of the other tales in being a self-revelatory dramatic monologue. In it, the Yeoman confesses how his involvement with the Canon changed his life. At the time of the Canterbury pilgrimage, he is at the end of the traditional term of apprenticeship, having lived with the Canon for seven years. Were this a legitimate craft, the Yeoman would have achieved mastery of the craft and the status of an independent tradesman, thus being rewarded for his seven years of effort. But since the pseudo-science of alchemy is futile, there can be no question of mastery of it. Not only has the apprentice made no progress, but he has actually "lost thereby" (VIII, G, 722). Before, he used to dress well, "be right fresh and gay / Of clothing and of other good *array*" (VIII, G, 724–725); now he dresses badly. Before, he had a "fresh and red" complexion; now, he is "wan and of a leaden hue" (VIII, G, 727–728). He has not, like other apprentices, learned how to make his living. Instead, he has lost all the money he had before, and more: he is so much in debt that he will never be able to repay it. All has been lost in pursuit of a "sliding science" (VIII, G, 732), an indefinite, elusive body of knowledge.

The "sliding science" of alchemy must at first have appeared to the Yeoman as a real body of learning. The Yeoman shows off the large number of technical terms he has acquired, "terms" that seem so *clergial*, or learned, so *queynte*, or complex (VIII, G, 752). Many lines are devoted to summarizing the vocabulary of alchemy (demonstrating Chaucer's keen interest in the subject as well). But all this learning of terms and processes is in vain, for nothing works:

> *Noght helpeth us; oure labour is in veyn.*
> *Ne eek oure spirites ascencioun,*
> *Ne oure materes that lyen al fix adoun,*

Mowe in oure werkyng no thyng us availle,
For lost is al oure labour and travaille;
And al the cost.

Nothing helps us; our labor is in vain.
Not our spirits' ascension,
Not our matters that lie all fixed down,
Nothing avails us in our working,
For lost is all our labor and travail,
And all the cost.

(VIII, G, 777–782)

What the alchemists are trying to do is to vaporize inert elements, thus causing the "ascension of spirits," or creation of a gas. The resulting chemical change, they hope, will lead to the discovery of the process that will cause the transmutation of base metals into gold. But Chaucer uses his alchemical language carefully here to suggest to the audience that the real root of the alchemists' failure is their futile concentration on heavy, fixed matter instead of light, airy spirit. Instead of concerning themselves as medieval Christians believed they should, with the ascension of their own spirits to heaven, they are engaged in a futile attempt to transform inert matter here on earth. No wonder, then, that matter lies down; it cannot rise as the spirit can. All their efforts are futile, and the price is not only monetary. The "labor and travail" spent on this futile quest diverts them from their proper life goal, their "spirit's ascension" to heaven.

If it were only these two involved in this vain labor, it would be bad enough. But the "elfish craft" (VIII, G, 751) requires that the Canon supplement his own funds with those of others:

And whan he thurgh his madnesse and folye
Hath lost his owene good thurgh jupartye,
Thanne he exciteth oother folk therto,
To lesen hir good as he hymself hath do.

And when, through his madness and folly
He has lost his own good through jeopardy,
Then he excites other folk to do the same,
To lose their good as he himself did do.

(VIII, G, 742–745)

The term "good," like the term "craft," has a double meaning in this tale. In fact, the meaning of words shifts and transmutes as if in imitation of the "sliding science" itself (VIII, G, 732). The "goods" that have been lost are not only monetary, but the spiritual progress lost through devoting one's best efforts to the lesser good of financial gain. The false learning embodied in the list of alchemical terms is "in vain" (VIII, G, 777). The true philosopher's stone is not a magical transmutational element; true philosophy, or love of wisdom, consists in transforming oneself.

In quest of earthly reward, alchemists risk loss of heaven. The Canon and his Yeoman are, like others involved in "this cursed craft" (VIII, G, 830), infused with the very savor of hell, "the smell of brimstone" (VIII, G, 885). The fires burning under the alchemical instruments are hellfires. Even though "the fiend does not show himself in our sight" (VIII, G, 916), he is with them in their laboratory. His function is to "infect" them all with an uncontrollable urge to continue in their futile enterprise—what moderns would call an obsession and what the Yeoman himself terms a "madness" (VIII, G, 889, 959). By the end of his introductory speech, the Yeoman seems to have freed himself from this illness of the spirit, at last realizing that "all things which shine like the gold / Are not gold" (VIII, G, 962–963).

The Yeoman's tale expands on the theme of deception and trickery employed in pursuit of an elusive and futile goal. In Part One, his introduction, he focuses on the machinations of "his" Canon; in Part Two, his tale, he transmutes (as if by an alchemical process) that character into another, equally evil canon. This second "canon of religion" (VIII, G, 972) perverts the nature of his calling by converting people not to faith but to his own obsessive quest for money. Like a fiend, he "would infect all a town" with his "sleights" and "infinite falseness" (VIII, G, 973, 976). The Yeoman apologizes to the ecclesiastics in the audience for speaking ill of a colleague, assuring them that his tale is an attack on "a singular man's folly" (VIII, G, 997) and is not a general condemnation. Despite this apology, his other character is yet another corrupt clergyman, an "annualeer" (VIII, G, 1012), a priest on an annual salary for saying masses. This easy, well-paid ecclesiastical sinecure is the kind of job to which lazy priests fled rather than meet the demands of a far-flung parish as did Chaucer's good Parson. The point of this detail is that this priest already has a comfortable life with "spending silver . . . right enough" (VIII, G, 1018). Nevertheless, like many already affluent people, he wants more.

The canon's complicated scam plays on the priest's deadly sin of covetousness. The canon asks the priest for a loan, which the canon repays in three days, as agreed. The canon's apparent reliability impresses the priest, as does the canon's affirmation of his own honesty:

"Trouthe is a thyng that I wol evere kepe
Unto that day in which that I shal crepe
Into my grave."

"Troth is a thing that I will ever keep
Until that day on which I shall creep
Into my grave."

                                                                    (VIII, G, 1044–1046)

To reward the priest for his generosity in loaning the money, the canon promises to share his secret knowledge, his "philosophy," or "mastery" (VIII, G, 1058, 1060). This apparent generosity, the audience knows, is just a cover for the canon's "dissimulation," his "fiendly thoughts" (VIII, G, 1073, 1071); the canon's real goal is to get the priest to fund his alchemical experiments.

In an aside, the Yeoman seems to be replying to a pilgrim's question as to whether this fictional canon was the same as his own Canon. No, replies the Yeoman; although his own Canon "has betrayed folks many time" (VIII, G, 1092), he is too embarrassed to recount episodes of deceptions in which he presumably played a part himself. He would indeed blush for shame, were it not for the fact that the chemical had "wasted . . . my redness" (VIII, G, 1100), turned his natural expression of embarrassment into an unnatural leaden hue. Medieval people believed that shame was a healthy emotion, calling one's attention to moral flaws. The inability to blush, then, indicates desensitization to appropriate feelings of guilt.

Resuming his tale, the Yeoman describes the canon's attempt to gull the priest. He tells the priest to send his man for quicksilver (an inexpensive metal). When it arrives, the canon urges the priest to put it into a crucible himself. With a magical secret substance, "a powder . . . that cost me dear" (VIII, G, 1133), the canon promises to transform the quicksilver into real silver. While the canon's alleged expensive powder is nothing but chalk or glass or "something else . . . not worth a fly" (VIII, G, 1150), the canon has another trick up his sleeve. To allay any suspicion the priest might have, the canon urges him to arrange the coals of the fire himself. In the coals, the canon has a false piece of charcoal with a hole drilled in it. Inside that hole he has placed silver filings, and "stopped . . . / This hole with wax" to keep the filings in (VIII, G, 1163–1164). Pretending to inspect the fire, the canon tells the priest that not only is the fire ill-made, but also that the priest himself is "right hot; I see how well you sweat!" (VIII, G, 1186). While feigning to rearrange the coals for a proper fire, the canon offers the priest a "cloth [to] wipe away the wet" (VIII, G, 1187). Taking advantage of the momentary distraction, the canon slips in the coal containing the silver. As if this were not enough deception, the canon also substitutes a small metal rod of silver and throws in the alleged magical powder as well.

The elaborateness of the whole scheme increases the priest's confusion (and the reader's), exploiting as it does the false reverence of the nonscientist for the (alleged) scientist. These elaborate and mysterious processes seem to lead to the transformation of inexpensive quicksilver into genuine silver. "This sotted priest, who was gladder than he?" (VIII, G, 1341). Get-rich-quick schemes have always appealed to the greedy. The sotted priest is now willing to buy the recipe for the powder for 40 pounds, a considerable sum in medieval money—4 pounds more than Chaucer's then-impressive annual salary in one of his best positions, the clerk of the King's Works. As might be expected, the canon first urges secrecy and then disappears. Ironically, secrecy is all but guaranteed, for the scam victim is unlikely to advertise his own greed and gullibility. Thus the canon, who seemed "friendly" but was in truth "fiendly," escapes to "bejape" and "beguile" yet another victim (VIII, G, 1302–1303, 1385).

The Yeoman thus concludes his tale, drawing an extended and complex moral based on two principles. "Multiplying" is wrong because it does not work; in fact, it leads to its opposite, "scarcity" (VIII, G, 1391, 1393). Though in the study of alchemy, many have been "burned," they still cannot "flee the fire's heat" (VIII, G, 1407–1408). Moderns would call this compulsion. Based on this reasoning and his own experience, the Yeoman advises his hearers to "meddle no more with that art" (VIII, G, 1424).

The Yeoman's second principle for condemning alchemy is more ambiguous. Alchemy involves "science" and "cunning," "private" and "secret" knowledge. In fact, the ultimate wisdom of the philosophers, or "lovers of wisdom," is the "secret of secrets" (VIII, G, 1446, 1447, 1452). The modern concept of scientific knowledge assumes wide dissemination of newly discovered information; but the alchemist's goal is secrecy. Secret knowledge is available only to one who knows science's special language, the "speech / Of philosophers" (VIII, G, 1443–1444). Complex technical language such as permeates the tale keeps knowledge secret, available only to a learned elite who vow to restrict its dissemination:

> "The philosophres sworn were everychoon
> That they sholden discovere it unto noon,
> Ne in no book it write."

"The philosophers were all sworn
That they should reveal it unto no one,
Nor write it in a book."

(VIII, G, 1464–1466)

Scientific knowledge must be kept secret because it is forbidden knowledge. To know what should be left unknown is a usurpation of the power of God:

"*For unto Crist it is so lief and deere*
That he wol nat that it discovered bee,
But where it liketh to his deitee
Men for t'enspire, and eek for to deffende
Whom that hym liketh."

"For unto Christ it is so beloved and dear
That he wills that it not be discovered,
Except when it pleases his godhood
To inspire men, and also to forbid
Whoever he pleases."

(VIII, G, 1467–1471)

Scientific knowledge, then, belongs to Christ, to reveal or conceal as he pleases. Man violates Christ's pleasure at man's peril.

The Yeoman's belief that the edge of scientific research encroaches on the domain of God is still held by many in modern times. Advances in fields such as genetics, where science manipulates the very stuff of human life, are often analyzed in similar terms today. The Yeoman advises that men "let it go," abandon the search for the "secret of secrets" (VIII, G, 1475, 1447): in our time, some would place similar restrictions on scientific research. Knotty ethical problems arise: Are there legitimate limits on human knowledge? Is there a point where the scientist makes "God his adversary" (VIII, G, 1476) by seeking forbidden knowledge?

The Yeoman thinks so; but he is a recent convert to this moral viewpoint, having only just left the Canon's service to join the Canterbury pilgrimage. Chaucer ends the Yeoman's speech with a certain ambiguity. Yes, the Yeoman does advise the pilgrims, in traditional moral terms, that his "multiplying" (VIII, G, 1479) has been sinful, and the only true rewards are conferred by Christ. But the Yeoman's final summation also suggests that he sees alchemy as evil only because it has not yet worked and that he nevertheless retains a fascination with the search for the "secret of secrets" (VIII, G, 1447).

Although alchemists like the Canon and his Yeoman failed, their desire to extend the frontiers of knowledge—in medieval terms, to invade God's privacy—laid the intellectual groundwork for later scientific experimentation. The quest for the philosopher's stone, undertaken out of mere greed, was transmuted into the search for scientific knowledge. That quest proved much more successful.

SUGGESTIONS FOR FURTHER READING

Cook, Robert. "The Canon's Yeoman and His Tale." *Chaucer Review* 22, no. 1 (1987): 28–40. Cook argues that the Yeoman is a "morally attractive person whose reform is likely to be permanent."

Hallissy, Margaret. "Poison and Infection in Chaucer's Knight's and Canon's Yeoman's Tales." *Essays in Arts and Sciences* 10, no. 1 (1981): 31–40. Hallissy shows how poison is a metaphor for the contagious nature of moral evil in both tales.

Hilberry, Jane. " 'And in Oure Madnesse Everemore We Rave': Technical Language in the *Canon's Yeoman's Tale*." *Chaucer Review* 21, no. 4 (1987): 435–443. Hilberry discusses the Yeoman's attraction to the "appealing poetic quality of alchemical language."

Longworth, Robert M. "Privileged Knowledge: St. Cecilia and the Alchemist in the *Canterbury Tales*." *Chaucer Review* 27, no. 1 (1992): 87–96. Longworth's thesis is that the relationship between the two tales is based on the common theme of transformation.

Lumiansky, R. M. *Of Sondry Folk: The Dramatic Principle in the Canterbury Tales*. Austin: University of Texas Press, 1955. 227–235. In support of his famous thesis, that the tales are developments of the characters of the tellers, Lumiansky argues that in this tale the Yeoman "unintentionally reveals more of his own state of mind than he intends."

Whittock, Trevor. *A Reading of the Canterbury Tales*. Cambridge: Cambridge University Press, 1968. 262–279. Whittock sees the tale as illustrating the "misuse of man's intelligence in the obsessive pursuit of false and meretricious goals."

The Manciple's Prologue and Tale

The word moot nede accorde with the dede.
If men shal telle proprely a thyng,
The word moot cosyn be to the werkyng.

The word must accord with the deed.
If men shall tell a thing properly,
The word must be cousin to the work.

(IX, H, 208–210)

The "Manciple's Tale" begins with a dialogue that is a structural hybrid, a cross between a prologue and a link. In joining his tales to each other and to the pilgrimage frame, Chaucer varied his methods. One method, allowing the character to introduce him- or herself in a dramatic monologue, then proceeding to a tale that further develops that character, is employed in the "Wife of Bath's Tale" and the "Pardoner's Tale." If this format were constantly repeated, it would probably become dull. Here, Harry Bailly, master of ceremonies, performs his structural function as a linking character (see Appendix I). Since his original choice, the Cook, cannot perform, the Host turns to the Manciple. The rapid dialogue between Host and Manciple serves to develop both their characters, to link the tale to the frame, and, most importantly, to introduce two apparently unrelated themes that will be expanded in the tale: base appetites and tale-telling.

The dialogue between Host and Manciple begins with a realistic reminder of the framing situation, the journey from London to Canterbury. The pilgrims are at a "little town," appropriately named "Bob-up-and-Down," as the rhythmic rocking motion of the ride has put the Cook to sleep (IX, H, 1–2). Harry Bailly attempts to wake him, with ribald suggestions of what nocturnal activities might have caused his extreme drowsiness. The Cook alleges that he doesn't know what made him so sleepy. But the Manciple has his own opinion. He tells the Cook, in the hearing of all, that his "breath . . . stinks"; he urges him to keep his mouth shut, since the odor "will infect us all" (IX, H, 32, 39). In short, says the Manciple, the Cook is thoroughly drunk. Angry, the Cook attempts to reply, but does indeed appear to be too drunk to do so. Instead, he falls off his horse.

In the visual arts of the Middle Ages, the image of a horse and rider reflected proper order in the universe, with the higher, rational mind (the rider) controlling the lower, animal impulses (the horse). In drunkenness, reason is lost or at least compromised; so man falls to a state lower than the animal's, precisely because man is supposed to be higher. A drunken man falling off his horse, then, is a powerful visual image of the negative consequences of yielding to base appetites. This idea of debasement through indulgence of fleshly appetites will recur in the tale.

The linking dialogue in the prologue also takes a dim view of one who would too precisely name the faults of others. The Host upbraids the Manciple for his overexplicit criticism of the Cook, reminding the Manciple that, since he too is flawed, the Cook may find occasion to criticize the Manciple in turn. This criticism causes the Manciple to back off—"I said it as a joke," he claims (IX, H, 81). Ironically, when the Manciple offers the Cook a drink of wine as a peace-offering, the Cook's rapid consumption of it proves the Manciple right. Seeing that the Cook will be in no condition to continue the tale-telling, the Host invites the Manciple to do so. This dialogue between Host, Manciple, and Cook serves the linking function and also highlights a theme of the subsequent tale: the disadvantages of frank truth-telling.

The central character of the "Manciple's Tale" is Phebus or Apollo, the sun god. When he was a mortal man, "as old books make mention" (IX, H, 106), he was a perfect example of the courtly gentleman. Not only was he "the most lusty bachelor / In all this world, and also the best archer" (IX, H, 107–108), but he was also famous for deeds of prowess (slaying the Python, a giant snake) and chivalric accomplishments (playing on musical instruments and singing). Every detail of the description is geared toward characterizing him as the epitome of his type, "the seemliest man / That is or was since the world began" (IX, H, 119–120). Full of "*gentilesse, / Of* honor, and of perfect worthiness," this "flower of bachelorhood" would seem to be the ideal catch for any woman—a man who could satisfy all legitimate desires (IX, H, 123–125).

"Now had this Phebus in his house a crow. . . . Now had this Phebus in his house a wife" (IX, H, 130, 139). In his house, this perfect Phebus has a pet crow and a wife. By the parallel phraseology, Chaucer suggests that there is some hidden similarity between the two, at least from Phebus' viewpoint. Phebus' two housemates are similar in that they are "had" by Phebus; they are his possessions, both kept in his house, and, as it later develops, both kept "in a cage" (IX, H, 131), albeit in two different sorts of cages. The crow, raised by Phebus, has three unusual features. It can speak like a jay; it can sing like a nightingale; and it is white like a swan. As the audience knows, all three traits are now uncharacteristic of the crow. Furthermore, since medieval people were given to ranking animals on a hierarchical scale, just as they ranked everything else, the audience would also know that the crow was considered inferior to the jay, the nightingale, and the swan. The crow, then, introduces a key idea: lower versus higher creatures.

In his house Phebus also has a wife, of whom he is jealous. The jealous husband, like Januarie in the "Merchant's Tale," is a figure of fun in medieval comedy. This stock character is usually old and unattractive, a dotard married to a nubile young woman. Phebus, however, is a "lusty bachelor" (IX, H, 107). Because Phebus has been described as perfect, his obsession with "keeping" his wife is out of character. Therefore the plot plays off the contrast between the two character types combined in Phebus: the jealous old husband and the ideal young "flower of bachelorhood" (IX, H, 125).

In medieval comedy, the plot involving the jealous husband is predictable. His best efforts to keep his wife faithful never suffice. The very effort is, as the Manciple points out, an exercise in futility:

> A good wyf, that is clene of werk and thoght,
> Sholde nat been kept in noon awayt, certayn;
> And trewely the labour is in vayn
> To kepe a shrewe, for it wol nat bee.

> A good wife, who is clean of work and thought,
> Should not be kept in suspicion, certainly;
> And truly the labor is in vain
> To keep a shrew, for it will not be.

                                                         (IX, H, 148–151)

"To keep": the connection between crow and wife hinges on this concept. The action of the verb indicates constraint of one being by another, more powerful being. The restrained creature, if it has any spirit at all, must by "nature" (IX, H, 161) try to break free. If it does, it may be ill-equipped to

use its newfound freedom wisely, for encagement is poor preparation for
liberty:

> *Taak any bryd, and put it in a cage,*
> *And do al thyn entente and thy corage*
> *To fostre it tendrely with mete and drynke*
> *Of all deyntees that thou kanst bithynke,*
> *And keep it al so clenly as thou may,*
> *Although his cage of gold be never so gay,*
> *Yet hath this brid, by twenty thousand foold,*
> *Levere in a forest that is rude and coold*
> *Goon ete wormes and swich wrecchednesse.*

> Take any bird, and put it in a cage,
> And carry out your intention wholeheartedly
> To foster it tenderly with meat and drink
> And every dainty food that you can think,
> And keep it all as cleanly as you may,
> Although his cage of gold be ever so gay,
> Yet this bird would, by twenty thousand fold,
> Rather live in a forest that is rude and cold
> And go eat worms and such wretchedness.

(IX, H, 163–171)

The image of a bird in a gilded cage is still used today to describe the wives
of wealthy husbands, trapped by that wealth in a loveless marriage. The
elegant home becomes a cage, a symbol not of sheltering love but of
imprisonment. Like a bird, such a woman would rather "go eat worms" as
an expression of desire to "escape out of [her] cage" (IX, H, 171, 173).
Chaucer has used the image of confinement in a cage in relation to a
woman before, in the "Miller's Tale." There, the jealous husband John the
carpenter is described as holding his young wife Alisoun "narrow in cage"
(I, A, 3224). But as Chaucer has observed in the "Franklin's Tale," "women,
by nature, desire liberty" (V, F, 768). As the medieval audience would
expect, attempts to confine only encourage rebellion.

As in the "Miller's Tale," so in the "Manciple's Tale." Rebellion against
entrapment often involves personal debasement. Not only birds but also
cats, she-wolves, and men behave in ways equivalent to "eating worms"
(IX, H, 171). Cats would rather eat mice than "every dainty that is in the
house"; a she-wolf lusts after "the lewdest wolf that she may find / Or least
of reputation"; men often have a "lecherous appetite" for women other than
their wives (IX, H, 179, 184–185, 189). So it is not surprising that Phebus'

wife expresses her desire to break free in a debased way: by taking as a lover "a man of little reputation" (IX, H, 199), inferior to Phebus in every way. Both animals and humans, then, are inclined to indulge base appetites.

The Manciple apologizes to the audience for his own frankness in calling the male companion of Phebus' wife's by the sexually explicit term *lemman*, lover (IX, H, 204). But, as the Manciple says in explanation,

> *The word moot nede accorde with the dede.*
> *If men shal telle proprely a thyng,*
> *The word moot cosyn be to the werkyng.*

> The word must accord with the deed.
> If men shall tell a thing properly,
> The word must be cousin to the work.

(IX, H, 208–210)

Accurate reporting, truth-telling, becomes an issue now in the tale as it was in the prologue, where the Host criticized the Manciple's frank speech about the Cook. The crow, too truthful, greets his master with cries of "Cuckoo!" or "Cuckold!" (IX, H, 243), that is, husband of an unfaithful wife. Questioned further, the crow reveals that he has seen Phebus' wife in bed with "one of little reputation" (IX, H, 253). Hearing this, Phebus, enraged, kills his unfaithful wife.

No sooner is she dead, however, than Phebus does an about-face; believing her guiltless, he blames the crow for his wife's death. Being a god, Phebus has the power to punish not only this crow but all his descendants as well:

> *And to the crowe, "O false theef!" seyde he,*
> *"I wol thee quite anon thy false tale.*
> *Thou songe whilom lyk a nyghtyngale;*
> *Now shaltow, false theef, thy song forgon,*
> *And eek thy white fetheres everichon,*
> *Ne nevere in al thy lif ne shaltou speke."*

> And he said to the crow, "O false thief!
> I will now pay back your false tale.
> You used to sing just like a nightingale;
> Now, false thief, you shall forego your song
> And also your white feathers every one,
> And you shall never speak again in your life."

(IX, H, 292–297)

Thus the crow loses all his positive features. He cannot sing or speak; and the darkness of his feathers would indicate to the medieval audience the low estate to which he has fallen, as have all subsequent crows along with him. For merely reporting base behavior, he has been debased himself.

The irony is that the crow, though tactless, told the truth: the wife *was* unfaithful, and Phebus *was* a cuckold. The tale emerges as a response to the Manciple's rebuke by the Host for his too-explicit comments on the Cook's drunkenness. Both prologue and tale illustrate what the Manciple was taught by his "dame," his mother, and what the episode with the Cook illustrates: that telling the truth can be unwise. The Manciple's mother's citation of several aphorisms on the subject reinforce the idea: "Keep well your tongue, and keep a friend"; "You should restrain your tongue / At all times"; "Much speaking is ill-advised" (IX, H, 319, 329–330, 335). In short, advises the Manciple's mother,

> "be noon auctour newe
> Of tidynges, wheither they been false or trewe.
> Whereso thou come, amonges hye or lowe,
> Kepe wel thy tonge and thenk upon the crowe."

> "be no new author
> Of tidings, whether false or true,
> Wherever you come, among the high or low,
> Keep your tongue well, and think about the crow."

> (IX, H, 359–362)

If consistently followed, this advice on speech would eliminate not only hurt feelings but tale-telling as well. The Manciple does not seem to realize that the tale itself disobeys his mother's injunctions. Twice he describes himself as "not textual" (IX, H, 235, 316), not book-learned. He only knows what he hears, then. But if, as his mother advised, no one told tales, how would he have heard this one? The implicit contradiction may be Chaucer's subtle jibe at the unlearned who think themselves wise, who take perverse pride in what they do not know.

But what of the base appetites that led Phebus' wife to adultery (and the Cook to drunkenness)? Birds, cats, she-wolves, men, and women flee entrapment; even if freedom is misused to "eat worms" (IX, H, 171), to debase oneself, it is a universal value transcending divisions of species. The crow, contented to be encaged, is somehow less worthy of respect than even the adulterous wife. Victim of a slave mentality, the crow sought rather to flatter his captor than to flee. Thus his debasement below jays, nightingales, and swans, worthier birds, is appropriate. His lower *estat* manifests his innate servility.

The use and abuse of speech are illustrated throughout the "Manciple's Tale" and its prologue. Called to account for his criticism of the Cook, the Manciple immediately withdraws his comments, terming them a "jest" (IX, H, 81). He apologizes for his use of precise terms in describing the relationship of Phebus' wife and her lover. He depicts the crow as being punished for truth-telling and Phebus as mistakenly believing the crow's tale. Finally, he repeatedly quotes his mother's advice not to tell a tale at all—advice that he has just disregarded. Through the "Manciple's Prologue and Tale" Chaucer explores the risks of truth-telling. Were everyone to emulate the crow, telling all, or Phebus, believing all, there would be no peace. On the other hand, were everyone to take the advice of the Manciple's mother, there would be no tales of Canterbury—or of anything else.

SUGGESTIONS FOR FURTHER READING

Howard, Donald R. *The Idea of the Canterbury Tales*. Berkeley: University of California Press, 1976. 298–304. Howard argues, against prevailing critical opinion, that the tale is not a "throwaway" but rather "prepares perfectly" for the concluding "Parson's Tale."

Lumiansky, R. M. *Of Sondry Folk: The Dramatic Principle in the Canterbury Tales*. Austin: University of Texas Press, 1955. 235–239. In support of his famous thesis, that the tales are developments of the characters of the tellers, Lumiansky sees the relationship between the Manciple and his tale as based on the concept of dishonesty.

Whittock, Trevor. *A Reading of the Canterbury Tales*. Cambridge: Cambridge University Press, 1968. 280–285. Whittock sees the "Manciple's Tale" as a contrast to the "Parson's Tale."

Chaucer's Retraction

Heere taketh the makere of this book his leve.
Here the maker of this book takes his leave.

(Subheading to "Retraction")

When a reader has completed *The Canterbury Tales*, Chaucer's "Retraction" comes as a shock, for in it, Chaucer revokes much of what is now considered his best work. So essential are career accomplishments to the modern sense of self that it is hard to imagine why Chaucer does this. But Chaucer's "Retraction" is crucial to understanding the poet as a man of his time. Throughout the tales, the poet has been represented by Geffrey the pilgrim. With the "Retraction" Chaucer drops that mask and speaks in his own voice. And it is the voice of a medieval Christian, whose religion taught him that his work in the world was nothing compared with the state of his soul before God. At the end of his own life's pilgrimage, Chaucer, the "maker of this book," must answer to his own Maker as to the use he made of his talents.

The theology of the "Retraction" places Chaucer firmly in the tradition of medieval penitential practice. Chaucer uses specific theological terms associated with the sacrament of Penance: sin, guilt, intent, grace, penitence, confession, satisfaction, forgiveness. The ritual of confession, as practiced in the Roman Catholic church to this day, involves the three elements Chaucer mentions: *penitence, confessioun, satisfaccioun*. A sinner preparing for confession should do so as if it were his last chance on earth. So, although students of the Chaucer texts cannot assure us that the poet actually wrote the "Retraction" at the end of his life, it does not matter; all confessions, whatever the age of the penitent, were to be made as if death were imminent. In this state of mind, the penitent reviewed his life. Sin was defined not only as obviously evil acts but also as preoccupation with "worldly vanities" (X, I,

1084), the things of the world as opposed to the things of God. Accusing oneself of sin aroused guilt, a salutary emotion that would lead the sinner to repent and to seek forgiveness through confessing his sins to a priest. Finally, the penitent must render satisfaction for any wrongs inflicted upon another. These three elements constitute the sacrament.

In the "Retraction," Chaucer follows the steps involved in receiving the sacrament of Penance when he accuses himself of composing "worldly vanities" (X, I, 1084), translations of secular poetry and any writing of his that might have tempted another to sin: *Troilus and Criseyde, The House of Fame, The Legend of Good Women, The Book of the Duchess, The Parliament of Fowls,* "the tales of Canterbury, those that lead to sin," and finally, another catch-all category for forgotten works, "many a song and many a lecherous lay" (X, I, 1085–1086). Moderns regard these as his best works, mainly because medievals and moderns disagree on the purpose of literature. To moderns, art is mainly for intellectual pleasure; to medievals art was for religious instruction.

Chaucer is theologically correct when he incorporates the same quote from St. Paul that he used in the "Nun's Priest's Tale": "All that is written is written for our doctrine" (X, I, 1083; VII, 3441–3442; Rom. 15:4). The purpose of all literature is to teach "doctrine," lessons conducive to salvation. Composing such works, Chaucer says, was his "intent." He may, however, have failed in some cases to measure up to his own standard. Intent is a crucial element in the definition of sin (a theme explored in the "Friar's Tale"). One cannot sin without intention; one cannot sin accidentally or, for that matter, through artistic inadequacy. As judged by this "doctrinal" norm, Chaucer's only valuable works, the only ones that measured up to his high intent, are his translation of Boethius' *Consolation of Philosophy* "and other books of legends of saints, and homilies" (X, I, 1087), works seldom read today except by Chaucer scholars. He apologizes, in effect, for the works that did not teach doctrine well enough.

If Chaucer indeed appears to be retracting his best work and retaining his worst, it is only by modern norms that this seems so. Having been given a special skill by God, he was obliged to use it to his own salvation and that of others. For after all, it is not, as he points out, the poet who acts through his own power, but rather God who acts through the poet. Chaucer humbly reminds "all who hearken unto this little treatise or read it," that if they "like anything in it," they should not credit the poet but rather "thank our lord Jesus Christ, of whom proceeds all wisdom and all goodness" (X, I, 1081). To Chaucer, Christ is the source of all that is wise and good, including Chaucer's own writing.

Now the sinful poet must reform his ways, repent of his sins and beseech Jesus and his mother Mary to "send me grace to bewail my guilt and to study the salvation of my soul" (X, I, 1089). Like literary talent, repentance is not a matter of unaided human ability but of grace, God's power working though man. What Chaucer seeks here is, in modern terms, a reversal of his priorities. He vows to devote himself to virtuous living, not literature. A new focus on the life of the spirit would constitute a sign that he had indeed received the "grace of true penitence" and was ready to be "one of them at the day of doom that shall be saved" (X, I, 1089, 1091). If at the Last Judgment his soul is not saved, it will do Chaucer little good to be judged as one of the greats of Western literature, whose works are read and discussed six centuries after his death. The life goal of the medieval Christian was not literary immortality but eternal life with the Trinity in heaven. To that end Chaucer concludes with a Latin prayer, invoking Christ and "the Father and the Holy Spirit who live and reign as one God forever and ever. Amen" (X, I, 1091).

With this vision of cosmic unity, Chaucer's penitential work is almost concluded. The medieval Christian believed that after death his soul was joined to the worshiping community of believers here on earth. The prayers of the living could benefit the dead who were enduring the temporary punishment of purgatory, a state of further cleansing before the soul is ready for full unity with God in heaven. Completing his "Retraction," Chaucer prays that Jesus Christ will have mercy on his soul, in effect hoping that his time in purgatory might be short, and giving his reader cause to hope so too, on his behalf. As centuries of readers repeat the poet's own words, they are, as he wished, praying for "Geoffrey Chaucer, on whose soul Jesus Christ have mercy. Amen" (X, I, 1092).

Yet despite the pious sentiments expressed in the "Retraction," Chaucer was apparently working on *The Canterbury Tales* right up to the time of his death. Like many confessions, Chaucer's did not really result in a change of behavior. Perhaps he saw himself as a relapsed sinner each time he returned to his writing. However guilty Chaucer may have felt about his work, however he may have retracted it, he did not destroy it. That may have been too hard a penance for the "maker of this book."

SUGGESTIONS FOR FURTHER READING

Boenig, Robert. "Taking Leave: Chaucer's Retraction and the Ways of Affirmation and Negation." *Studia Mystica* 12, nos. 2–3 (1989): 21–28. Boenig provides a theological explanation of Chaucer's simultaneously rejecting and validating his life's work.

Dean, James. "Chaucer's Repentance: A Likely Story." *Chaucer Review* 24, no. 1 (1989): 64–76. Dean argues that the sentiments expressed in the "Retraction" are comparable to those expressed in other fourteenth-century works operating within the same penitential conventions.

Howard, Donald R. *The Idea of the Canterbury Tales.* Berkeley: University of California Press, 1976. 56–67. Howard shows the relationship of the "Retraction" to the idea of the book in the Middle Ages.

Appendix I

The Links

Although a first-time reader of *The Canterbury Tales* may be tempted to skim or skip the links, they are important to Chaucer's design. *The Canterbury Tales* is an unfinished work; possibly Chaucer might have made changes, had he lived. But it is clear from what we have that Chaucer had begun to link each tale to the one before it, mainly by interspersing scraps of conversation between the pilgrims. The links show that his intention was not to assemble an anthology of disparate works, a medieval short-story collection, but to build a larger work consisting of a group of short narratives within and united to an overarching structure. For all their relative brevity, the links between the tales serve several purposes: they tie the tales to each other and to the pilgrimage frame; they provide dramatic continuity; they develop the character of certain pilgrims; they allow some characters to act as literary critics; and they establish Harry Bailly as a key principle of unity.

In the frame story, a group of individual shorter narratives are contained within a longer overall narrative, or frame. The pilgrimage to Canterbury, the overarching plot, constitutes the frame; the individual stories are like pictures within that frame. The premise of *The Canterbury Tales* is that each pilgrim will tell two tales going to and two tales coming from Canterbury. Had Chaucer lived to finish his massive project according to plan, the pilgrims would have reached Canterbury and then returned to London, completing the frame. At that point the work would have been vast; the audience would often have needed to be reminded of the relationship between the individual tales and the frame. First and foremost, the links serve this purpose: they join the parts to the whole.

It is obvious from Chaucer's careful work on the links between the first three tales, those of the Knight, the Miller, and the Reeve, that he also intended the links to provide linear continuity. The dramatic interaction between the pilgrims in the links causes the three tales to flow together and thus to move the overall plot along. In the opening set of tales, each tale is knitted firmly to its predecessor by means of the interaction between the characters in the links. In the first three tales, the link is *quyting*, requital or "paying back." The Knight having finished his tale, Harry Bailly wants the Monk to tell the next tale, to *quyte* the Knight with as good a tale or better. Harry's choice of words reminds the audience of the element of competition in the tale-telling: this is a contest, with only one winner. When the drunken Miller disrupts the Host's orderly plan, Harry Bailly tries to silence him by protesting that a "better man" (I, A, 3130) should speak next. Since the Host's plan depends on social rank, a universally accepted organizing principle in medieval life, the Miller is a rebel against Harry's established order. But he does accept the concept of *quyting*, responding to the Knight's high-style romance with a low "churl's" tale (I, A, 3169), a *fabliau* using contrasting characters. Because the butt of the Miller's vulgar humor is a carpenter, the Reeve, himself a carpenter, is angry and *quytes* the Miller with a still more vulgar tale. Thus the three tales are joined. The care with which Chaucer interweaves these tales suggests that he may have planned to create more similarly linked subgroups as an important principle of organization in the work as a whole.

The interaction of the Miller and Reeve with each other and of both with Harry Bailly is a means of developing the characters of all three. Characters are developed in *The Canterbury Tales* in three ways: by their description from the narrator Geffrey's point of view in the "General Prologue"; by their self-revelation in their own prologues and tales; and by their dialogue in the links. In the links we learn that the Reeve hates growing old; that the Merchant is unhappily married; that the Cook drinks too much and has bad breath; that the Franklin is disappointed in his son; that the Summoner and the Friar hate each other as much as do the Miller and the Reeve. As might happen with any group of people spending time together, characters reveal themselves in conversation. The links provide a realistic situation in which character revelation can take place; any travelers might behave as these do.

It is most natural that they would comment on each other's tales. The links provide an opportunity for the pilgrims to be a built-in audience. They agree with, reflect on, and criticize the tales, weighing them carefully against their own life experiences. Two pilgrims are well-read and comment on their reading: the Clerk says he is adapting his tale from the work of the fourteenth-century Italian poet Petrarch, and the Man of Law is familiar with, though not totally enthusiastic about, the works of a poet named

Geoffrey Chaucer. Several times the pilgrims register strong reactions to
the tales: Miller and Reeve, Friar and Summoner become angry at each
other, and the Host is profoundly moved by the Physician's story of the
martyred Virginia. When the pilgrims dislike a story, the links give them a
chance to say so. Twice stories are interrupted by a disapproving member
of the pilgrim audience. The incomplete "Squire's Tale" is not one of these,
because the favorable comments in the links suggest that Chaucer meant
to complete it. But the "Tale of Sir Thopas" and the "Monk's Tale" are
clearly written to be interrupted. The Host stops the "Tale of Sir Thopas"
with derogatory remarks about Geffrey's ineptitude at rhyme. The Knight,
whose own tale is long enough, cuts off the Monk in his ever-growing series
of examples of the fall of great men. Both these interruptions also serve to
suggest Chaucer's negative opinion of two literary forms already overdone
in his day: the long-winded tales of the adventures of the knight-errant;
and the repetitive exemplary tales of the fall from fortune. Perhaps Chaucer
was no more enthusiastic about finishing these tales than his fictional
audience was about hearing them; and the links provide an opportunity for
him to incorporate his own critical judgment through his characters.

The prime literary critic and central character in the links is Harry Bailly,
the Host. Since he has no "General Prologue" description or tale of his own,
the links provide the sole, but effective, source of his characterization.
Outgoing, chatty, and funny, he is well-suited by nature to his trade of
innkeeper. He is fond of entertaining people, often encouraging a funny tale
and discouraging a serious one. As is also predictable of an innkeeper, he is
adept at managing the flow of conversation and relating to a diverse group
of people. He is fluent in the jargon of many trades. With the Parson, he
jokes about religion; with the Physician, he shows off his medical vocabulary; with the Clerk, he discusses rhetoric; with the Cook, food. The reader
can easily imagine lively, gregarious Harry behind the bar at the Tabard.

Not only does Harry Bailly facilitate communication within the group,
but also, like several other characters, he reveals bits of himself. He has a
rocky relationship with his wife, Goodelief, and wishes she had heard the
"Tale of Melibee" so that she could imitate the patient Prudence. His vivid
description of a marital spat in the Bailly household in the prologue to the
"Monk's Tale" (VII, 1891–1923) is a small comic masterpiece, and suggests
that Harry's unsatisfactory marriage might account for his willingness to
drop everything and go on pilgrimage.

Harry's character is also revealed in his opinions of other pilgrims. At
the end of the "Pardoner's Tale," the Host reacts with violent anger and
unquotable language to the Pardoner's attempt to gull the Canterbury

pilgrims. For a moment, Harry's wrath causes him to step out of his mediator role, and the Knight must intervene to restore peace. But though Harry is crass, he is right about the Pardoner. Vulgar speech might nevertheless be true speech, as Harry's is, providing a needed corrective to the smooth-talking deceptiveness of the Pardoner.

In the links, Harry Bailly serves an important function as the principle of unity linking the tales to each other and to the frame. At the Tabard Inn in London, it was agreed that Harry Bailly would be the organizer and judge of the tale-telling competition. As master of ceremonies, Harry keeps the conversation flowing, inviting and cajoling the speakers, nudging them along. He resolves conflicts between the pilgrims so that the tale-telling does not degenerate into bickering. When orderly progress is interrupted by the unexpected arrival of the Canon's Yeoman, it is Harry's role to weave this unexpected character into the pattern of the narrative. Harry uses both questions and facilitating conversational tags ("tell me . . . let me talk to you" [VIII, G, 639, 663]) to draw out the Canon's Yeoman's story, allowing this new character to describe himself as the other characters were described in the "General Prologue." That done, the newcomer becomes part of the design. Organization and execution of the overall scheme is Harry's basic function in the tales.

Another way of looking at the character of Harry Bailly is as the embodiment of the principle of order. All medieval institutions functioned on the basis of the higher overseeing and commanding the lower. Thus even in this small and temporary society, a leader is needed, and Harry Bailly is that leader. He is king and pope of this group; as the Clerk reminds him, "You have of us for now the governance" (IV, E, 23). But like all representatives of authority, Harry Bailly must constantly battle against the forces of disorder inherent in any group. Not all the pilgrims obey him as they should. The Miller speaks out of turn; the Monk tells a series of boring tragedies when Harry requested "merry . . . cheer" (VII, 1924). Harry is in charge of restoring order, of sustaining motion along the right path. Order is crucial to the success of this pilgrimage as of the larger pilgrimage of human life.

The links, then, are the main structural device holding the individual tales to the frame of the pilgrimage. One of Chaucer's characters, Alisoun of Bath, is a weaver; weaving was a popular art form as well as a useful trade in the Middle Ages. To understand the function of the links, it is useful to think of them in terms of the metaphor of weaving. The links contribute to the overall tapestry by joining part to part, while at the same time adding colors and designs of their own.

Appendix II

The Cook's Tale and the Squire's Tale

Like *The Canterbury Tales* themselves, the tales of the Cook and Squire are fragmentary. Even in their unfinished state, however, memorable characters and interesting situations are created. The reader can only speculate why Chaucer abandoned these two tales which begin so auspiciously.

Each tale eminently suits its teller. The Cook's tale of an apprentice food-seller is a *fabliau*, like the tales of the Miller and the Reeve, a bawdy tale featuring lower-class characters and physical, earthy themes. The Squire's tale, in contrast, is a romance; like his father, the Knight, the Squire tells of high-born characters who experience only the most lofty emotions. With the suitability of teller to tale, the resemblance between the two fragments ends.

In its brief space, the "Cook's Tale" develops a memorable character: Perkin. An apprentice food-seller who "loved the tavern better than the shop" (I, A, 4376), Perkin is a partygoer, a "reveller" (I, A, 4371). Since he often neglects his work, his master is glad to be rid of him when his apprenticeship ends. When this occurs, Perkin sends all his possessions to a companion like himself, who "loved dice and revel and entertainment" (I, A, 4420). Apparently, he intends to move in with this companion, and with his wife, who kept a shop for the sake of appearances and "*swyved* for her sustenance" (I, A, 4422). Since the Middle English verb *swyve* is a vulgarism referring to sexual intercourse, the companion's wife must be a prostitute. Here, teasingly, the tale ends; for whatever reason, Chaucer abandoned the interesting triangle of Perkin Reveller, the comrade, and the *swyvyng* wife.

The "Squire's Tale," a romance, has no such vulgar characters. It is set in the kingdom of the noble Cambuskan; Cambuskan is a perfect king, famous for his excellence as a king, admirable in every regal quality, a perfect exemplar of monarchy. He has three children: two sons, Algarsyf and Cambalo, and a daughter, Canace. Canace, a conventionally beautiful romance heroine, is the focus of the romance plot.

The action of the story begins when King Cambuskan proclaims a feast to celebrate his birthday. It is springtime, the conventional time in medieval romance for beginning any sort of adventure. The king's birthday feast is a typical medieval banquet, characterized by stately ritual and lavish display of food. In the middle of this feast, a knight enters, mounted upon a brass horse and bearing three gifts: a mirror, a ring, and a sword. This mysterious knight rides to the high board, the high table or dais at which the king sits, and addresses him. The king of Araby and of India has sent the horse and three gifts, all magical, for the noble Cambuskan. The horse, mirror, ring, and sword each have distinctive features. The mirror's power allows a man looking into it to tell the future, to foresee "any adversity / Unto your reign or unto yourself also" (V, F, 134–135). If a woman looks into the mirror, however, she can see if her lover will be false or true. The mirror and the ring are gifts for Canace. The power of the ring is such that if she puts it on her thumb or in her purse, she can understand and speak the language of birds. The third gift, the sword, can, if used against an enemy, "carve and bite" (V, F, 158) through any armor. But if the wound made by the sword is touched with the sword's flat, the wound heals. The brass steed on which the knight rides becomes a fourth gift, to bear the king through the air to any destination he chooses.

Having bestowed the gifts, the knight spends a typical pleasant medieval evening with the folks at Cambuskan's court. In the morning, Canace, excited about her two gifts, rises early and walks out into the lovely spring day wearing the ring. Because of the ring's power, she understands the speech of a falcon crying with "piteous voice" (V, F, 412). This female or peregrine falcon has obviously suffered; she swoons, as if from loss of blood, to the point that she nearly falls from the tree. Stirred to pity because of her gentle heart, Canace asks how the peregrine became so woebegone.

The peregrine tells a story of betrayal in love. She loved a tercelet, a male falcon, who "seemed the well of all *gentilesse*," or gentlemanly behavior (V, F, 505). Appearances were deceiving, however, because in fact the tercelet was "full of treason and falseness" (V, F, 506), a serpent, a hypocrite. A trusting soul, the peregrine had given him all her love, had made herself subject to him: "my will was his will's instrument" (V, F, 568). As fortune willed, however, the tercelet had to leave the place where the falcon was. At first she believed that he regretted this as much as she did and that he would return soon.

Chaucer had worked with the theme of a trusting woman abandoned by a duplicitous male before, in his *Legend of Good Women*. The basic plot line in the legends is similar to this one: good woman loves bad man; bad man leaves her for another woman; good woman, now abandoned, suffers forever. So it is here. The tercelet leaves the peregrine and falls in love, suddenly, with a kite, a scavenger, an ignoble bird; the action embodies the theme of the debasement of the sensual appetites (as in the "Manciple's Tale"). The tercelet's abandonment of the loyal peregrine breaks her heart and causes the suffering in which Canace finds her. Canace, moved to pity, nurses the peregrine, wrapping her in plasters to cure her. The peregrine has injured herself with her own beak, suggesting that she is punishing herself for her inability to retain the love of the duplicitous tercelet. "Thus," the narrator says, "I leave Canace, keeping her hawk" (V, F, 651); he then begins to develop another plot strand, probably the adventures of another member of the Cambuskan family with another magic gift. At this point, with an approving comment by the Franklin, the tale ends.

The reader can only speculate as to what caused Chaucer to abandon these two tales, which seem to begin as auspiciously as any of his others. One possible explanation is that Chaucer was seeking a variety of story types in *The Canterbury Tales*, and both types, the *fabliau* and the romance, had already been used. Perhaps Chaucer abandoned these tales on the grounds that repetition of these narratives would detract from rather than add to the diversity he wanted in his *Canterbury Tales*.

Appendix III

The Tale of Sir Thopas

The "Tale of Sir Thopas" can be seen as an extended joke played by the poet Chaucer on his character Geffrey. The plan of the Canterbury pilgrimage is that each pilgrim tell two tales going to Canterbury and two tales coming back. According to this plan, at some point Geffrey will have to step out of his role as observer and step into the role of tale-teller. The "Tale of Sir Thopas" is that point.

Chaucer describes his alter ego Geffrey as a comical fellow. According to Harry Bailly, Geffrey is shaped in the waist just like the Host himself, and, in the "General Prologue," Harry is described as a large man. In the illustrations of Chaucer in early manuscripts, Chaucer is depicted as a small plump man, just as he describes himself in his poetry. Such a man is not a natural-born lover. (Harry says Geffrey would, in a woman's embrace, be a *popet* [VII, 701], a little doll—hardly an impressive image of masculinity.) Such a man is rather a comedian, fit to tell a "tale of mirth" (VII, 706). So Harry Bailly invites him to do just that. When Geffrey's turn comes, the audience would naturally expect great things from him, standing as he does in place of the poet.

What we do get is a clever satire on the courtly romance. Satire mocks the conventions of a particular form of literature. Like all satire, the "Tale of Sir Thopas" depends on a knowledge of the literary form being satirized. The romance, a tale of love and courage, is a long narrative composed of individual episodes. It recounts the brave deeds of young knights concerned with proving themselves and taking their places in a society of mature knights. In the romance, the knight does manly deeds and has all sorts of improbable adventures. Each element in the "Tale of Sir Thopas" plays off the audience's expectations of this highly conventional form.

Geffrey's tale begins as conventional romances do, by summoning the audience to "Listen, lords, in good intent," to a true story (VII, 712), a tale of "mirth" and of "solace" (VII, 714), a tale of a fair and gentle knight who, the audience would expect, will proceed to demonstrate manly prowess in adventures, in battles, and in tournaments. This knight, Sir Thopas, was born in a faraway country, in Flanders beyond the sea. The remoteness of his birthplace lends an air of mystery and exoticism. As is typical of the courtly romance, the knight and his equipment are described in detail. The audience learns that he has a "seemly nose" (VII, 729), and that he has good leather shoes, brown stockings, and an elegant robe. While it is typical of the characters in the courtly romance to be dressed in costly *array*, it is not typical for the narrator to estimate its actual cost, as Geffrey does; the price estimate, then, is a joke. In his expensive shoes, stockings, and robe, Sir Thopas engages in conventional knightly activities: hunting, hawking, archery, and wrestling. Knights about to go on a quest, a journey in pursuit of honor or fame, were supposed to be pure, like the Arthurian character Galahad, who can only succeed in his quest for the Holy Grail because he is a virgin. In keeping with this tradition, Sir Thopas is described as "chaste and no lecher" (VII, 745). Thus far, Sir Thopas is a typical exemplar of the *estat* of knighthood.

The traditional romance plot involves such a knight setting forth from a place of relative security and stability, usually a castle, to a symbolic wilderness, in which he will undergo a test of his manly virtue. So Sir Thopas rides out upon his grey steed through a fair forest. Descriptions of the natural world through which he rides—flowers growing and birds singing—are like those found in virtually every medieval romance. The spring setting is conventionally connected with love, and the romance hero by definition needs a lover. Therefore it is fitting that Sir Thopas experience an attack of "love-longing" (VII, 772) so severe that he has to lie down on the soft grass. There he dreams of falling in love with a supernatural being, "an elf-queen," who lives in "the country of Faery / So wild" (VII, 788, 802–803). Love between a human and a supernatural being is a common element in the romances, lending excitement and mystery. Naturally, the audience would expect, from this heavy foreshadowing, that the hero would now meet this elf-queen from the country of Faery.

Instead, he meets a great giant, named Sir Oliphaunt (Sir Elephant). A fight with a giant, another typical romance episode, gives the hero a chance to prove his manly prowess by overcoming the giant against all odds, as David slew Goliath. Anyone familiar with the medieval romance would expect Sir Elephant to do exactly what he does, which is to challenge Sir Thopas, threatening to kill him and his steed. The audience would also expect Sir Thopas, as befits a manly man, to respond to this challenge by issuing his own counterchallenge and engaging in immediate battle. Instead, Sir Thopas promises to fight "tomorrow . . . / When I have my armor" (VII, 818–819). But the ideal romance knight would not defer a fight until he was better prepared for it, Indeed, his very lack of preparation would be an incentive, since his triumph would be the greater under such adverse circumstances. And why would a knight on a quest be without his armor in the first place? Thopas' behavior is the opposite of expectations for the romance knight. So it is no surprise that the encounter ends in an undignified rout:

> *Sire Thopas drow abak ful faste;*
> *This geant at hym stones caste*
>   *Out of a fel staf-slynge.*
> *But faire escapeth child Thopas.*

> Sir Thopas drew back very quickly.
> This giant cast stones at him
>   Out of a fearsome slingshot.
> But child Thopas escaped quite well.

(VII, 827–830)

The term *child* in Middle English meant a knight in training; if Sir Thopas is going to act like this, bolting and running at the first challenge, he will never become a full-fledged knight.

Thus ends the first *fit*, or section. The second *fit* begins as the first one did, with another exhortation to the audience to listen to a merry tale. The hero, this time described as having a slender waist (unlike his creator, the narrator Geffrey, or *his* creator, the poet Chaucer), rides forth in search of another adventure. This new episode involves fighting a giant with three heads (not the same giant who routed him in the previous fit). Because Sir Thopas is much concerned with his own reputation as it will be recorded in literature, he summons minstrels and jesters to tell his tale. A key element in such tales is the description of the arming of the knight, to which five stanzas are now devoted. Such descriptions are characteristic of courtly romance, but here the effect is to suggest that the hero is wearing many, many layers of knightly garb. Indeed, he seems to be equipped with every possible kind of device that a knight might wear upon setting forth in search of adventure.

Having thus elaborately armed himself, however, Sir Thopas does nothing. So far, in the first fit, Sir Thopas runs away from a fight with a giant; in the second, he arms himself but does not set forth. Not only Sir Thopas but this narrative is going nowhere. The third fit begins as the other two did, exhorting the audience to listen to a tale of adventure. At this point the Canterbury audience, though accustomed to the slow pace of the courtly romance, must notice that the pace of this romance is even slower. Geffrey summarizes a variety of adventures that his audience might have read and promises to tell the audience a new adventure involving Sir Thopas. Romances, once under way, were exceedingly long, and this romance runs the risk of never even getting under way. It seems as if Geffrey is finally about to set his hero on his path to adventure when he is interrupted by the Host.

"No more of this," protests the Host (VII, 919). As a literary critic, Harry Bailly is clearly impatient with a story told with such apparent ineptitude. He hates Geffrey's "doggerel rhyme" (VII, 925), the poem's jangling meter and mechanical rhyme. The effect of the doggerel rhyme is clear in both Middle and modern English:

> Hymself drank water of the well,
>   As dide the knyght sire Percyvell.

> Himself drank water of the well,
>   As did the knight, Sir Percival.
>
>   (VII, 915–916)

Harry Bailly judges such "rhyming . . . not worth a turd" (VII, 930). To Harry, the plot is bad and the style is worse.

The net effect of the "Tale of Sir Thopas" is that Chaucer depicts his alter ego Geffrey as a literary incompetent. In reality, however, the tale is sophisticated satire. Like all satire, it depends for its humor on intimate knowledge of the object of the satire. Anyone familiar with the conventions of the medieval romance would find the "Tale of Sir Thopas" brilliantly funny. Perhaps the joke is on Harry Bailly. As a middle-class man, he cannot be expected to be familiar with the courtly romance genre.

Since Harry Bailly dislikes Geffrey's rhyming, he asks him to tell a tale in prose instead. If poetry is the language of romance and adventure, prose is the medium of history and instruction. Geffrey agrees to "tell a little thing in prose . . . a moral tale virtuous" (VII, 937, 940), and that is the "Tale of Melibee."

Appendix IV

The Tale of Melibee

Like the "Tale of Sir Thopas," the "Tale of Melibee" is told by Geffrey the pilgrim. Geffrey has been brought up short by the Host for producing, in the "Tale of Sir Thopas," poetry so bad that it made his "ears ache" (VII, 923), and is asked to tell a tale in prose instead. Since prose was considered the vehicle of instruction, Geffrey chooses to tell a "moral tale virtuous" (VII, 940). Moral and virtuous though it is, however, the "Tale of Melibee" is hardly lively reading. Like the "Parson's Tale," it is a piece of didactic literature. Where the "Parson's Tale" is a typical medieval sermon, the "Tale of Melibee" is another favorite medieval didactic form, an allegory. Medieval people were fond of allegory, a literary form in which characters representing religious and moral concepts engage in obviously symbolic activities. Allegory's purpose is not to entertain but to teach virtuous behavior.

The premise of the "Tale of Melibee" is that one day while Melibee was away from home, his wife and daughter, whom he had left there, were attacked by his enemies. Though the doors to Melibee's house were "fast shut" (VII, 969), the foes entered by setting ladders against the walls and climbing through the windows. Once inside, the foes "beat his wife, and wounded his daughter with five mortal wounds in five sundry places,— / this is to say, in her feet, in her hands, in her ears, in her nose, and in her mouth—and left her for dead, and went away" (VII, 971–972). Melibee is distraught: "he, like a mad man tearing his clothes, began to weep and cry" (VII, 975). But his wife urges him to moderate his distress over the injury inflicted on his daughter:

Youre doghter, with the grace of God, shal warisshe and escape. / And, al were it so that she right now were deed, ye ne oughte nat, as for hir deeth, youreself to destroye. / Senek seith: "The wise man shal nat take to greet disconfort for the deeth of his children, / but, certes, he sholde suffren it in pacience as wel as he abideth the deeth of his owene propre persone."

Your daughter, with the grace of God, shall recover and escape [from death]. / And, even if she were dead right now, you ought not, on account of her death, destroy yourself. / Seneca says: "The wise man shall not take too great discomfort for the death of his children, / but surely, he should suffer it in patience as well as he endures his own death." (VII, 982–985)

To the modern reader, the response given by Melibee's wife seems peculiar. Calmly quoting the Roman philosopher Seneca (4 B.C.–A.D. 65), she is too rational in response to Melibee's emotionalism, too cool in responding to a "mortal" injury inflicted on her child. Gender roles seem blurred as well: the audience might well expect a mother to be at least as upset as a father in this situation.

How can this be the "moral tale virtuous" that Geffrey promised? The answer lies in the nature of allegory. Allegorical characters are not realistic. Much as Uncle Sam in a Fourth of July pageant is not expected to demonstrate individuality but rather to represent American identity, allegorical characters personify abstract qualities. In the "Tale of Melibee," the initiating incident has an allegorical meaning that gradually becomes clear.

Melibee's house represents the human body. The foes laying siege to the house are the "three enemies of mankind . . . the flesh, the devil, and the world" (VII, 1420), the three principal sources of temptation, according to medieval theology: sensual pleasure, the devil himself, and attachment to earthly as opposed to spiritual values. These foes seek to penetrate the house. The windows in the walls signify areas of vulnerability to temptation, weak points through which the foes may enter. Because Melibee/man has "not defended [himself] sufficiently against their assaults and their temptations" (VII, 1422), the foes can get in and injure the soul. Melibee's daughter is the soul. She should be well protected (within the walls of the house), but Melibee's carelessness has left her vulnerable to temptation. So she has been mortally injured in her five senses, and Melibee must decide how to respond.

To help him decide, Melibee calls a council of advisors, a "great congregation of folk," including doctors and lawyers, "old folk and young," even "old enemies reconciled" to him (VII, 1003–1004). He asks them for advice, for "in [his] heart he bore a cruel ire, ready to do vengeance upon his foes" (VII, 1008). Each advisor responds according to the dictates of his own nature. The old men advise against war. The young urge immediate retaliation. The physicians propose to solve the problem by curing

Melibee's injured daughter. The lawyers hesitate and stall for time. Melibee is left with conflicting advice. Which would be the more prudent course of action?

True to the conventions of allegory, a character emerges as the personification of the very virtue Melibee needs: his wife Prudence. But like all medieval men, Melibee is influenced by the misogynistic belief that women's advice is untrustworthy. This commonplace of the age was espoused by learned theologians and passed down to humble believers as absolute truth. Melibee cites authorities to the effect that "all women are wicked and none of them are good" (VII, 1056). This overgeneralization, like all of its kind, can be disproved by only one example to the contrary, which Prudence does, competently and at great length. Prudence, a more solemn version of the Wife of Bath, is learned like her and knows what learned men were taught in the schools. She marshals quotations aplenty from authoritative sources of women who were "discreet and wise in counseling" (VII, 1096). So convincing is she that Melibee, praising the "great sapience [wisdom]," and "great truth" of her "sweet words" (VII, 1113), changes his mind. The resolution of this improbable tale is peace. Melibee's flaws—immoderation and anger—are corrected, and Prudence triumphs as Melibee's/man's first and best advisor.

In the "Tale of Melibee," Geffrey delivers what he promised: a moral tale. Few modern readers regard this as an interesting tale. But for its time, the tale advances an innovative thesis: that those who would silence women by discounting the value of their opinions are wrong, and that those who would listen to women might well learn something. Chaucer uses these ideas to better advantage when creating the Wife of Bath.

Appendix V

The Monk's Tale

In his role as master of ceremonies, the Host invites the Monk to tell his tale, urging him to be "merry of cheer" (VII, 1924). In addition, Harry Bailly, like Geffrey the pilgrim, admires the Monk's manliness. It seems from the conjunction of the two qualities—merriness and manliness—that the Monk might tell a *fabliau*. But Harry Bailly's expectations are, in this instance, wrong. The Monk tells a tale belonging to a popular but solemn genre—the *exemplum*.

The *exemplum*, or example story, illustrates a moral lesson. Medieval people loved collections of stories illustrating the same point; the more stories were told to make the point, the more effectively the point was considered to have been made. The Monk's examples define tragedy as would most theoreticians of medieval literature:

> "Tragedie is to seyn a certeyn storie,
> As olde bookes maken us memorie,
> Of hym that stood in greet prosperitee,
> And is yfallen out of heigh degree
> Into myserie, and endeth wrecchedly."

> "Tragedy is, to say, a certain story,
> As old books make us remember,
> Of him who stood in great prosperity,
> And is fallen out of high degree
> Into misery, and ends wretchedly."

(VII, 1973–1977)

In those authoritative old books that medieval people loved, tragic tales were told of those who rose to the top of the world, stood in great prosperity, and then fell.

Medieval people would imagine the tragic hero as being on top of Fortune's wheel (see photo 2). Inevitably, the blindfolded goddess would spin her wheel, so for those on top there was no way to go but down. Men who attempt to achieve high position, whether "popes, emperors or kings" (VII, 1986), in religious or secular life, risk falling from it. The "Monk's Tale," then, is a collection of stories from history, the Bible, and mythology of men of "high degree" who fell from "great prosperity" (VII, 1975–1976). Remembering that medieval people believed that the older an idea was, the truer it was, it is only logical that the Monk should begin with the original cosmic disasters: the biblical stories of the fall of Lucifer and the fall of Adam. These examples, like all the others, follow the same pattern and illustrate the same thesis: the inevitability of sorrow after joy.

Lucifer, created as the best and the brightest of God's angels, could not accept his subordination to God. His rebellion against God led to his fall. Similarly, Adam, the man who had everything, fell through his own "misgovernance" (VII, 2012). Because he ate the apple, he was "driven out of his high prosperity / To labor, and to Hell, and to mischance" (VII, 2013–2014). These two ancient stories are the model for all the example stories that follow. One tale with which the modern reader might be familiar through William Shakespeare's play is the description of the fall of Julius Caesar.

Julius Caesar is the archetypal tragic hero in that he rose to his high position by his own abilities and efforts, by his "wisdom, manhood and great labor" (VII, 2671). At the height of his achievement, he had conquered "all the West by land and sea" (VII, 2674). Inevitably, having reached the pinnacle of success, Caesar must fall. When he returns to Rome triumphant, a villain awaits: Brutus Cassius. Chaucer fuses the two conspirators, who are separate characters in Shakespeare, and provides a suitable motive: "envy" of Caesar's "high *estat*" (VII, 2698). When Brutus Cassius climbs onto Fortune's wheel, Caesar must be thrown down. Thus great Caesar dies, stabbed to death in the capitol; thus all the mighty fall.

The Monk can multiply many examples of this same cyclical pattern of rise and fall (he says in his prologue that he has a hundred of them). While medieval people liked these example stories much more than the modern reader typically does, it is clear by the time the Monk finishes his seventeenth example that everyone has had enough. The Monk is interrupted and is not allowed to finish with his hundred. The interruptor is not even the brash Host, Harry Bailly; it is the *gentil* Knight. The Knight thinks the Monk's story has been too serious, too "heavy" (VII, 2769), for the pilgrims to endure any longer. The purpose of the tale-telling is to pass the travel time more pleasantly, and the purpose is defeated with boring stories such as these.

The Knight's interruption and comment redirect the course of the story-telling into a lighter vein. Tragedy is, the Knight says, "a great disease" (VII, 2771), a great source of dis-ease. On the other hand,

> *"the contrarie is joye and greet solas,*
> *As whan a man hath been in povre estaat,*
> *And clymbeth up and wexeth fortunat,*
> *And there abideth in prosperitee.*
> *Swich thyng is gladsom, as it thynketh me."*

> "the contrary is joy and great solace,
> As when a man has been in poor estate,
> And climbs up and waxes fortunate,
> And there abides in prosperity.
> Such a thing is gladsome, I think."

(VII, 2774–2778)

A "gladsome thing" is what the Knight wants to hear on the Canterbury pilgrimage.

The Knight's literary criticism, diverting the subject matter of the tales from tragedy to comedy, ties the "Monk's Tale" to the "Nun's Priest's Tale," which follows. What the Nun's Priest does is to take the Monk's motif, the fall from high position, and transform it into a "merry" story (VII, 2817) by applying the same heroic pattern to the fate of a rooster.

Appendix VI

The Parson's Tale

In his portrait in the "General Prologue," the Parson is described as "a learned man, a clerk, / Who would preach Christ's gospel truly" (I, A, 480–481). Since preaching the gospel—after first following it himself—is the main duty of a good priest, it is not surprising that the "Parson's Tale" should be a sermon. Although Harry Bailly asked him for a "fable" (X, 1, 29), a light, merry tale, the Parson replies that the Canterbury pilgrims will "get no fable told by me" (X, 1, 31). Instead, the Parson explains the moral purpose of literature.

Citing Paul's letter to Timothy in the New Testament, the Parson reminds his pilgrim audience that fables, worldly tales, are only "wretchedness" when compared to "soothfastness," or truth-telling (X, 1, 33–34). To medieval people, the true purpose of literature was didactic: to teach moral and ethical lessons. If a story pleased its readers, that feeling of pleasure was praiseworthy only if it contributed to the communication of truth. The Parson uses a key medieval image to describe the relationship between literature and moral truth: the wheat and the chaff. The "draff," or chaff (X, 1, 35), is the external covering of the grain of wheat, that which is thrown away. The "wheat" (X, 1, 36) is the kernel, the crucial part, that which is retained. To medieval people, the chaff of a story is its surface narrative, which captures the reader's interest and motivates him or her to read the story through to its conclusion. But the true purpose of literature is the "wheat," the "morality and virtuous matter" (X, 1, 38) within the work of art.

Thus, the Parson's idea of "a merry tale in prose" (X, 1, 46) is one that teaches a lesson that will help the Canterbury pilgrims, not just to pass the time on their journey to Canterbury, but also

To shewe yow the wey, in this viage,
Of thilke parfit glorious pilgrymage
That highte Jerusalem celestial.

To show you the way, on this journey,
Of this perfect, glorious pilgrimage
That is called celestial Jerusalem.

(X, 1, 49–51)

The image of the journey is central to *The Canterbury Tales*, and the sermon is a road map on that journey. The goal of any sermon is to show the Christian believer the right way, the true way, to heaven. So the "Parson's Tale" instructs the Christian pilgrim on "the good way, / and walking in that way" (X, 1, 76–77), the right path to heaven. The success of one's earthly pilgrimage is consequent upon turning away from sin, the wrong path, and following virtue, the right path. Repentance is the redirection of one's life path. To rejoin the pilgrimage to the celestial city, the medieval Christian needed to be sensitized to his own sinfulness. Thus the Parson preaches on the Seven Deadly Sins: pride, envy, anger, sloth, avarice, gluttony, and lechery. The Parson describes all of these, with specific examples.

As one might expect in a sermon preached by a learned clerk, the "Parson's Tale" is a fabric of interwoven references to scriptures and the Fathers of the Church, those early church theologians who glossed, or commented on and explained, the scriptures. Having learned from these authorities, as transmitted to them through their parish priest, the medieval Christian was ready to formalize his repentance by going to confession. Confession is the process of telling one's sins to a priest to obtain forgiveness from God through the agency of that priest. The priest would offer suggestions to the penitent as to how to remedy these flaws or defects in his life. In keeping with that procedure, the "Parson's Tale" follows up on the detailed descriptions of the particular sins with suggested remedies for each of them, much as would happen in confession. The concepts of sin and repentance in penitential practice were seen as analogous to the concepts of illness and treatment in medicine. If a fever is treated with cold compresses, then, they reasoned, since the physical mirrors the spiritual, a sin is remedied by its contradictory virtue. The way this principle operates is most obvious in the Parson's discussion of the deadly sin of gluttony.

According to the hierarchical thought processes characteristic of me-dieval people, the spirit is superior to the flesh. Reason, by which man is linked to God, is superior to any of the fleshly appetites that link him to the beasts. Therefore it is proper that all base appetites be governed by reason. Gluttony is a sin precisely because it is the triumph of appetite over reason. The Parson defines gluttony as the "unmeasurable appetite to eat or to drink" (X, 1, 817). The negative term "unmeasurable" is crucial here:

its opposite, *mesure*, is a term of approval for the moderate, reasonable control of appetites. The glutton is immoderate; so is the person who starves himself. Virtue lies as a mean or measure between those two extremes. Like Adam, placing his desire to eat the apple before his duty of obedience to God, the glutton makes his belly his god. If spirit is superior to the flesh, then he who "savors earthly things" (X, 1, 819) worships a lesser god. Inversion of proper hierarchical values is most conspicuous in the sin of drunkenness, a subspecies of gluttony. Drunkenness, according to the Parson, is the "horrible sepulchre [tomb] of man's reason. . . . When a man is drunk he has lost his reason, and this is deadly sin" (X, 1, 821). It is sinful to lose one's reason because reason is a higher power; it is sinful to identify with the lower portion of one's nature.

According to the principle that devotion to the pleasures of the body is equivalent to neglecting the well-being of the soul, many medieval food customs were also considered sinful. When a man "devours his meat and has no rightful manner of eating" (X, 1, 824), he is a glutton; greedy table manners alone constitute a sin against moderation. Abusing the body by consuming too much food, so that the "humours," or vital fluids of the body, become "distempered" or disordered, is a sin (X, 1, 825). Furthermore, it is a sin if a man seeks "too delicate meat or drink" (X, 1, 828) as would a modern gourmet. This form of immoderation also demonstrates another character flaw, termed "curiosity" (X, 1, 829): excessive concern for the things of the world.

The remedy for the sin of gluttony is the contrary virtue, temperance. Temperance "holds the mean in all things" (X, 1, 833), maintains moderation. The temperate man "seeks no rich meats nor drinks and attaches no importance to the outrageous apparelling of meat" (X, 1, 833). *Mesure*, or moderation, "restrains by reason the enslaved appetite of eating" (X, 1, 834), thus maintaining proper hierarchical order. Moderation even requires that one should not sit too long at table; those elaborate medieval meals that extended over a good part of the day probably encouraged overindulgence in food and drink. Controlling one's appetite for food and drink is conducive to the "health of the body" (X, 1, 830); the virtue of temperance, analogously, is conducive to the health of the soul.

The Parson's analysis of gluttony is a typical discussion of each of the Seven Deadly Sins: he describes the characteristic features of the sin and then prescribes a remedy for it. The entire tale can be read from this point of view. Each sin is a deviation from the mean, the middle course that constitutes virtue. To cure oneself of the excess of a particular sin, one must diligently practice the opposing virtue. A greedy man must learn generosity, a lustful man purity. Thus can the medieval Christian find his way back to the right path.

At the end of his sermon, the Parson reminds his audience once again that the goal of the earthly pilgrimage is "the endless bliss of Heaven" (X, 1, 1076). Just as the pilgrims journey toward Canterbury Cathedral, so the Christian pilgrim journeys toward the celestial city, the heavenly Jerusalem. There, all harms are healed:

ther as the body of man, that whilom was foul and derk, is moore cleer than the sonne; ther as the body, that whilom was syk, freele, and fieble, and mortal, is inmortal, and so strong and so hool that ther may no thyng apeyren it; / ther as ne is neither hunger, thurst, ne coold, but every soule replenyssed with the sighte of the parfit knowynge of God.

there, the body of man, that once was foul and dark, is more clear than the sun; there, the body that once was sick, frail and feeble, and mortal, is immortal and so strong and so whole that nothing may harm it; / there is neither hunger, thirst, nor cold, but every soul is replenished with the sight of the perfect knowledge of God. (X, 1, 1078–1079)

This state of perfection is the goal of the earthly pilgrimage. And again, like the Canterbury pilgrimage itself, it is not only an individual but also a communal goal. Chaucer's vision of the "blissful company that rejoice evermore" (X, 1, 1077) encompasses his Canterbury pilgrims, his medieval audience, and his modern audience as well.

Character Index

General Index

"Ages of Man," 175, 192

Aging. *See* "Merchant's Tale"; *Senex amans*; "Wife of Bath's Prologue and Tale"

Alchemy, 270–281

Allegory, 93, 95–96, 99, 102

Anger, 149–150

Animals, 27–29, 79, 88, 216, 284–289. *See also* "Manciple's Tale"; "Nun's Priest's Tale"

Apprenticeship, 275–276

Argument, 113–124, 128–134

Aristotle, 253

Array (clothing): in "Canon's Yeoman's Prologue and Tale," 273, 275; in "Clerk's Tale," 157, 159–160, 164–168; defined, 4–5; of Doctor of Physic, 41–42; of Friar, 34; of Guildsmen, 39; of Knight, 24; in "Man of Law's Tale," 100; of Monk, 29–30; of Prioress, 28–29; of Sergeant of the Law, 36–37; in "Shipman's Tale," 226, 229, 233, 234; of Squire, 24; of Wife of Bath, 42–43; in "Wife of Bath's Prologue," 103–104; of Yeoman, 24

Astrology, 200

Auctoritee (authority): in "Clerk's Tale," 155–172; defined, 4; in

"Franklin's Tale," 196–197; and Friar, 33; and Monk, 31–32; in "Nun's Priest's Prologue and Tale," 249–251; in "Pardoner's Tale," 215; in "Physician's Tale," 207–208, 210; in "Second Nun's Tale," 261, 266; in "Wife of Bath's Prologue and Tale," 105–108, 110, 120, 122–124, 126–134

Authority. *See Auctoritee*

Avarice, 213–214, 216, 271, 277, 279

Aventure. See Fortune

Avicenna, 221

Beast fable, 246, 253. *See also* "Nun's Priest's Tale"

Becket, Thomas, 18–19

Blindness, 186–187, 191–192

Boethius, 71–72, 252, 253, 292

Books: and *auctoritee*, 114, 120–125, 132–134, 260, 263; Chaucer and his own work, 292–293; and education, 35–36, 76, 105–108, 288; and organization of *Canterbury Tales*, 20; and Wife of Bath, 114, 120–125, 132–134

"Canon's Yeoman's Prologue and Tale": alchemy in, 270–281; ap-

About the Author

MARGARET HALLISSY is Professor of English at C.W. Post College, Long Island University, where her specialty is Chaucer and medieval literature. She is the author of *Clean Maids, True Wives, Steadfast Widows: Chaucer's Women and Medieval Codes of Conduct* (Greenwood Press, 1993) and *Venomous Woman: Fear of the Female in Literature* (Greenwood Press, 1987).